W9-CTX-231

The School of Life

Alain de Botton is a philosopher and writer.
He is the bestselling author of fifteen books, including
How Proust Can Change Your Life, *The Consolations
of Philosophy*, *The Art of Travel* and *The Course
of Love*. He is the founder of The School of Life
(www.theschooloflife.com), an organization devoted to
helping people lead more resilient and fulfilled lives.
The School of Life: An Emotional Education is the
ultimate guide to how we might achieve
emotional maturity and self-understanding.

The School of Life

An Emotional Education

By Alain de Botton
and The School of Life

PENGUIN BOOKS

PENGUIN BOOKS

UK | USA | Canada | Ireland | Australia
India | New Zealand | South Africa

Penguin Books is part of the Penguin Random House group of companies
whose addresses can be found at global.penguinrandomhouse.com.

First published by Hamish Hamilton 2019
Published in Penguin Books 2020
005

Copyright © The School of Life, 2019

This is an anthology of materials drawn from the work of The School of Life Press and The School of Life
Blog (www.theschooloflife.com/thebookoflife). These materials have previously been, and may continue to
be, published or otherwise made available elsewhere by the copyright holder.

The right of Alain de Botton to be identified as the author of this work has been asserted by him in accordance
with the Copyright, Designs and Patents Act 1988.

The permissions on pp. 299–300 constitute an extension of this copyright page.

The passage referencing Bernard Mandeville on pp. 238–9 appeared in a slightly different form in
Alain de Botton's *Status Anxiety* (Penguin, 2004) – and is included here with full permission.

The moral right of the copyright holders has been asserted

Typeset by Jouve (UK), Milton Keynes
Printed and bound in Great Britain by Clays Ltd, Elcograf S.p.A.

A CIP catalogue record for this book is available from the British Library

ISBN: 978–0–241–98583–0

www.greenpenguin.co.uk

Penguin Random House is committed to a
sustainable future for our business, our readers
and our planet. This book is made from Forest
Stewardship Council® certified paper.

Contents

Introduction

EDUCATION

Modern societies are collectively deeply committed to education, and have in place the mechanisms needed to teach every conceivable profession and to cover every topic of enquiry. We reliably educate pilots and neurosurgeons, actuaries and dental hygienists; we offer lessons in the irregularities of the French pluperfect and textbooks on the conductive properties of metal alloys. We are not individually much cleverer than the average animal, a heron or a mole, but the knack of our species lies in our capacity to transmit our accumulated knowledge down the generations. The slowest among us can, in a few hours, pick up ideas that it took a few rare geniuses a lifetime to acquire.

Yet what is distinctive is just how selective we are about the topics we deem it possible to educate ourselves *in*. Our energies are overwhelmingly directed towards material, scientific and technical subjects – and away from psychological and emotional ones. Much anxiety surrounds the question of how good the next generation will be at maths; very little around their abilities at marriage or kindness. We devote inordinate hours to learning about tectonic plates and cloud formations, and relatively few fathoming shame and rage.

The assumption is that emotional insight might be either unnecessary or in essence unteachable, lying beyond reason or method, an unreproducible phenomenon best abandoned to individual instinct and intuition. We are left to find our own path around our unfeasibly complicated minds – a move as striking (and as wise) as suggesting that each generation should rediscover the laws of physics by themselves.

ROMANTICISM

That we think so well of untrained intuition is because (perhaps without realizing it) we are the troubled inheritors of what can be defined as a Romantic view of emotions. Starting in Europe in the eighteenth century and spreading widely and powerfully ever since, Romanticism has been deeply committed to casting doubt on the need to apply reason to emotional life, preferring to let spontaneous feelings play an unhampered role instead.

In our choice of whom to marry, Romanticism has counselled that we be guided by immediate attraction. In our working lives, we are prompted to choose our jobs by listening to our hearts. We are, above all else, urged never to think too much – lest cold reason overwhelm the wisdom of feeling.

The results of a Romantic philosophy are everywhere to see: exponential progress in the material and technological fields combined with perplexing stasis in the psychological one. We are as clever with our machines and technologies as we are simple-minded in the management of our emotions. We are, in terms of wisdom, little more advanced than the ancient Sumerians or the Picts. We have the technology of an advanced civilization balancing precariously on an emotional base that has not developed much since we dwelt in caves. We have the appetites and destructive furies of primitive primates who have come into possession of thermonuclear warheads.

EMOTIONAL INTELLIGENCE

Emotional intelligence remains a peculiar-sounding term, because we are wedded to thinking of intelligence as a unitary capacity, rather than what it actually is: a catch-all word for what is in fact a range of skills directed at a number of different challenges. There is mathematical intelligence and culinary intelligence, intelligence around literature and intelligence towards animals. What is certain is that there is no such thing as an intelligent person per se – and probably no entirely dumb one either. We are all astonishingly capable of messing up our lives, whatever the prestige of our university degrees, and are never beyond making a sincere contribution, however unorthodox our qualifications.

When we speak of emotional intelligence, we are alluding – in a humanistic rather than scientific way – to whether someone understands key components of emotional functioning. We are referring to their ability to introspect and communicate, to read the moods of others, to relate with patience, charity and imagination to the less edifying moments of those around them. The emotionally intelligent person knows that love is a skill, not a feeling, and will require trust, vulnerability, generosity, humour, sexual understanding and selective resignation. The emotionally intelligent person awards themselves the time to determine what gives their working life meaning and has the confidence and tenacity to try to find an accommodation between their inner priorities and the demands of the world. The emotionally intelligent person knows how to hope and be grateful, while remaining steadfast before the essentially tragic structure of existence. The emotionally intelligent person knows that they will only ever be mentally healthy in a few areas and at certain moments, but is committed to fathoming their inadequacies and warning others of them in good time, with apology and charm.

Sustained shortfalls in emotional intelligence are, sadly, no minor matter. There are few catastrophes, in our own lives or in those of nations, that do not ultimately have their origins in emotional ignorance.

SECULARIZATION

For most of human history, emotional intelligence was – broadly – in the hands of religions. It was they that talked with greatest authority about ethics, meaning, community and purpose. It was they that offered to instruct us in how to live, love and die well. Religions were natural points of reference at times of personal crisis; in agony, one generally called first for the priest.

When belief went into decline in north-western Europe in the middle of the nineteenth century, many commentators wondered where humanity would – in an increasingly secular future – find the guidance that religions had once provided. Where would ethical counsel come from? How would self-understanding be achieved? What would determine our sense of purpose? To whom would we turn in despair?

One answer – hesitantly and then increasingly boldly articulated – came to the fore: culture. *Culture could replace scripture*. There was, it was proposed, a convincing set of substitutes for the teachings of the faiths within the canon of culture. The plays of Sophocles and Racine, the paintings of Botticelli and Rembrandt, the literature of Goethe and Baudelaire, the philosophy of Plato and Schopenhauer, the musical compositions of Liszt and Wagner: these would provide the raw material from which an adequate replacement for the guidance and consolation of the faiths could be formulated.

With this idea in mind, an unparalleled investment in culture followed in many ever-less faithful nations. Vast numbers of libraries, concert halls, university humanities departments and museums were constructed around the world with the conscious intention of filling the chasm left by religion.

Lest we miss the point, in 1854 the designers of the British Museum's new Reading Room specified that its vast central dome should have precisely the same circumference as St Peter's in Rome.

When commissioning its new national museum in the 1870s, the Netherlands entrusted the task to the foremost church architect of the day, Pierre Cuypers, whose Rijksmuseum was indistinguishable from a place of worship. Museums were – as the rallying crying put it – to be our new cathedrals.

Culture will replace scripture:
the Reading Room at the British Museum, 1854.

Cathedrals of secularism: the Rijksmuseum, 1885.

That culture might replace scripture remains a theoretically intriguing and emotionally deeply compelling concept. And yet it has, to all intents and purposes, been entirely ignored. Culture has *not* in any way replaced scripture. Our museums are not our new cathedrals. They are smart filing cabinets for the art of the past. Our libraries are not our homes for the soul. They are architectural encyclopedias. And if we were to show up at any university humanities department in urgent search of purpose and meaning, or were to break down in a museum gallery in a quest for forgiveness or charity, we would be swiftly removed and possibly handed over to psychiatric authorities. The intensity of need and the emotional craving that religions once willingly engaged with have not been thought acceptable within the contemporary cultural realm. The implication is that any moderately educated and sensible person already knows how to manage the business of living and dying well enough – without the need for a nanny.

Those who have produced culture may have sought to transform and inspire us; those who guard and interpret it have restricted themselves to a sober and curatorial interpretation of its function.

No wonder we might still be casting around for ways to arrange our minds in the wake of religion's ebb.

SELF-HELP

It is notable that, within the upper echelons of culture, there is no genre more maligned or discredited than self-help. The entire self-help category has become synonymous with sentimentality, idiocy and hucksterism.

To go by many of its examples, this caustic verdict is not especially unfair. The book covers are frequently garish and the promises overblown. But to dismiss the idea that underpins self-help – that one might at points stand in urgent need of solace and emotional education – seems an austerely perverse prejudice.

Ancient Greek and Roman culture recognized and honoured our

needs with greater dignity. The noblest minds – Aristotle, Epicurus, Cicero, Seneca and Marcus Aurelius – all turned their hands to what were unmistakably works of self-help. The applied philosophical tradition in which they operated continued beyond the fall of Rome. Michel de Montaigne's *Essays* (1580) amounted to a practical compendium of advice on helping us to know our fickle minds, find purpose, connect meaningfully with others and achieve intervals of composure and acceptance. Marcel Proust's *In Search of Lost Time* (1913) was, with equally practical ambition, a self-help book intent on delineating the most sincere and intelligent way that we might stop squandering and start to appreciate our too brief lives.

The problem should not, therefore, be assumed to lie with the idea of self-help per se, only with the manner in which the genre has, in modern times, been interpreted and explored. In reality, there could be few more serious tasks for any literary work than guiding and consoling us and weakening the hold that confusion and error have on us.

Progress towards a better kind of self-help depends on reviewing the potential of a widely debased genre, and in keeping faith with the essential seriousness of the project of emotional education.

SELF-DEVELOPMENT

As children, when someone asked our age, we might have said, 'I'm four', and added, with great solemnity, 'and a half'. We didn't want anyone to think we were only four. We had travelled so far in those few months, but then again we were modest enough to sense that the huge dignity of turning five was still quite far away. In other words, as children, we were hugely conscious of the rapidity and intensity of human development and wanted clearly to signal to others and ourselves what dramatic metamorphoses we might undergo in the course of our ordinary days and nights.

It would nowadays sound comic or a touch mad for an adult to say proudly, 'I'm twenty-five and a half' or 'forty-one and three-quarters' – because, without particularly noticing, we've drifted away from the notion that adults, too, are capable of evolutions.

Once we're past eighteen or so, our progress is still monitored but it is envisaged in different terms: it is cast in the language of material and professional advancement. The focus is on what grades have been achieved, what career has been chosen and what progress has been made in the corporate hierarchy. Development becomes largely synonymous with promotion.

But emotional growth still continues. There won't be a simple outward measure: we're no taller, we've not boosted our seniority at work and we've received no new title to confirm our matriculation to the world. Yet there have been changes nevertheless. We may, over two sleepless nights, have entirely rethought our attitude to envy or come to an important insight about the way we behave when someone compliments us. We may have made a momentous step in self-forgiveness or resolved one of the riddles of a romantic relationship.

These quiet but very real milestones don't get marked. We're not given a cake or a present to mark the moment of growth. We're not congratulated by others or viewed with enhanced respect. No one cares or even knows how caring might work. But inside, privately, we might harbour a muffled hope that some of our evolutions will be properly prized.

In an ideal world, we might have in our possession maps of emotional progress against which we could plot our faltering advance towards more sustained maturity. We might conceive of our inner developments as trips around a region, each one with distinct landmarks and staging posts, and as significant in their way as the cities of Renaissance Italy or the beauty spots on the Pacific Highway – and which we might be equally proud to have reached and come to understand our way around.

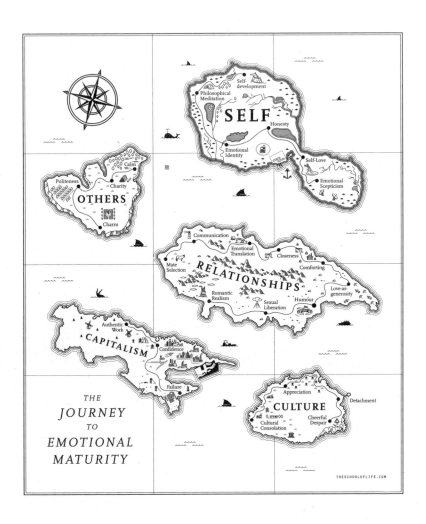

THE
JOURNEY
TO
EMOTIONAL
MATURITY

AKRASIA

The contemporary education system proceeds under two assumptions about how we learn. First, it believes that *how* we are taught matters far less than *what* we are taught. What educates students is – it's believed – the soundness of certain arguments, not especially the manner of their delivery. Teaching should not rely on gloss and charm. It is not, and should never be, a branch of the entertainment industry.

Second, the education system assumes that once we understand something, it will stick in our minds for as long as we need it to. These minds are envisaged as a little like computer hard drives: unless violently knocked, they will hold on to data for the long term. This is why we might imagine that education could stop at the age of twenty-two, once the important things have been imbibed.

But an emotional education may require us to adopt two different starting points. For a start, *how* we are taught may matter inordinately, because we have ingrained tendencies to shut our ears to all the major truths about our deeper selves. Our settled impulse is to blame anyone who lays our blind spots and insufficiencies bare – unless our defences have first been adroitly and seductively appeased. In the face of critically important insights, we get distracted, proud or fidgety. We may prefer to do almost anything other than take in information that could save us.

Moreover, we forget almost everything. Our memories are sieves, not robust buckets. What seemed a convincing call to action at 8 a.m. will be nothing more than a dim recollection by midday and an indecipherable contrail in our cloudy minds by evening. Our enthusiasms and resolutions can be counted upon to fade like the stars at dawn. Nothing much sticks.

It was the philosophers of ancient Greece who first identified these problems and described the structural deficiencies of our minds with a special term. They proposed that we suffer from *akrasia*, commonly translated as 'weakness of will', a habit of not listening to what we accept should be heard and a failure to act upon what we know is right. It is because of akrasia that crucial information is frequently lodged in our minds without being active in them and it is because of akrasia that we often both understand what we should do and resolutely omit to do it.

There are two solutions to these fragilities of mind that a successful emotional education must draw upon: the first is art, the second is ritual.

ART

We are so used to understanding the purpose of art in Romantic terms, as the fruit of individual artistic genius, that we forget that for most of history art had a plainer and more direct purpose: it was a tool of education. The point of art was to render tough or knotty lessons easier to absorb; to nudge our recalcitrant minds towards accepting ideas that we might nod along to but then ignore if they were not stated in especially varnished and graceful terms.

Christianity, for example, devoted so much attention to art (architecture, music, painting, etc.) not because it cared for beauty per se, but because it understood the power of beauty to persuade us into particular patterns of thought and habits of the heart. In fifteenth-century Florence, the teacher and scholar Marsilio Ficino set out on an explicit mission to educate his city in the truths of Christian theology. He wished, with the help of the powerful and wealthy Medici family, to teach Florence about the Christly virtues of charity and compassion, courage and dignity of spirit. But he also understood that any such lessons would be largely ineffective if they were simply articulated in workmanlike prose on the pages of a book or delivered in a monotone voice from the front of a classroom. Ideas would have to be amplified by art in order to work their way properly into our muffled intelligence.

Beauty in the service of education:
Sandro Botticelli, *Madonna of the Book*, c. 1480.

One of Ficino's foremost protégés was Sandro Botticelli. His works may now be celebrated for their visual skill, but they were at the outset honoured for their educative power. The *Madonna of the Book* was not seeking idly to charm the eye but to impress upon viewers the value of maternal care, sacrifice and sorrowful contemplation. Expressed in blunt words, the instruction would – Ficino and Botticelli knew – have gone nowhere. It needed, in order to carry deep into our minds, the help of an azure sky, the dance of a rich gold filigree, an adorable child and an exceptionally tender maternal figure; ideas, however noble, tend to require a little help from beauty.

RITUAL

Our problem isn't just that we are in the habit of shirking important ideas. We are also prone to forget them immediately even if we have in theory given them our assent. For this, humanity invented ritual. Ritual can be defined as the structured repetition of important concepts, made resonant through the help of formal pageantry and ceremony. Ritual takes thoughts that are known but unattended and renders them active and vivid once more in our distracted minds. Unlike standard modern education, ritual doesn't aim to teach us anything new; it wants to lend compelling form to what we believe we already know. It wants to turn our theoretical allegiances into habits.

It is, not coincidentally, also religions that have been especially active in the design and propagation of rituals. It is they that have created occasions at which to tug our minds back to honouring the seasons, remembering the dead, looking inside ourselves, focusing on the passage of time, empathizing with strangers, forgiving transgressions or apologizing for misdeeds. They have put dates in our diaries to take our minds back to our most sincere commitments.

We might interpret rituals negatively, as symbols of an old-fashioned attempt to control and direct our thoughts by appointment.

However, the best rituals don't so much impose upon us ideas that we are opposed to but take us back to ideas that we are in deep agreement with yet have allowed to lapse: they are an externally mandated route to inner authenticity.

In the course of secularizing our societies, we may have been too hasty in doing away with rituals. An education system alive to the wisdom of religions would perceive the role of structured lessons that constantly repeat what we know full well already – and yet so arduously and grievously forget. A good 'school' shouldn't tell us only things we've never heard of before; it should be deeply interested in rehearsing all that is theoretically known yet practically forgotten.

FIRST WORLD PROBLEMS

Part of what stops us addressing our emotional knots is a background belief that they are too small to be worth bothering with. Our will to tackle what may, in reality, destroy our lives is sapped by a background fear of being self-indulgent. A lingering puritanism kicks in at precisely the wrong moment.

But there is (sadly) nothing especially laughable about the problems unfolding in the world's richest countries. People may not starve, life expectancy is high and child mortality almost eradicated, but populations remain beleaguered. The issues are not the sob stories of the well-to-do, begging for sympathy on account of an incorrectly chilled wine, but comprise extremes of loneliness, anxiety, relationship breakdown, rage, humiliation and depression – problems that culminate in the greatest indictment of advanced societies: their exceptionally high suicide rates.

The priority of modern politics is economic growth. But humanity's struggle towards material security will only be worthwhile if we understand and find ways to attenuate the psychological afflictions that appear to continue into, and are sometimes directly fostered by, conditions of abundance. The problems of the thirty or so rich countries described as First World are the ones that the whole of our species will, according to current trajectories, be facing in 300 years' time. The issues that currently wreck people's lives in Switzerland and Norway, Australia and the Netherlands are the problems that will be rife around the globe in 2319. First World problems aren't an unnecessary oddity. They are a form of time travel. They are a glimpse into what will one day bedevil all humankind – unless we learn to view them as more than the tantrums of the spoilt.

IMPERFECTION

The single greatest enemy of contemporary satisfaction may be the belief in human perfectibility. We have been driven to collective rage through the apparently generous yet in reality devastating idea that it might be within our natural remit to be completely and enduringly happy.

For thousands of years, we knew better. We might have been superstitious and credulous, but not without limit. All substantial endeavours – marriage, child-rearing, a career, politics – were understood to be sources of distinctive and elaborate misery. Buddhism described life itself as a vale of suffering; the Greeks insisted on the tragic structure of every human project; Christianity interpreted each of us as being marked by a divine curse.

First formulated by the philosopher St Augustine in the closing days of the Roman Empire, 'original sin' generously insisted that humanity was intrinsically, rather than accidentally, flawed. That we suffer, feel lost and isolated, are racked with worry, miss our own talents, refuse love, lack empathy, sulk, obsess and hate: these are not merely personal flaws, but constitute the essence of the human animal. We are broken creatures and have been since our expulsion from Eden, damned – to use the resonant Latin phrase – by *peccatum*

Peccatum originale – original sin

Of course we are sad: detail from Lucas Cranach
the Elder, *Adam and Eve*, 1526.

originale. Even without subscribing to the precise details of Augustine's logic, we can appreciate his conclusion.

This should feel not like a punishing observation, but more like relief from the pressures of 200 years of scientifically mandated faith in the possibility of progress.

There can wisely be no 'solutions', no self-help, of a kind that removes problems altogether. What we can aim for, at best, is consolation – a word tellingly lacking in glamour. To believe in consolation means giving up on cures; it means accepting that life is a hospice rather than a hospital, but one we'd like to render as comfortable, as interesting and as kind as possible.

A philosophy of consolation directs us to two important salves: understanding and companionship. Or grasping what our problem is – and knowing that we are not alone with it. Understanding does not magically remove the pain but it has the power to reduce a range of secondary aggravations and fears. At least we know what is racking us and why. Our worst fears are held in check, and tears may be turned into bitter knowledge.

It helps immensely too to know that we are in company. Despite the upbeat tone of society in general, there is solace in the discovery that everyone else is, in private, of course as bewildered and regretful as we are. This is not *Schadenfreude*, simply profound relief that we are not the only ones.

SANE INSANITY

Basic sanity should also be assumed to be beyond us. There are too many powerful reasons why we lack anything like an even keel. We have complex histories, we are heading towards the ultimate catastrophe, we are vulnerable to devastating losses, love will always leave us wanting, the gap between our hopes and our realities is always going to be unbridgeable. In the circumstances, it makes no sense to aim for sanity; we should fix instead on the goal of achieving a wise, knowledgeable and self-possessed relationship with our manifold insanities, or what can be termed 'sane insanity'.

What separates the sane insane from the simply insane is the honest, personable and accurate grasp they have on what is not entirely right with them. They may not be wholly balanced, but they don't have the additional folly of insisting on their normalcy. They can admit with good grace – and no particular loss of dignity – that they are naturally deeply peculiar at myriad points. They do not go out of their way to hide from us what they get up to in the night, in their sad moments, when anxiety strikes, or during attacks of envy. They can – at their best – be drily funny about the tragedy of being human. They lay bare the fears, doubts, longings, desires and habits that don't belong to the story we commonly tell ourselves about who we are.

The sane insane among us are not a special category of the mentally unwell; they represent the most evolved possibility for a mature human being.

IN PRAISE OF MELANCHOLY

Melancholy is not rage or bitterness; it is a noble species of sadness that arises when we are properly open to the idea that suffering and disappointment are at the heart of human experience. It is not a disorder that needs to be cured; it is a tender-hearted, calm, dispassionate acknowledgement of how much agony we will inevitably have to travel through.

Modern society's mania is to emphasize buoyancy and cheerfulness. It wishes either to medicalize melancholy states – and therefore 'solve' them – or to deny their legitimacy altogether. Yet melancholy springs from a rightful awareness of the tragic structure of every life. We can, in melancholy states, understand without fury or sentimentality that no one truly understands anyone else, that loneliness is universal and that every life has its full measure of shame and sorrow. The melancholy know that many of the things we most want are in tragic conflict: to feel secure and yet to be free; to have money and yet not to have to be beholden to others; to be in close-knit communities and yet not to be stifled by the expectations and demands of society; to explore the world and yet to put down deep roots; to fulfil the demands of our appetites for food, sex and sloth and yet stay thin, sober, faithful and fit.

The wisdom of the melancholy attitude (as opposed to the bitter or angry one) lies in understanding that our suffering belongs to humanity in general. Melancholy is redolent with an impersonal perspective on suffering. It is filled with a soaring pity for our condition. There are melancholy landscapes and melancholy pieces of music, melancholy poems and melancholy times of day. In them, we find echoes of our own griefs, returned back to us without some of the personal associations that, when they first struck us, made them particularly agonizing. The task of culture is to turn rage and forced jollity into melancholy. The more melancholy a culture can be, the less its individual members need to be persecuted by their own failures, lost illusions and regrets.

THE SIMPLE AND THE OBSCURE

We could expect humans to display a powerful reflex for simple over obscure explanations. Yet in many areas of intellectual and psychological life, we observe a stranger, more unexpected phenomenon: a prejudice in favour of abstruseness, density, enigma and the esoteric. Our respect for explanations that come close to incomprehensible, that provoke puzzlement, that employ uncommon words suggests an implicit belief that the truth should not come in a form that is easily fathomable. We too readily assume that we are approaching a person of genius when we stop understanding anything of what they're saying.

It is problematic, therefore, that so many of the central truths of emotional life have an elemental simplicity to them that violates our predilections for difficulty and maintains some of the innocent plainness of a parable. To hear that we should understand rather than condemn, that others are primarily anxious rather than cruel, that every strength of character we admire bears with it a weakness we must forgive: these are both key laws of psychology and entirely familiar truisms of the sort that we have been taught to disdain. Yet despite their so-called obviousness, simple-sounding emotional dynamics are aggressively capable of ruining extended periods of our lives. Three decades devoted to the unhappy pursuit of wealth and status may turn out to be driven by nothing more or less than a forgotten desire to secure the attention of a distracted parent more interested in an older sibling. The failure of a fifteen-year relationship, a thousand nights of pain and fury, might have originated in an avoidant pattern of attachment established in one's fourteenth month on earth. Emotional life is never done with showing us how much we might have to suffer for 'small' things.

We should gracefully acknowledge how much of what nourishes and guides us, how much of what we should be hearing is astonishingly, almost humiliatingly, simple in structure. We should not compound our problems by insisting on elevated degrees of mystery, or allow our emotional intelligence to be clouded by a murkiness that would be legitimate only in the advanced sciences. Our vulnerability to basic psychological error is no more absurd, and no less poignant, than the fact that an adult can be killed by a well-aimed pebble or that we can die for want of a glass of water. Simplicity should never insult our intelligence; it should remind us to be nimble in our understanding of what intelligence comprises.

We need to be sophisticated enough not to reject a truth because it sounds like something we already know. We need to be mature enough to bend down and pick up governing ideas in their simplest guises. We need to remain open to vast truths that can be stated in the language of a child.

THE SCHOOL OF LIFE

There is a deliberate paradox in the term 'the school of life'. School is meant to teach us what we need to know to live and yet, as the phrase ruefully suggests, it is most often life – by which we really mean painful experience – that does the bulk of the instruction for us. The real institution called the School of Life therefore carries within it a hope and a provocation. It dares to believe that we might learn, in good time and systematically, what we might otherwise acquire only through many decades of stumbling. And it gently criticizes the current way we set about equipping ourselves with the skills we need to thrive.

We aren't ever done with the odd business of becoming that most extraordinary and prized of things, an emotionally mature person – or, to put it a simpler way, an almost grown-up adult. In an ideal society, it would be not only children who were known to need an education. All adults would recognize that they inevitably required continuing education of an emotional kind and would remain active followers of a psychological curriculum. Schools devoted to emotional intelligence would be open for everyone, so that children would feel that they were participating in the early stages of a lifelong process. Some classes – about anger or sulking, blame or consideration – would have seven-year-olds learning alongside fifty-five-year-olds, the two cohorts having been found to have equivalent maturities in a given area. In such a society, the phrase 'I've finished school' would sound extremely strange.

We have collectively left to chance some of what it is most important to know; we have denied ourselves the opportunity to systematically transmit wisdom – reserving our belief in education to technical and managerial skills. The School of Life is a modest attempt to try to spare us a bit of time.

I : Self

1 *Strangers to Ourselves*

THE DIFFICULTY OF SELF-KNOWLEDGE

One of our greatest challenges is to understand the peculiar content of own minds. We may look like the ultimate owners of our skulls but we remain practical strangers to too much of what unfolds within them. A casual acquaintance may, in a few minutes of conversation, deduce more about our psyches than we have been able to determine across many decades. We are frequently the very last people to know what is at work within 'us'.

We suffer because there is no easy route to introspection. We cannot open a hatch and locate 'ourselves'. We are not a fixed destination, but an eternally mobile, boundless, unfocused, vaporous spectre whose full nature can only be retrospectively deduced from painfully recollected glimpses and opaque hints. There is no time or vantage point from which to securely decode our archives of experience. There is too much data entering us at every moment for us to easily sift and arrange our sensations with the care and logic they deserve.

Symptoms of our self-ignorance abound. We are irritable or sad, guilty or furious, without any reliable sense of the origins of our discord. We destroy a relationship that might have been workable under a compulsion we cannot account for. We fail to know our professional talents in time. We pass too many of our days under mysterious clouds of despair or beset by waves of persecution.

We pay a very high price for our self-ignorance. Feelings and desires that haven't been examined linger and distribute their energy randomly across our lives. Ambition that doesn't know itself re-emerges as panic; envy transforms itself into bitterness; anger turns into rage; sadness into depression. Disavowed material buckles and strains the system. We develop pernicious tics: a facial twitch, impotence, a compulsion, an unbudgeable sadness. Much of what destroys our lives can be attributed to emotions that our conscious selves haven't found a way to understand or to address in time.

It is logical that Socrates should have boiled down the entire wisdom of philosophy to one simple command: 'Know yourself.'

EMOTIONAL SCEPTICISM

Yet he also added, 'I am wise not because I know, but because I know I don't know.' The eventual result of a quest for self-knowledge might be presumed to be a confident understanding of the corridors of the mind. But a truly successful outcome might involve something rather different. The more closely we introspect, the more we start to appreciate the range of tricks our minds play on us – and therefore the more we appreciate the extent to which we will continually misjudge situations and the feelings they provoke. A successful search for self-knowledge may furnish us not with a set of newly mined rock-solid certainties, but with an admission of how little we do – and ever can – properly know ourselves.

This critical attitude towards our own thought processes can be called emotional scepticism. It was the ancient Greek philosophical sceptics (from the Greek word *skepsis*, meaning 'questioning' or 'examination') who first concentrated on showing up how flawed and unreliable our minds can be, in both large and small ways. The average pig is – as Pyrrho, the founder of the sceptical movement, liked to point out – cleverer, sharper, kinder and distinctly happier than its human counterpart.

The sceptics emphasized a range of cognitive malfunctions and blind spots. We are notoriously bad judges of distances, wildly misreading how far away a distant island or mountain might be, and easily fooled in our estimations by small changes of light and moisture in the air. Our sense of time is highly inaccurate, influenced chiefly by the novelty or familiarity of what happens rather than by strict chronological duration. We desire excessively and inaccurately. Our sexual drives wreak havoc on our sense of priorities. Our whole assessment of the world can be transformed according to how much water we have drunk or sleep we have had. The instrument through which we interpret reality, our 1,260 or so cubic centimetres of brain matter, has a treacherous proclivity for throwing out faulty readings.

For the sceptics, understanding that we may be repeatedly hoodwinked by our own minds is the start of the only kind of intelligence of which we are ever capable; just as we are never as foolish as when we fail to suspect we might be so.

We take the first steps towards maturity by determining some of the ways in which our emotional minds deny, lie, evade, forget and obsess, steering us towards goals that won't deliver the satisfaction of which we're initially convinced. A readiness to mitigate the worst of our everyday foolishness contributes to the highest kind of emotional intelligence of which we may ever be capable.

THE PAST IN THE PRESENT

One of the characteristic possessions of all European nobles for many centuries was an elaborate depiction of their family tree, showing lineage down the generations. The person at the foot of the tree would see themselves as the product of, and heir to, all who had come before them.

Aristocratic genealogy may seem a quaint preoccupation, but the idea behind it rests upon a universally relevant concern: irrespective of the status details of our families, each of us is the recipient of a large and complex emotional inheritance that is decisive in determining who we are and how we will behave. Furthermore, and at huge cost, we mostly lack any real sense of what this powerful inheritance might be doing to our judgement.

The presence of the unknown past colours, and sharply distorts, all our responses to the present. We interpret what is happening in the here and now – what a friend meant by their silence, what we are responsible for, how much permission we need – through expectations fostered in long years whose real nature we have forgotten.

Psychology has built up a humbling array of tests that show up the presence of the unknown past and, with it, a tendency to impose – or, as the technical term puts it, to 'transfer' – old assumptions and patterns of thinking on to contemporary reality. The best known of such tests, devised in the 1920s by the Swiss psychiatrist Hermann Rorschach, presents us with groups of ambiguous images generated by spilt ink, upon which we're asked to reflect without inhibition, expressing freely what we feel of their atmosphere and identity.

Naturally, Rorschach's images have no predetermined meaning; they aren't about anything in particular, but are suggestive in a vast array of directions, so that the atmospheres we see in them depend upon what our pasts most readily predispose us to feel. To an individual who inherited from their parents a kindly and forgiving conscience, the image shown here might be viewed as a sweet mask, with eyes, floppy ears, a covering for the mouth and wide flaps extending from the cheeks. Another, hounded across childhood by a domineering father, could equally readily view it as a powerful figure seen from below, with splayed feet, thick legs, heavy shoulders and a head bent forward as if poised for attack.

With similar intent, a few years later, the psychologist Henry Murray and Christiana Morgan, a lay psychoanalyst, created a set of drawings that presented people in deliberately indeterminate situations and moods. In one example, two figures are positioned close to each other, their faces open to a host of interpretations. 'It's perhaps a mother and daughter, mourning together for a shared loss,' one respondent who has had a close relationship with a bereaved

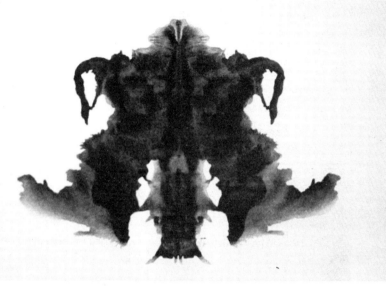

Scary dad or cute bunny? Hermann Rorschach, inkblot test, 1932.

Catching our own past in our interpretations of ambiguous images:
Henry Murray, *Thematic Apperception Test*, 1943.

parent might say. Or another, bearing the burden of a punitive past, might assert, 'It's a jealous old crone in the process of undermining a talented young employee who has failed at an important task.' A third, wrestling with a legacy of censured homosexuality, might venture, 'I feel something unholy is going on out of the frame: the older woman knows a sexual secret about the younger person, a highly effeminate man, who is embarrassed but perhaps also somehow turned on . . .'

Yet one thing is certain: the picture doesn't show any of these things. The elaboration is coming from the person who looks at it, and the way they elaborate, the kind of story they tell, necessarily reveals far more about their emotional inheritance than it ever does about the image itself.

Further in this vein, from the 1940s, the American psychologist Saul Rosenzweig devised tests that tease out our inherited ways of dealing with humiliation. His 'Picture-Frustration Study' (1948 for children, 1978 for adults) shows a range of situations to which our psychological histories will give us very different templates of responses.

One kind of person, the bearer of a solid emotional inheritance, will tend to be resilient when someone hurts or behaves badly towards them. It won't be a catastrophe, just a few unpleasant moments. But such a verdict would feel entirely alien to someone who has been bequeathed a backdrop of shame and self-contempt, always looking to reconfirm itself in contemporary incidents.

Maturity involves accepting with good grace that we are all – like marionettes – manipulated by the past. And, when we can manage it, it may also require that we develop our capacity to judge and act in the ambiguous here and now with somewhat greater fairness and neutrality.

Saul Rosenzweig, *Picture-Frustration Study*, 1978.

2 *Knowing the Past*

PRIMAL WOUNDS

Almost universally, without anyone intending this to happen, somewhere in our childhood our trajectory towards emotional maturity can be counted upon to have been impeded. Even if we were sensitively cared for and lovingly handled, even if parental figures approached their tasks with the highest care and commitment, we can be counted upon not to have passed through our young years without sustaining some form of deep psychological injury – what we can term a set of 'primal wounds'.

Childhood opens us up to emotional damage in part because, unlike all other living things, *Homo sapiens* is fated to endure an inordinately long and structurally claustrophobic pupillage. A foal is standing up thirty minutes after it is born. A human will, by the age of eighteen, have spent around 25,000 hours in the company of its parents. A female grouper will unsentimentally dump up to 100 million eggs a year in the sandy banks off the north Atlantic seaboard, then swim away without bothering to see a single one of her offspring again. Even the blue whale, the largest animal on the planet, is sexually mature and independent by the age of five.

But, for our part, we dither and linger. It can be a year till we take our first steps and two before we can speak in a whole sentence. It is close to two decades before we are categorized as adults. And in the meantime, we are at the mercy of that highly peculiar and distorting institution we call home and its even more distinctive overseers, our parents.

Across the long summers and winters of childhood, we are

intimately shaped by the ways of the big people around us. We come to know their favourite expressions, their habits, how they respond to a delay, the way they address us when they're cross. We know the atmosphere of home on a bright July morning and in the afternoon downpours of mid-April. We memorize the textures of the carpets and the smells of the clothes cupboards. As adults, we can still recall the taste of a particular biscuit we liked after school and know intimately the tiny distinctive sounds a mother or father will make as they concentrate on something in the newspaper. We can return to our original home for a holiday when we are parents ourselves and find, despite our car, our responsibilities and our lined faces, that we are eight once more.

During our elongated gestation, we are at first, in a physical sense, completely at the mercy of our caregivers. We are so frail, we could be tripped up by a twig; the family cat is a tiger. We need help crossing the road, putting on our coat, writing our name.

But our vulnerability is as much emotional. We can't begin to understand our strange circumstances: who we are, where our feelings come from, why we're sad or furious, how our parents fit into the wider scheme and behave as they do. We necessarily take what the big people around us say as an inviolable truth; we can't help but exaggerate our parents' role on the planet. We are condemned to be enmeshed in their attitudes, ambitions, fears and inclinations. Our upbringing is fundamentally always particular and peculiar.

We can brush so little of it off. We are without a skin. If a parent shouts at us, the foundations of the earth tremble. We can't tell that some of the harsh words weren't perhaps entirely meant, or had their origins in a tricky day at work, or were the reverberations of the adult's own childhood. It simply feels as if an all-powerful, all-knowing giant has decided, for certain good (if as yet unknown) reasons that we are to be annihilated.

Nor can we understand, when a parent goes away for the weekend, or relocates to another country, that they haven't left us because we did something wrong or because we are unworthy of their love but because even adults aren't always in control of their destinies.

If parents are in the kitchen raising their voices, it can seem as though these two people must hate one another inordinately. To children, an overheard altercation (there was a slammed door and several swear words) may feel catastrophic, as though everything safe is about to disintegrate imminently. There is no evidence anywhere in the child's grasp that arguments are a normal part of relationships; and that a couple may be entirely committed to a lifelong union and at the same time forcefully express a wish that the other might go to hell.

Children are equally helpless before the distinctive theories of the parents. They can't understand that an insistence that they do not mix with another family from school, or that they follow particular dress codes or hate a given political party or worry about dirt or arrive no less than four hours early for a flight, represents a very partial perspective on human priorities and reality.

Children can't go elsewhere. They have no extended social network. Even when things are going right, childhood is a gentle open prison.

As a result of the peculiarities of our early years, we lose balance. Things within us start to develop in wayward directions. We may find that we can't trust easily, or need to keep any sign of dirt at bay, or get unusually scared around people who raise their voices. No one needs to do anything particularly shocking, illegal, sinister or wicked to us for serious distortions to unfold. The causes of our primal wounds are rarely outwardly dramatic but their effects are rarely insignificant. Such is the fragile base of childhood that nothing outwardly appalling needs to have happened to us for us to wind up inwardly profoundly scrambled.

We know the point well enough from tragedy. In the tragic tales of the ancient Greeks, it is not enormous errors and slips that unleash drama but the tiniest, most innocent of mistakes. From seemingly minor starting points, terrible consequences unfurl. Our emotional lives are similarly tragic in structure. Everyone around us may have been trying to do their best and yet we end up now, as adults, nursing certain major hurts which ensure that we are so much less than we might be.

IMBALANCES

The imbalances go in endless directions. We are too timid or too assertive; too rigid or too accommodating; too focused on material success or excessively lackadaisical. We are obsessively eager around sex or painfully wary and nervous in the face of our own erotic impulses. We are dreamily naive or sourly down to earth. We recoil from risk or embrace it recklessly. We emerge into adult life determined never to rely on anyone or are desperate for another to complete us. We are overly intellectual or unduly resistant to ideas. The encyclopedia of emotional imbalances is a volume without end.

Yet because we are reluctant historians of our emotional pasts, we too easily take our temperament as our destiny. We believe we simply are, in and of ourselves, people who micromanage or can't get much pleasure out of sex, scream a lot when someone contradicts us or run away from lovers who are too kind to us. It may not be easy, but it is not alterable or up for enquiry.

The truth is likely to be more hopeful – though, in the short term, a great deal more uncomfortable. We are a certain way because we were knocked off a more fulfilling trajectory years ago. In the face of a viciously competitive parent, we took refuge in underachievement. Having lived around a parent disgusted by the body, sex became frightening. Surrounded by material unreliability, we had to overachieve in relation to money and social prestige. Hurt by a dismissive parent, we fell into patterns of emotional avoidance. A volatile parent pushed us towards our present meekness. Early overprotectiveness inspired timidity and, around any complex situation, panic. A continually busy, inattentive parent was the catalyst for a personality marked by exhausting attention-seeking behaviour.

There is always a logic and there is always a history.

We can tell that our imbalances date from the past because they reflect the ways of thinking and instincts of the children we once were. Our way of being unbalanced tends towards a fundamental immaturity, bearing the marks of what was once a young person's attempt to grapple with something utterly beyond their capacities.

For example, when they suffer at the hands of an adult, children almost invariably take what happens *to* them as a reflection of something that must be very wrong *with* them. If someone humiliates, ignores or hurts them, it must – so it seems – be because they are, in and of themselves, imbecilic, repugnant and worth neglecting. It can take many years, and a lot of patient inner exploration, to reach an initially far less plausible conclusion: that the hurt was essentially undeserved and that there were inevitably a lot of other things going on, offstage, in the raging adult's interior life, for which the child was entirely blameless.

Similarly, because children cannot easily leave an offending situation, they are prey to powerful, limitless longings to fix the broken person they so completely depend on. It becomes, in the infantile imagination, the child's responsibility to mend the anger, addiction or sadness of the grown-up they adore. It may be the work of decades to develop a wiser power to feel sad about, rather than eternally responsible for, those we love but cannot change. And perhaps, at points, in the interests of self-preservation, to move on.

Communication patterns are beset by comparable childhood legacies. When something is very wrong, children have no innate capacity to explain its cause. They lack the confidence, poise and verbal dexterity to get their points across with the calm and authority required. They tend to experience dramatic overreactions instead: insisting, nagging, exploding, screaming. Or else excessive under-reactions: sulking, sullen silence, avoidance. We may be well into middle age before we can shed our first impulses to explode at or flee from those who misunderstand our needs, and more carefully and serenely strive to explain them instead.

It is another feature of the emotional wounds of childhood that they tend to provoke what are in effect large-scale generalizations. Our wounds may have occurred in highly individual contexts: with one particular adult who hit his particular partner late at night in one particular terraced house in one town near the border. Or the wound may have been caused by one specific parent who responded with intense contempt after a specific job loss in one specific factory. But these events give rise to expectations of other people and life more broadly. We grow to expect that everyone will resort to violence, that every partner may turn on us and every money problem will unleash disaster. The character traits and mentalities that were formed in response to one or two central actors of childhood become our habitual templates for interpreting pretty much anyone. The always jokey and slightly manic way of being that we evolved so as to keep a depressed, listless mother engaged becomes our second nature. Even when she is long gone, we remain people who need to shine at every meeting, who require a partner to be continually focused on us and who cannot listen to negative or dispiriting information of any kind. We are living the wide-open present through the narrow drama of the past.

It is a complicating factor that our imbalances don't cleanly reveal their origins, either to our own minds or, consequently, to the world at large. We aren't really sure why we run away as we do, or are so often angry, or have a proud, haughty air, or break every deadline, or cling excessively to people we love. And because the sources of our imbalances escape us, we miss out on important sources of possible sympathy. We are judged on the behaviours that our wounds inspire, rather than on the wounds themselves. The damage may have begun with a feeling of invisibility, a poignant enough phenomenon, but to the world that doesn't care to know more, we now just come across as somewhat sickening in our search for attention. Maybe the damage began with a truly unwarranted let-down, but now we simply appear unreasonable and controlling. Perhaps it started with a bullying, competitive father; now it seems as if we are just spineless.

We make our lives tougher than they should be because we insist on thinking of people, ourselves and others, as inept and mean rather than, as is almost invariably the case, primarily the victims of what we have all in some ways travelled through: an immensely tricky early history.

AMNESIA AND DENIAL

We can recall the basic facts and a few incidents of course, but in terms of grasping in detail, with visceral emotion, how our present is influenced by the personalities and circumstances of our early years, we're often novices, or simply resolutely sceptical about the point of a close look backwards. It wouldn't – in many cases – be too strong to speak of willed amnesia.

The urge to forget the primal wounds is not hard to understand. It is deeply implausible, but also humiliating, to imagine that events from so long ago might be influencing the bulk of our feelings and actions in the here and now. Blunt and cliché-sounding psychological determinism negates our hopes for a life of dignified adult liberty. It seems crushing and, from certain perspectives, plain daft to suppose that our personalities might remain forged by incidents that unfolded before our fifth birthday.

Towards the past, we tend to adopt a sentimental attitude which is far more attentive to the occasional endearing exception than the more challenging norm. Family photos, almost always snapped at the happier junctures, guide the process. There is much more likely to be an image of one's mother by the pool, smiling with the expression of a giddy young girl, than of her slamming the veranda door in a rage at the misery of conjugal life; there will be a shot of one's father genially performing a card trick, but no visual record of his long, brutal mealtime silences. A lot of editing goes on, encouraged by all sides.

With age, we naturally look at the world through the eyes of an adult rather than going to the trouble of recovering the distinctive and peculiar perspective of the child. To any grown-up, it is immediately obvious that a three-year-old having a tantrum in a hotel restaurant is irritating, theatrical and bad-mannered. But that is chiefly because we lack the encouragement or empathetic energy to try to recreate the strange inner world of a small person in which she might feel monumentally tired and bewildered, fearful that an unfamiliar dish was going to be forced on her, or lonely and humiliated by being the smallest person in a large and lugubrious dining room, far away from Lanky, the stuffed rabbit left by mistake on the floor in the room upstairs.

Or when an adult locks a kitchen door to ensure silence during an hour-long business call, it is far from normal to picture the scene from the viewpoint of the very young child on the other side, for whom this endless exclusion may seem proof that everything good and kind has mysteriously suddenly died. It becomes difficult for us to keep in mind how much in all our characters was marked by what are (from a grown-up perspective) almost laughably minor yet hugely potent emotions.

But it's not simply that we've idly forgotten the past. We could in principle re-enter the emotional spaces we once inhabited. It is for deeper reasons that we push the memories aside and actively restrict reflection on our histories.

We keep away from ourselves because so much of what we could discover threatens to be agony. We might discover that we were, in the background, deeply furious with, and resentful about, certain people we were meant only to love. We might discover how much ground there was to feel inadequate and guilty on account of the many errors and misjudgements we have made. We might recognize how much was compromised and needed to be changed about our relationships and careers.

SELF-DECEPTION

We don't only have a lot to hide, we are liars of genius. It is part of the human tragedy that we are natural self-deceivers. Our techniques are multiple and close to invisible:

- We get addicted. Not necessarily to heroin or whisky, but to everyday innocuous activities that attract no alarm or suspicion. We are hooked on checking the news or tidying the house, exercising or taking on fresh projects at work. It can look to the world as if we are just being productive, but the clue to our compulsiveness lies in our motives. We are checking the news to keep the news from ourselves at bay; we are working on a project as an alternative to working on our psyches. What properly indicates addiction is not *what* someone is doing, but their way of doing it, and in particular their desire to avoid any encounter with certain sides of themselves. We are addicts whenever we develop a manic reliance on something, anything, to keep our darker and more unsettling feelings at bay.

- We lie by being very cheerful. It sounds, conveniently, almost indistinguishable from happiness. But with its remorseless and insistent upbeat quality, aggressive jolliness has very little to do with true satisfaction. The person who is relentlessly jolly doesn't just want the mood to be happy; they can't tolerate that it might in any way be sad, so unexplored and potentially overwhelming are their own background feelings of disappointment and grief.

- We lie by attacking and denigrating what we love but haven't managed to get. We dismiss the people we once wanted as friends, the careers we hoped at the start one day to have, the lives we tried to emulate. We reconfigure what a desired but painfully elusive goal meant to us in the hope of not having to register its loss properly.

- We lie through a generalized cynicism, which we direct at everything and everyone so as to ward off misery about one or two things in particular. We say that all humans are terrible and every activity compromised, so that the specific causes of our pain do not attract scrutiny and shame.

- We lie by filling our minds with impressive ideas which blatantly announce our intelligence to the world but subtly ensure that we won't have much room left to rediscover long-distant feelings of ignorance or confusion upon which the development of our personalities may nevertheless rest.

   We write dense books on the role of government bonds in the Napoleonic Wars or publish extensively on Chaucer's influence on the mid-nineteenth-century Japanese novel. We secure degrees from institutes of advanced study or positions on editorial boards of scientific journals. Our minds are crammed with arcane data. We can wittily inform a dining table of guests who wrote the *Enchiridion* (Epictetus) or describe the life and times of Dōgen (the founder of Zen Buddhism). But we don't remember very much at all about how life was long ago, back in the old house, when our father left, our mother stopped smiling and our trust broke in pieces.

   We deploy knowledge and ideas that carry indubitable prestige to stand guard against the emergence of more humble but essential knowledge from our emotional past. We bury our personal stories beneath an avalanche of expertise. The possibility of a deeply consequential intimate enquiry is deliberately left to seem feeble and superfluous next to the grander task of addressing a conference on the political strategies of Dona Maria I or the life cycle of the Indonesian octopus.

We lean on the glamour of being learned to limit all that we might really need to learn about.

■ We lie by pretending that we are simpler than we actually are and that too much psychology might be nonsense. We lean on a version of robust common sense to ward off intimations of our own awkward complexity. We imply that not thinking very much is, at base, evidence of a superior kind of intelligence.

In company, we deploy bluff strategies of ridicule against more complex accounts of human nature. We sideline avenues of personal investigation as unduly fancy or weird, implying that to lift the lid on inner life could never be fruitful or entirely respectable. We use the practical mood of Monday morning 9 a.m. to ward off the complex insights of 3.a.m. the previous night, when the entire fabric of our existence came into question. Deploying an attitude of vigorous common sense, we strive to make our moments of radical disquiet seem like aberrations, rather than the central occasions of insight they might actually be.

We appeal to the understandable longing that our personalities be non-tragic, simple and easily comprehended, so as to reject the stranger but more useful facts of our real, intricate selves.

A defence of emotional honesty has nothing to do with high-minded morality. It is ultimately cautionary and egoistic. We need to tell ourselves a little more of the truth because we pay too high a price for our concealments. We cut ourselves off from possibilities of growth. We shut out large portions of our minds and end up uncreative, tetchy and defensive, while others around us have to suffer our irritability, gloom, manufactured cheerfulness or defensive rationalizations.

THE EMOTIONALLY HEALTHY CHILDHOOD

We can sometimes be so modest about our power to know what is good for others or ourselves that we forget it might be possible to hazard a few generalizations about what constitutes an emotionally healthy childhood. It can't be pure idiosyncrasy or good luck; there are distinct themes and goals to identify. With a map of optimal development in mind, we could more clearly appreciate where dislocation begins, what we have to be grateful for and what there is to regret. At a collective level, we would have a greater sense of what might need to be done to generate a more emotionally privileged, and therefore slightly saner, world.

With that in mind, we could expect some or all of the following to occur:

■ In an emotionally healthy childhood, someone will put themselves profoundly at our service. If as adults we have even a measure of mental health, it is almost certainly because, when we were helpless infants, there was a person (to whom we essentially owe our lives) who pushed their needs to one side for a time in order to focus wholly on ours. They interpreted what we could not quite say, they guessed what might be ailing us, they settled and consoled us. They kept the chaos and noise at bay and cut the world up into manageable pieces for us.

They did not, all the while, ask that we thank them, understand them or show them sympathy. They didn't demand that we enquire how their days went or how they were sleeping at night (they weren't much). They treated us like royalty, so that we would later on be able to submit to the rigours and humiliations of an ordinary life. This temporarily one-sided relationship guaranteed our eventual ability to form a two-sided kind.

We may think of egoists as people who have grown sick from too much love, but in fact the opposite is the case: an egoist is someone who has not yet had their fill. Self-centredness has to have a clear run in the early years if it isn't to haunt and ruin the later ones. The so-called narcissist is simply a benighted soul who has not had a chance to be inordinately and unreasonably admired and cared for at the start.

■ In an emotionally healthy childhood, we're given the benefit of the doubt. We are assessed by what we might one day be, not by exactly what we are right now. Someone is on hand to put the best possible spin on our behaviour. Someone is kind.

A harsh judge might, for example, say that we were 'attention-seeking'. Our caregiver imagines that we just stand in need of some encouraging words. We might have acted rather meanly. Our caregiver adds that we must, in the background, have been feeling threatened. It looked as if we were negligent; the caregiver remembers that tiredness might account for the lion's share of the explanation.

Our carer constantly searches beneath the surface for a more sympathetic set of reasons. They help us to be on our own side, to like ourselves and therefore, eventually, not to be too defensive about our own flaws, the existence of which we grow strong enough to accept.

■ In an emotionally healthy childhood, the relationship with our caregiver is steady, consistent and long-term. We trust that they will be there tomorrow and the day after. They are boringly predictable. As a result, we are able to believe that what has gone well once can go well again and to let such an expectation govern our pick of available adult partners. We aren't mesmerized by people who are offhand and frustrating; we don't relish being punished. We can locate candidates who are kind and nurturing – and don't judge them as weak or deficient for being so.

And if trouble strikes with our kindly partners, we don't panic or turn away. We can confidently set about trying to repair a love we know we deserve.

- In an emotionally healthy childhood, we aren't always required to be wholly good boys or girls. We are allowed to get furious and sometimes a bit revolting – at certain points to say 'absolutely not' and 'because I feel like it'. The adults know their own flaws and do not expect a child to be fundamentally better than they are. We do not have to comply at every turn to be tolerated. We can let others in on our shadow sides.

  This period of freedom prepares us to submit one day to the demands of society without having to rebel in self-defeating ways (rebels being, at heart, people who have had to obey too much too early). We can knuckle down and toe the line when it's in our long-term interest to do so. At the same time, we're not overly cowed or indiscriminately obedient either. We find a sound middle ground between slavish compliance on the one hand and self-destructive defiance on the other.

- In an emotionally healthy childhood, our carer isn't jealous of or competitive with us. They can allow themselves to be overtaken and superseded. They have had their moment in the limelight, or are having it elsewhere beyond the family. They can be proud rather than rivalrous of the achievements of the child.

  Equally, the good carer isn't overly ambitious on the child's behalf. They want them to do well, but for their own sake and in their own way. There is no particular script the child has to follow in order to be loved; the child isn't required to support the carer's frayed self-belief or burnish their self-image in the eyes of strangers.

- In an emotionally healthy childhood, the child learns that things which break can be fixed. Plans can go awry, but new ones can be made. You can fall over and start anew. The carer models how to plough on and remain hopeful. A voice of resilience, originally external, becomes the way the child learns to speak to themselves. There are alternatives to panic.

In the seventeenth century, the Dutch developed a tradition of painting that depicted ships in violent storms. These works, which hung in private homes and in municipal buildings around the Dutch Republic, had an explicitly therapeutic purpose: they were delivering a moral to their viewers, who lived in a nation critically dependent on maritime trade, about confidence in seafaring and life more broadly. Ludolf Bakhuysen painted *Warships in a Heavy Storm* around 1695. The scene looks chaotic in the extreme: how could the ships survive? But they were designed for just such situations. Their hulls had been minutely adapted through long experience to withstand the tempests of the northern oceans. The crews practised again and again the manoeuvres that could keep their vessels safe. They knew about taking down sails at speed and ensuring that the wind would not shred the mast. They understood about shifting cargo in the hull, tacking to the left and then abruptly to the right, and pumping out water from the inner chambers. They knew to remain coolly scientific in responding to the storm's wilful, frantic motions. The picture pays homage to decades of planning and experience. One can imagine the older sailors on the ship saying to a terrified novice, with a laugh, that just last year, off the coast of Jutland, there was an even bigger storm – and slapping him on the back with paternal playfulness as the youth was sick overboard. Bakhuysen wanted us to feel proud of humanity's resilience in the face of apparently dreadful challenges. His painting implies that we can all cope far better than we think; that what appears immensely threatening may be highly survivable. All this the caregiver teaches, usually without reference to ships and Dutch art – just by their way of keeping on.

Ludolf Bakhuysen, *Warships in a Heavy Storm*, c. 1695.

- Importantly, in an emotionally healthy childhood plenty goes wrong. No one has staked their reputation on rendering the whole story perfect. The carer does not see it as their role to remove every frustration. They intuit that a lot of good comes from having the right, manageable kind of friction, through which the child develops their own resources and individuality. In contact with bearable disappointment, the child is prompted to create their own internal world, in which they can dream, hatch fresh plans and build up their own resources.

- In an emotionally healthy childhood, the child can see that the good carer isn't either entirely good or wholly bad and so isn't worthy of either idealization or denigration. The child accepts the faults and virtues of the carer with melancholy maturity and gratitude – and in doing so, by extension, becomes ready to accept that everyone they like will be a mixture of the positive and the negative. They won't as adults fall deeply in love and then grow furious at the first moment of let-down. They will have a realistic sense of what can be expected of life alongside another flawed, good enough human.

Soberingly, despite all our advances in technology and material resources, we are not much more advanced in the art of delivering emotionally healthy childhoods than generations before us. The number of breakdowns, inauthentic lives and broken souls shows no marked signs of decline.

We are failing to offer one another tolerable childhoods not because we are sinful or indifferent, but because we still have so far to go before we know how to master that improbably complicated subject: love.

THE MARKERS OF EMOTIONAL HEALTH

One way to start assessing how badly we have been knocked by our early years – and where we might therefore need to direct most of our repair work and attention – is to identify a range of markers of emotional health and imagine how we fare in relation to them. At least four central ones suggest themselves.

Self-Love

Self-love is the quality that determines how much we can be friends with ourselves and, day to day, remain on our own side.

When we meet a stranger who has things we don't, how quickly do we feel ourselves pitiful, and how long can we remain assured by the decency of what we have and are? When another person frustrates or humiliates us, can we let the insult go, able to perceive the senseless malice beneath the attack, or are we left brooding and devastated, implicitly identifying with the verdict of our enemies? How much can the disapproval or neglect of public opinion be off-set by the memory of the steady attention of significant people in the past?

In relationships, do we have enough self-love to leave an abusive union? Or are we so down on ourselves that we carry an implicit belief that harm is all we deserve? In a different vein, how good are we at apologizing to a lover for things that may be our fault? How rigidly self-righteous do we need to be? Can we dare to admit mistakes or does an admission of guilt or error bring us too close to our background sense of nullity?

In the bedroom, how clean and natural or alternatively disgusting and unacceptable do our desires feel? Might they be a little odd, but not for that matter bad or dark, since they emanate from within us and we are not wretches?

At work, do we have a reasonable, well-grounded sense of our worth and so feel able to ask for (and properly expect to get) the rewards we are due? Can we resist the need to please others indiscriminately? Are we sufficiently aware of our genuine contribution to be able to say no when we need to?

Candour

Candour determines the extent to which difficult ideas and troubling facts can be consciously admitted into the mind, soberly explored and accepted without denial. How much can we admit to ourselves about who we are even if, or especially when, the matter is not especially pleasant? How much do we need to insist on our own normality and wholehearted sanity? Can we explore our own minds, and look into their darker and more troubled corners, without flinching overly? Can we admit to folly, envy, sadness and confusion?

Around others, how ready are we to learn? Do we always need to take a criticism of one part of us as an attack on everything about us? How ready are we to listen when valuable lessons come in painful guises?

Communication

Can we patiently and reasonably put our disappointments into words that, more or less, enable others to see our point? Or do we internalize pain, act it out symbolically or discharge it with counter-productive rage?

When other people upset us, do we feel we have the right to communicate or must we slam doors and fall silent? When the desired response isn't forthcoming, do we ask others to guess what we have been too angrily panicked to spell out? Or can we have a plausible second go and take seriously the thought that others are not merely wilfully misunderstanding us? Do we have the inner resources to teach rather than insist?

Trust

How risky is the world? How readily might we survive a challenge in the form of a speech we must give, a romantic rejection, a bout of financial trouble, a journey to another country or a common cold?

How close are we, at any time, to catastrophe? Of what material do we feel we are made?

Will new acquaintances like or wound us? If we are a touch assertive, will they take it or collapse? Will unfamiliar situations end in a debacle? Around love, how tightly do we need to cling? If they are distant for a while, will they return? How controlling do we need to be? Can we approach an interesting-looking stranger? Or move on from an unsatisfying one?

Do we, overall, feel the world to be wide, safe and reasonable enough for us to have a legitimate shot at a measure of contentment – or must we settle, resentfully, for inauthenticity and misunderstanding?

It isn't our fault or, in a sense, anyone else's that many of these questions are so hard to answer in the affirmative. But, by entertaining them, we are at least starting to know what kind of shape our wounds have and so what kind of bandages might be most urgently required.

3 *Therapies*

PSYCHOTHERAPY

In the arena of self-knowledge, psychotherapy may be the single most useful intervention of the last 200 years. It is a tool and, like all tools, it finds its purpose in helping us to overcome an inborn weakness and to extend our capacities beyond those originally gifted to us by nature. It is, in this sense, not metaphysically different from a bucket, which remedies the problem of trying to hold water in our palms, or a knife, which makes up for the bluntness of our teeth.

Therapy is an invention devised to correct the substantial difficulties we face understanding ourselves, trusting others, communicating successfully, honouring our potential and feeling adequately serene, confident, authentic, direct and unashamed.

For such an important invention, psychotherapy is low on overt signs of innovation. Technically speaking, it requires only a comfortable room free of any interruptions, fifty minutes, possibly twice a week for a year or so and two chairs. But at the level of training, the psychotherapist needs to undertake a period of extensive education in the workings of our minds which – in the more responsible jurisdictions – has some of the rigour, intellectual ambition and periods of hands-on experience demanded by the acquisition of a pilot's licence.

To deliver on its promises, psychotherapy relies on at least eight distinct moves.

Witnessing

Most of what we are remains a secret to the world, because we are aware of how much of it flouts the laws of decency and sobriety we would like to live by. We know that we would not last long in society if a stream of our uncensored inner data ever leaked out of our minds.

A lot of what is inside us can seem daft: how we felt a strange impulse to burst into tears when reading a children's book (about an elephant befriending a baby sparrow); how we sometimes imagine acquiring the power to go back in time and correct the missed opportunities of adolescence. Some of it is, from a harsh angle, distinctly pathetic: how worried we are about asking where the bathroom is; how envious we are of a close acquaintance; how much we worry about our hair. A significant part is alarming and quasi-illegal: our fantasies about a work colleague and a family member; our plans for what we'd ideally do to an enemy.

In response to our isolation, we are often told about the importance of friends. But we know that the tacit contract of any friendship is that we will not bother the incumbent with more than a fraction of our madness. A lover is another solution, but it is – likewise – not in the remit of even a highly patient partner to delve into, and accept, more than a modest share of what we are.

In every social interaction, we sensibly ensure that there remains a large and secure divide between what we say and what is truly going on inside our minds.

The exception can be psychotherapy. Here, remarkably, we are allowed to divulge pretty much everything we feel – and indeed, if the process is to work, should strive to do so. We don't have to impress the therapist or reassure them of our sanity. We need to tell them what is going on. There is no need to stop them thinking we are perverted, odd or terrified. We can gingerly hint at some very dark things about us and will find that our interlocutor isn't horrified or offended but, on the contrary, calmly interested. We're not – we're learning – monsters or freaks. We arrive at the opposite of loneliness.

This may be the first (and perhaps the last) human we are ever properly honest with.

Worldliness

Therapists know a lot about the unvarnished truths of human nature. They have close-up experience of the greatest traumas – incest and rape, suicide and depression – as well as the smaller pains and paradoxes: a longing provoked by a glance at a person in a library that took up the better part of twenty years, an otherwise gentle soul who broke a door, or a handsome, athletic man who can no longer perform sexually.

They know that inside every adult there remains a child who is confused, angry, hurt and longing to have their say and their reality recognized. They appreciate that this child has to get to know themselves again and will want to be heard, perhaps through tears or near-incomprehensible mutterings, which might be utterly at odds with the surface maturity and self-command normally associated with the grown-up sitting in the therapeutic chair.

Therapists know the human heart, not primarily through books, but by being courageous about exploring their own nature. They may not share our fantasies exactly, but they accept that their own are as colourful and as complex. They don't have our precise anxieties, but they know well enough the powerful and peculiar fears that hold us all hostage.

They can start to help us because they have an accurately broad grasp of what it means to be normal – which is, of course, far from what we insist on pretending it might be. They don't require us to be conventionally good or typical to shore up their fragile sense of self or reality. Their only hope is that we will be able to admit, at last, without too much defensiveness, to some of what is really going on inside us.

Kindness

They are, furthermore, and very gratifyingly, on our side. Without ill intention, most people are not quite; they are intermittently jealous, bored, vindictive, keen to prove a point or distracted by their own lives. But the therapist brings a focused, generous attention to our case. Their room is set aside from day-to-day pressures. They're sorry that we suffered. They understand that it must have been worrying, enraging or exciting. They know we didn't do it on purpose or that if we did we had our reasons. Without flattering us in a rote way, they strive to enter into our experience and to side with it. They look at reality through our eyes so that they can start to correct a legacy of shame and isolation.

At the same time, their kindness makes ours a bit less necessary. Normal life requires that we constantly weigh the impact of our words on other people. We have to consider their priorities, ask how their children are and hold their concerns in mind.

Here there is no such call. Like a parent who doesn't need a small child to reciprocate, the therapist voluntarily forgoes equality in the relationship; they won't talk of their regrets or insist on their anecdotes. They simply want to help us find what is best for us, understood on our terms. They won't have a preconceived view of how we're meant to live, just a great deal of sympathy for the complexities and the suffering we've endured already.

That said, kindness is not merely pleasant. Knowing that we have someone on our side is designed to lend us the courage to face up to experiences we normally evade. In a sufficiently calm, reassuring and interested environment, we can look at areas of vulnerability we are otherwise too burdened to tackle. We can dare to think that perhaps we were wrong or that we have been angry for long enough; that it might be best to outgrow our justifications or halt our compulsion to charm others indiscriminately.

The kindness of another gives us the security needed to probe constructively at our scared, puzzling, evasive minds.

Listening

It's one of the structural flaws of these minds that it is immensely hard for us to think deeply and coherently for any length of time. We keep losing the thread. Competing, irrelevant ideas have a habit of flitting across the mental horizon and scrambling our tentative insights. Every now and then, consciousness goes entirely blank. Left to our own devices, we quickly start to doubt the value of what we are trying to make sense of and can experience overpowering urges to check the news or eat a biscuit. And as a result, some of the topics we most need to examine – where our relationship is really going, what we might do next at work, how we should best answer a letter, what bothers us so much about the way our partner returns our hand after an attempt at a caress – founder into the mental sands, to our grave psychological cost.

What helps enormously in our attempts to know our own minds is, surprisingly, the presence of another mind. For all the glamour of the solitary seer, thinking usually happens best in tandem. It is the curiosity of someone else that gives us the confidence to remain curious about ourselves. It is the application of a light pressure from outside us that firms up the jumbled impressions within. The requirement to verbalize our intimations mobilizes our flabby reserves of concentration.

Occasionally a friend might be unusually attentive and ready to hear us out. But it isn't enough merely for them to be quiet. The highest possibilities of listening extend beyond the privilege of not being interrupted. To be really heard means being the recipient of a strategy of 'active listening'.

From the start, the therapist will use a succession of very quiet but significant prompts to help us develop and stick at the points we are circling. These suggest that there is no hurry but that someone is there, following every utterance and willing us on. At strategic points, the therapist will drop in a mission-critical and hugely benign 'do say more' or an equally powerful 'go on'. Therapists are expert at the low-key positive sound: the benevolent, nuanced 'ahh' and the potent 'mmm', two of the most significant noises in the aural repertoire of psychotherapy which together invite us to remain faithful to what we were starting to say, however peculiar or useless it might at first have seemed.

As beneficiaries of active listening, our memories and concerns don't have to fall into neat, well-formed sentences. The active listener contains and nurtures the emerging confusion. They gently take us back over ground we've covered too fast and prompt us to address a salient point we might have sidestepped; they will help us chip away at an agitating issue while continually reassuring us that what we are saying is valuable.

They're not treating us like strangely ineffective communicators; they're just immensely alive to how difficult it is for anyone to piece together what they really have on their minds.

Time

Therapy is built on the understanding that we will not be able to transmit our key experiences in one or two self-contained blocks. We live in time and have to decode ourselves at different periods. Things emerge, sometimes very slowly, over months. We can't be in all the moods we need to access on every occasion. Some weeks will find us readier than others to investigate particular memories or consider certain viewpoints. So long as we keep showing up and sharing, we'll drop enough clues to assemble – eventually – a psychological portrait of the self, like an ancient vase slowly being pieced together from fragments scattered across miles of sand.

Interpretation

The therapist's active listening is not meandering: what underpins it is an attempt to understand – for our sake – how the subterranean operations of the past are affecting the present.

We arrive in therapy with questions. We have a presenting problem which hints at, but does not fully capture, the origins of our suffering. Why, for instance, do we appear so repeatedly to fall for people who control and humiliate us? How can we be so convinced we need to leave a job and yet have remained unable to locate a more satisfying replacement for so long? Why are we paralysed by anxiety in every public context? Why do we sabotage sexual possibilities?

By their questions and their attention, their careful probing and investigative stealth, the therapist tries – harder than anyone may yet have done – to discover how our presenting problem might be related to the rest of our existence and, in particular, to the turmoils of childhood. Over many sessions, a succession of small discoveries contributes to an emerging picture of the sources of our emotional wounds and of the way in which our character evolved defences in response to them in a manner that hampers our possibilities today.

We may, for example, start to sense how a feeling of rivalry with a parent led us to retire early from workplace challenges in order to hold on to their love, as well as seeing, perhaps for the first time, that the logic of our self-sabotage no longer holds. Or we might perceive the way an attitude of aggressive cynicism, which restricts our personalities and our friendships, might have had its origins in a parent who let us down at a time when we couldn't contain our vulnerability, and thereby turned us into people who try at every juncture to disappoint themselves early and definitively rather than risk allowing the world to turn down our hopes at a time of its own choosing.

But it is no good stating any of this too starkly. An interpretation – delivered in its bare bones – will be anticlimactic and bathetic and most likely prompt resistance or aggression. For the interpretation to work its effect, we as clients need to move from merely assenting to it intellectually to having an internal experience of the emotions it refers to. We need to feel for ourselves, rather than take on trust, the poignant drama undergone by the person we once were. There is, in this setting, no point in being too clever.

An intellectual understanding of the past, though not wrong, won't by itself be effective in the sense of being able to release us from our symptoms. For this, we have to edge our way towards a far more close-up, detailed, visceral appreciation of where we have come from and what we have suffered. We need to strive for what we can call an emotional understanding of the past, as opposed to a top-down, abbreviated, intellectual one.

We will have to re-experience at a novelistic level of detail a whole set of scenes from our early life in which our problems around fathers and mothers and authority were formed. We will need to let our imaginations wander back to certain moments that have been too unbearable to keep alive in a three-dimensional form in our active memories (the mind liking, unless actively prompted, to reduce most of what we've been through to headings rather than the full story, a document which it shelves in remote locations of the inner library). We need not only to know that we had a difficult relationship with our father, but to relive the sorrow as if it were happening to us today. We need to be back in his book-lined study when we were not more than six; we need to remember the light coming in from the garden, the corduroy trousers we were wearing, the sound of our father's voice as it reached its pitch of heightened anxiety, the rage he flew into because we had not met his expectations, the tears that ran down our cheeks, the shouting that followed us as we fled out into the corridor, the feeling that we wanted to die and that everything good was destroyed. We need the novel, not the essay.

Psychotherapy knows that thinking is hugely important – but on its own, within the therapeutic process itself, it is not the key to fixing our psychological problems. It insists on a crucial difference between broadly recognizing that we were shy as a child and re-experiencing, in its full intensity, what it was like to feel cowed, ignored and in constant danger of being rebuffed or mocked; the difference between knowing, in an abstract way, that our mother wasn't much focused on us when we were little and reconnecting with the desolate feelings we had when we tried to share certain of our needs with her.

Therapy builds on the idea of a return to live feelings. It's only when we're properly in touch with our feelings that we can correct them with the help of our more mature faculties – and thereby address the real troubles of our adult lives.

Oddly (and interestingly) this means intellectual people can have a particularly tricky time in therapy. They get interested in the ideas. But they don't so easily recreate and exhibit the pains and distresses of their earlier, less sophisticated selves, though it's actually these parts of who we all are that need to be encountered, listened to and – perhaps for the first time – comforted and reassured.

A Relationship

The ongoing contact between ourselves and the therapist, the weekly sessions that may continue over months or years, contribute to the creation of something that sounds, in a professional context, distinctly odd: a relationship.

We are almost certain to have come to see a therapist in the first place because, in some way, having relationships has become beset with difficulties: maybe we try to please people at once, secure their admiration, but then feel inauthentic and inwardly numb and so pull back. Perhaps we fall in love very powerfully, but then always discover a major flaw in a partner that puts us off and makes us end the story and restart the cycle. Perhaps we are simply very lonely.

The relationship with the therapist may have little in common with the unions of ordinary life. We won't ever go shopping together or watch T V side by side in bed. But unavoidably and conveniently, we will bring to our encounters with the therapist the very tendencies that are likely to emerge in our relations with other people in our lives. Without intending this, in the therapist's office we will play out our characteristic moves: we may be seductive but then cold; or full of idealization but then manifest a strong wish to flee; we'll be preternaturally polite but full of hidden contempt. Except that now, in the presence of the therapist, our tendencies will have a chance to be witnessed, slowed down, discussed, sympathetically explored and – in their more damaging manifestations – overcome. The relationship with the therapist becomes a litmus test of our behaviour with people in general and thereby allows us, on the basis of greater self-awareness, to modify and improve, in the direction of greater kindness, trust, authenticity and joy, the way we typically relate to others.

In the therapy room, all our proclivities and habits are noticed and can be commented on – not as reproaches but as important information about our character that we deserve to become aware of. The therapist will gently point out that we're reacting as if we had been attacked, when they only asked a question; they might draw our attention to how readily we seem to want to tell them impressive things about our finances (yet they like us anyway) or how we seem to rush to agree with them when they're only trying out an idea which they themselves are not very sure of (we could dare to disagree and not upset them). They will signal where we are prone to pin to them attitudes or outlooks that they don't actually have. They may note how invested we seem to be in the idea that they are disappointed in us, or find us boring, or are revolted by our sexuality. They will with stealth point out our habit of casting people in the present in roles that must derive from the past and will search with us for the origins of these attributions, which are liable to mimic what we felt towards influential caregivers and now shape what we expect from everyone.

Through a relationship with someone who will not respond as ordinary people will, who will not shout at us, complain, say nothing or run away – in other words, with a proper grown-up – we can be helped to understand our immaturities. This may be for us the first properly healthy relationship we have had, one in which we learn to hold off from imposing our assumptions on the other and trust them enough to let them see the larger, more complex reality of who we are, without too much intervening shame or embarrassment. It becomes a model – earned in a highly unusual situation – that we can then start to apply in the more humdrum but consequential setting of daily life, with our friends and our partners. We are given some tools with which to start to have adult relationships of our own.

Inner Voices

Somewhere in our minds, removed from the day to day, there sit judges. They watch what we do, study how we perform, examine the effect we have on others, track our successes and failures – and then, eventually, they pass verdicts. These determine our levels of confidence and self-compassion, they lend us a sense of whether we are worthwhile beings or, conversely, should not really exist. The judges are in charge of our self-esteem.

The verdict of an inner judge doesn't follow an objective rule book or statute. Two individuals can end up with wildly different verdicts on the esteem they deserve even though they may have done and said much the same thing. Certain judges simply seem more predisposed than others to lend their audiences an essentially buoyant, warm, appreciative and generous view of themselves, while others encourage them to be hugely critical, disappointed and sometimes close to disgust or ready for self-destruction.

The origin of the voice of the inner judge is simple to trace: it is an internalization of the voices of people who were once outside us. We absorb the tones of contempt and indifference or charity and warmth that we will have heard across our formative years. Sometimes a voice is positive and benign, encouraging us to run those final few yards. But frequently the inner voice is not very nice at all. It is defeatist and punitive, panic-ridden and humiliating. It doesn't represent anything like our best insights or most mature capacities.

An inner voice was always an outer voice that we have – imperceptibly – made our own. We've absorbed the tone of a kind and gentle caregiver who liked to laugh indulgently at our foibles and had endearing names for us. Or else we have taken in the voice of a harassed or angry parent, never satisfied with anything we achieved and full of rage and contempt.

We take in these voices because at certain moments in the past they sounded so compelling and irresistible. The authority figures repeated their messages over and over until they got lodged in our own way of thinking and became a part of our minds.

A good internal voice is rather like (and just as important as) a genuinely decent judge: someone who can separate good from bad but who will always be merciful, fair, accurate in understanding what's going on and interested in helping us deal with our problems. It's not that we should stop judging ourselves, rather that we should learn to be better judges of ourselves.

Part of improving how we judge our lives involves learning – in a conscious, deliberate way – to speak to ourselves in a new and different tone, which means exposing ourselves to better voices. We need to hear constructive, kindly voices often enough and around tricky enough issues that they come to feel like normal and natural responses – so that, eventually, they become our own thoughts.

When things don't go as we want, we can ask ourselves what a benevolent fair judge would say, and then actively rehearse to ourselves the words of consolation they would most likely have offered (we'll tend to know immediately).

We need to become better friends to ourselves. The idea sounds odd, initially, because we naturally imagine a friend as someone else, not as a part of our own mind. But there is value in the concept because of the extent to which we know how to treat our own friends with a sympathy and imagination that we don't apply to ourselves. If a friend is in trouble our first instinct is rarely to tell them that they are fundamentally a failure. If a friend complains that their partner isn't very warm to them, we don't tell them that they are getting what they deserve. In friendship, we know instinctively how to deploy strategies of wisdom and consolation that we stubbornly refuse to apply to ourselves.

The good friend is compassionate. When we fail, as we will, they are understanding and generous around our mishaps. Our folly doesn't exclude us from the circle of their love. The good friend deftly conveys that to screw up is what humans do. The good friend brings, as a starting point, their own and humanity's vivid experience of messing up as key points of reference. They're continually telling us that though our specific case might be unique the general structure is common. People don't just sometimes fail. Everyone fails, as a rule; it's just we seldom know the details.

It is ironic – yet essentially hopeful – that we usually know quite well how to be a better friend to near strangers than to ourselves. The hopefulness lies in the fact that we already possess the relevant skills of friendship, it's just that we haven't as yet directed them to the person who probably needs them most – namely, of course, ourselves.

Part of what therapy offers us is a chance to improve how we judge ourselves and the voices we hear in our heads. It can involve learning – in a conscious, deliberate way – to speak to ourselves in the manner the therapist once spoke to us over many months. In the face of challenges, we can imaginatively enquire what the therapist would say now. And because we will have heard them for so long and over so many issues, we will know; their way of thinking will have become a part of our own thoughts.

HOW PSYCHOTHERAPY MIGHT CHANGE US

What sort of person, then, might we be after therapy, if the process goes as well as could be hoped?

Evidently, still – quite often – unhappy. People will continue to misunderstand us; we'll meet with opposition; there will be things it would be nice to have that will be out of reach; success will come to people who don't appear to deserve it and much that's good about us won't be fully appreciated by others. We'll still have to compete and submit to the judgement of others; we'll still be lonely sometimes; and therapy won't stop us having to watch the people we love pass away, and falling ill and eventually dying ourselves. Therapy can't make life better than it truly is.

But with these caveats in place, there are some low-key but in truth very substantial benefits we can expect. We'll have slightly more freedom. A key feature of the defences we build up against our primal wounds is that they are rigid and so limit our room for manoeuvre. For example, we may have very distinctive but unfortunate characters we go for in love; or we can't be touched in certain places; or we feel we have to be constantly cynical or else insistently jolly. Our sense of who we are allowed to be and what we can do is held prisoner by the shocks of the past.

But the more we understand the original challenges and the logic of our responses to them, the more we can risk deviating from whom we once felt we had to be in order to survive. Perhaps we can, after all, afford to hope; or be less afraid, or go on top, or spend some time alone, or try a new professional path.

We realize that what we had believed to be our inherent personality was really just a position we had crouched into in order to deal with a prevailing atmosphere. And having taken a measure of the true present situation, we may accept that there could, after all, be other, sufficiently safe ways for us to be.

We can be readier to explain ourselves. We had learned to be ashamed and silent. But the therapist's kindness and attention encourage us to be less disgusted by ourselves and furtive around our needs. Having once voiced our deeper fears and wishes, they become ever so slightly easier to bring up again with someone else. There may be an alternative to silence.

With a greater sense of our right to exist, we may become better able to articulate how it feels to be us. Instead of just resenting another person's criticism, we might explain why we believe they have been unjust to us. If we are upset by our partner, we don't need to accuse them of being evil and slam doors. We'll know to explain how (perhaps strangely) sensitive we are and how much reassurance we need to feel secure in their affection. Instead of trying to pretend that nothing is ever our fault, we can offer a candid explanation of one or two of our (unfortunate) limitations.

We can be more compassionate. We will inevitably, in the course of therapy, realize how much we were let down by certain people in the past. A natural response might be blame. But the eventual, mature reaction (building on an understanding of how our own flaws arose) will be to interpret others' harmful behaviour as a consequence of their own disturbance. The people who caused our primal wounds almost invariably didn't mean to do so; they were themselves hurt and struggling to endure. We can develop a sad but realistic picture of a world in which sorrows and anxieties are blindly passed down the generations. The insight isn't only true with regard to experience; holding it in mind will mean there is less to fear. Those who wounded us were not superior, impressive beings who knew our special weaknesses and justly targeted them. They were themselves highly frantic, damaged creatures trying their best to cope with the litany of private sorrows to which every life condemns us.

PHILOSOPHICAL MEDITATION

To understand ourselves, we need not only to learn of our past but also to take regular stock of what is flowing through our consciousness in the present.

In so far as there is public encouragement of the idea, it tends to be according to practices collectively referred to under the term 'meditation'. In meditation, we strive to empty consciousness of its normal medley of anxieties, hurts and excitements, and concentrate on the sensations of the immediate moment, allowing even events as apparently minor but as fundamental as the act of breathing to be noticed. In a bid for serenity and liberation, we still the agitations of what the Buddhists evocatively term our 'monkey minds'.

But there is another approach to consider, this one based not on

Eastern thought but on ideas transmitted to us via the Western tradition. In 'philosophical meditation', instead of being prompted to sidestep our worries and ambitions, we are directed to set aside time to untangle, examine and confront them.

It is a basic, distinctive quirk of our minds that few of the emotions we carry in them are properly acknowledged, understood or truly felt, that most of our affective content exists in an 'unprocessed' form within us. Philosophical meditation seeks to lend us a structure within which to sieve the confused content that muddies our stream of consciousness.

Key to the practice is regularly to turn over three large questions. The first asks what we might be anxious about right now.

We are rarely without a sizeable backlog of worries, far greater than we tend consciously to recognize. Life, properly felt, is an infinitely alarming process even in its apparently calmer stretches. We face a medley of ongoing uncertainties and threats. Even ordinary days contain concealed charges of fear and challenge: navigating through a train station, attending a meeting, being introduced to a new colleague, being handed responsibility for a task or a person, keeping control over our bodies in public settings – all contain the grounds for agitation that we are under pressure to think should not be taken seriously. We need, during our meditative sessions, to give every so-called small anxiety a chance to be heard, for what lends our worries their force is not so much that we have them but that we don't allow ourselves the time to know, interpret and contextualize them adequately. Only by being listened to in generous, almost pedantic detail will anxieties lose their hold on us. At almost any time, within our minds, a chaotic procession flows which would make little sense if recorded and transcribed: . . . *biscuits to the train why earrings deal they can't do it I have to Milo phone list do it the bathroom now I can't do, 11.20, 33 per cent it a 10.30 tomorrow with Luke why invoices separately detailed why me trees branches sleep right temples* . . . But such streams can gradually be tamed, drained, ordered and evaporated into something far less daunting and illogical. Each word can be encouraged to grow into a paragraph or page and thereby lose its hold on us. We can force ourselves to imagine what might happen if our vague, catastrophic forebodings truly came to pass. We can refuse to let our concerns covertly nag at us and look at them squarely until we are no longer cowed. We can turn a jumble of worries into that most calming, and intellectually noble, of documents: a list.

A philosophical meditation moves on to a second enquiry: what am I upset about right now? This may sound oddly presumptuous, because we frequently have no particular sense of having been upset by anything. Our self-image leans towards the well defended. But almost certainly we are somewhere being too brave for our own good. We are almost invariably carrying around with us pulses of regret, loss, envy, vulnerability and sorrow. These may not register in immediate consciousness, not because they don't exist, but because we have grown overly used to no one around us giving a damn and have dutifully taken heed, along the course of our development, to recommendations that we toughen up a little. Yet a life among others exposes us daily to small darts and pinpricks: a meeting ends abruptly, a call doesn't come, an anticipated reunion feels disappointingly distant, someone doesn't touch us when we need reassurance, news of a friend's latest project leaves us envious. We are mental athletes at shrugging such things off, but there is a cost to our stoicism. From small humiliations and slights, large blocks of resentment eventually form that render us unable to love or trust. What we call depression is in fact sadness and anger that have for too long not been paid the attention they deserve.

But during a philosophical meditation we can throw off our customary, reckless bravery and let our sadness take its natural, due shape. There may not be an immediate solution to many of our sorrows, but it helps immeasurably to know their contours. We might, as we turn over our griefs, large and small, imagine that we are sharing them with an extremely kind, patient figure who gives us the chance to evoke hurt in detail, someone with whom there is no pressure to rush, be grown up or impressive, and who allows us to admit without fear to the many curious things that have pained and diminished us in the previous hours.

The third question to consider within a philosophical meditation is: what am I ambitious and excited about right now?

A part of our mind is forever forward-thinking and hopeful, seeking to maximize opportunities and develop potential. Much of this energy registers as vague tension about new directions we might take. We could experience this inchoate restlessness when we read an article, hear of a colleague's plans or glimpse an idea about next year flit across our mental landscape as we lie in the bath or walk around a park. The excitement points indistinctly to better, more fulfilled versions of ourselves. We should allow our minds to wonder at greater length than usual about what the excitement (it could be a view, a book, a place, an insight) might want to tell us about ourselves. In a poem written in 1908, the German poet Rilke described coming across an ancient statue of the Greek god Apollo. It had had its arms knocked off at the shoulders but still manifested the intelligence and dignity of the culture that had produced it. Rilke felt an unclear excitement, and as he meditated upon and investigated his response, he concluded that the statue was sending him a message, which he announced in the final, dramatic line of his short poem, 'Archaic Torso of Apollo':

Du mußt dein Leben ändern.
[You must change your life.]

Under the unhealthy sway of German Romanticism, Rilke realized that he had developed an abstruse way of thinking and expressing himself. Now the Greek statue was being recognized by one part of his mind as a symbol of the intellectual clarity of ancient Greece, which his conscience knew he needed to pay more attention to. By decoding his excitement, Rilke was catching sight of an alternative way of being.

The case may be particular, but the underlying principle is

universal. We each face calls, triggered by chance encounters with people, objects or ideas, to change our lives. Something within us knows far better than our day-to-day consciousness permits us to realize the direction we need to go in in order to become whom we could really be.

A daily period of philosophical meditation does not so much dissolve problems as create an occasion during which the mind can order and understand itself. Fears, resentments and hopes become easier to name; we grow less scared of the contents of our own minds – and less resentful, calmer and clearer about our direction. We start, in faltering steps, to know ourselves slightly better.

A MORE NORMAL NORMALITY

If part of the reason we don't look more regularly into ourselves is our shame and fear at the unusual nature of what we may find there, then a crucial collective resource in the path to self-knowledge is a redrawn sense of what is normal.

Our picture of acceptability is – very often – way out of line with what is actually true and widespread. Many things that we might assume to be uniquely odd or disconcertingly strange about us are in reality wholly ubiquitous, though simply rarely spoken of in the reserved and cautious public sphere.

Any idea of the normal currently in circulation is not an accurate map of what is customary for a human to be. We are – each one of us – far more compulsive, anxious, sexual, tender, mean, generous, playful, thoughtful, dazed and at sea than we are encouraged to accept.

The misunderstanding begins with a basic fact about our minds: that we know through immediate experience what is going on inside us, but can only know about others from what they choose to tell us – which will almost always be a very edited version of the truth. We know our somewhat shocking reality from close up; we are left to guess about other people's from what their faces tell us, which is not very much.

We simply cannot trust that sides of our deep selves will have counterparts in those we meet, and so remain silent and shy, struggling to believe that the imposing, competent strangers we encounter can have any of the vulnerabilities, perversions and idiocies we're so intimately familiar with inside our own characters.

Ideally, the task of culture would be to compensate for the failings of our brains. It should assist us to a more correct vision of what other people are normally like – by taking us, in realistic and sensitive ways, into the inner lives of strangers. Novels, films and songs should constantly be defining and evoking states of mind we thought we were alone in experiencing but that belong to the typical lot of humankind. We should put down the average novel wondering – with relief – how the novelist had come to know so much about us. We should begin to understand that an average stranger is always far more likely to be as we know we are – with all our quirks, fragilities, compulsions and surprising aspects – than they are to resemble the apparently 'normal' person their exterior implies.

We need culture to take on the task because we cannot do it all by ourselves. In order to know ourselves well, we rely on the level of self-awareness, courage and honesty circulating in society as a whole. We will be as hypocritical as the most representative voices around us and we will, conversely, be freed by what society is prepared to countenance as acceptable.

There is, at present, so much we pretend not to feel. Starting in childhood, we have instilled in us, so subtly we don't even notice, strong notions about what is and is not permissible to experience. Traditionally, boys were not allowed to acknowledge that they felt like crying and girls weren't allowed to entertain certain kinds of ambitions. We might not have such obviously naive prohibitions today, but other, equally powerful ones have taken their place. We may have picked up covert but forceful indications that no decent person could be enthusiastic about making money or unable to cope at work, tempted by an affair or still upset over a break-up.

Furthermore, despite the apparently sexually liberated spirit of the times, the lion's share of our sexual impulses remains impossible to avow. There is still a great deal we are not meant to feel in order to fit that most desirable of categories: a good boy or girl.

The way to greater honesty follows some of the techniques evident from the rehabilitation of the people who commit crimes. We must reduce the shame and danger of confession. We need a broader, more reassuring sense of what is common. Of course it is normal to be envious, crude, sexual, weak, in need, childlike, grandiose, terrified and furious. It is normal to desire random adventures even within loving, committed unions. It is normal to be hurt by 'small' signs of rejection, and to be made quickly very insecure by any evidence of neglect by a partner. It is normal to harbour hopes for ourselves professionally that go far beyond what we have currently been able to achieve. It is normal to envy other people, many times a day, to be very upset by any kind of criticism of our work or performance, and to be so sad we regularly daydream of flight or a premature end.

The journey to self-knowledge needs to begin with a better map of the terrain of normality.

THE IMPORTANCE OF A BREAKDOWN

One of the great problems of human beings is that we're far too good at keeping going. We're experts at surrendering to the demands of the external world, living up to what is expected of us and getting on with the priorities defined by others around us. We keep showing up and doing our tasks – and we can pull off this magical feat for up to decades at a time without so much as an outward twitch or crack.

Until suddenly, one day, much to everyone's surprise (including our own), we break. The rupture can take many forms. We can no longer get out of bed. We fall into silence. We develop all-consuming social anxiety. We refuse to eat. We babble incoherently. We lose command over part of our body. We are compelled to do something extremely scandalous and entirely contrary to our normal behaviour. We become wholly paranoid in a given area. We refuse to play by the usual rules in our relationship, we have an affair, ramp up the fighting, or otherwise poke a very large stick in the wheels of daily life.

Breakdowns are hugely inconvenient for everyone and so, unsurprisingly, there is an immediate rush to medicalize them and attempt to excise them from the scene, so that business as usual can resume.

But this is to misunderstand what is going on when we break down. A breakdown is not merely a random piece of madness or malfunction, it is a very real – albeit very inarticulate – bid for health and self-knowledge. It is an attempt by one part of our mind to force the other into a process of growth, self-understanding and self-development which it has hitherto refused to undertake. If we can put it paradoxically, it is an attempt to jump-start a process of getting well, properly well, through a stage of falling very ill.

The danger, therefore, if we merely medicalize a breakdown and attempt to shift it away at once is that we will miss the lesson embedded within our sickness. A breakdown isn't just a pain, though it is that too of course; it is an extraordinary opportunity to learn.

The reason we *break* down is that we have not, over years, *flexed* very much. There were things we needed to hear inside our minds that we deftly put to one side; there were messages we needed to heed, bits of emotional learning and communicating we didn't do, and now, after being patient for so long, far too long, the emotional self is attempting to make itself heard in the only way it now knows how. It has become entirely desperate – and we should understand and even sympathize with its mute rage. What the breakdown is telling us above anything else is that it must no longer be business as usual; that things have to change or (and this can be properly frightening to witness) that death might be preferable.

Why can't we simply listen to the emotional need calmly and in good time, thus avoiding the melodrama of a breakdown? Because the conscious mind is inherently lazy and squeamish and so reluctant to engage with what the breakdown eventually has to tell it with brutality. For years, it refuses to listen to a particular sadness, or is in flight from a dysfunction in a relationship, or pushes desires down very far beneath the surface.

A good mental physician tries hard to listen to rather than censor the illness. They detect within its oddities a plea for more time for ourselves, for a closer relationship, for a more honest, fulfilled way of being, for acceptance for who we really are sexually . . . That is why we started to drink, or to become reclusive, or to grow entirely paranoid or manically seductive.

A crisis represents an appetite for growth that hasn't found another way of expressing itself. Many people, after a horrific few months or years of breakdown, will say, 'I don't know how I'd ever have got well if I hadn't fallen ill.'

In the midst of a breakdown, we often wonder whether we have gone mad. We have not. We're behaving oddly no doubt, but beneath the agitation we are on a hidden yet logical search for health. We haven't become ill; we were ill already. Our crisis, if we can get through it, is an attempt to dislodge us from a toxic status quo and constitutes an insistent call to rebuild our lives on a more authentic and sincere basis. It belongs, in the most acute and panicked way, to the search for self-knowledge.

II : Others

1 *Kindness*

CHARITY OF INTERPRETATION

At its most basic, charity means offering someone something they need but can't get for themselves. This is normally and logically understood to mean something material. We overwhelmingly associate charity with giving money. But, in its widest sense, charity stretches far beyond financial donations. Charity involves offering someone something that they may not entirely deserve and that it is a long way beyond the call of duty for us to provide: sympathy.

We are often in trouble of a distinctive sort. We're not quite in a ditch; we may even have a little money, but we are in difficulties nevertheless, as much at the mercy of strangers as if we were beggars – and equally unappealing to the hard-nosed and impatient. Just like the most scabrous of panhandlers, we have lost any claim on the respect of the righteous.

We may have done something highly foolish or disreputable. We may have been inconsiderate or hasty. We may have lied or lost our temper. Perhaps our deficiency is one of temperament: under the pressure of disappointment, our personalities have grown sour or boastful. Or we come across as dispiritingly shy or cynical in our dealings with others.

We need charity, but not of the usual kind; we need what we might term a 'charity of interpretation': that is, we require an uncommonly generous assessment of our idiocy, weakness, eccentricity or deceit.

We need onlookers who can provide some of the rationale we have grown too mute, cowed or ashamed to proffer. Even when they do not know any of the details, generous onlookers must make a stab at picturing the overall structure of what might have happened to the wretched being before them. They must guess that there will be sorrow and regret beneath the furious rantings, or a sense of intolerable vulnerability behind the pomposity and snobbishness. They must intimate that early trauma and let-down must have formed the backdrop to later transgressions. They will remember that the person before them was once a baby too.

The charitable interpreter holds on also to the idea that sweetness must remain beneath the surface, along with the possibility of remorse and growth. They are committed to mitigating circumstances; to all the bits of the truth that can cast a less catastrophic light on folly.

In cases of financial charity, the gifts tend to go in one direction only, from the rich to the poor. Those who give may be generous, but they tend to experience only one side of the equation, remaining for all their lives the donor rather than the recipient. They can be reasonably sure that they won't ever be in material need, which is what can lend a somewhat unimaginative or aloof tone to their generosity. But when it comes to the gift of charitable interpretation, none of us is ever committedly beyond need. Such is our proclivity for error and our vulnerability to reversals of fortune, we are all on the verge of needing someone to come to our imaginative aid. And therefore, if for no other reason, we have a duty to remain constant providers of generous interpretations of the lives of others. We must be kind in the sense not only of being touched by the remote material suffering of strangers, but also of being ready to do more than condemn and hate the sinful around us, hopeful that we too may be accorded a tolerable degree of sympathy in our forthcoming hour of failure and shame.

LOSERS AND TRAGIC FAILURES

Our societies are very interested in winners but don't really know what to do about losers – of which there are always, by definition, a far greater number.

For a long time, around success and failure, the rhetoric tends to be upbeat. We hear about resilience, bouncing back, never surrendering and giving it another go. But there's only so long this kind of talk can go on. At some point, the conclusion becomes inevitable: things won't work out. The political career isn't going to have a come-back. There'll be no way of getting finance for the film. The novel won't be accepted by the thirty-second publisher. The criminal charges are forever going to taint one's reputation.

Where does responsibility for success and failure lie? Nowadays, the answer tends to be: squarely with the individual concerned. That's why failure isn't just hard (as it has always been), it is a catastrophe. There is no metaphysical consolation, no possibility of appealing to the idea of 'bad luck', no one to blame but oneself. Suicide rates climb exponentially once societies become modern and start to hold people profoundly responsible for their biographies. Meritocracies turn failure from a misfortune to an unbudgeable verdict on one's nature. We trust that the world is more or less just – and that, the odd exception aside, people will secure roughly what they deserve. Those who are condemned and broken did something wrong; those who succeeded worked hard and were good. The status of a person has to be a more or less reliable indicator of their effort and decency.

But not all societies and eras have seen success and failure in such a stark and forbidding light. In ancient Greece, another rather remarkable possibility – ignored by our own era – was envisaged: you could be good and yet fail. To keep this idea at the front of the collective imagination, the ancient Greeks developed a particular art form: tragic drama. They put on huge festivals, which all the citizens were expected to attend, to act out stories of appalling, often grisly, failure: people were seen to break a minor law, or make a hasty decision, or sleep with the wrong person and the results were ignominy and death. Yet what happened was shown to be to a large extent in the hands of what the Greeks called 'fate' or 'the gods'. It was the Greeks' poetic way of saying that things often work out randomly, according to dynamics that simply don't reflect the merits of the individuals concerned.

The great Greek tragedians – Aeschylus, Euripides and Sophocles – recounted stories of essentially respectable, intelligent and honest men and women who, on account of a minor and understandable error or omission, unleashed catastrophe and ended up in a very short time dead or ruined. The way in which these stories of downfall were told was intended to leave audiences stunned by the recognition of how easily any life might be undone and how a small mistake can require us to pay the ultimate price. They were to walk out of the theatre afraid for themselves and filled with pity for the cruelty of the fate dealt out to the unknowing and unfortunate heroes soaked in blood on stage. Having followed the slow unfurling of events from prosperity and esteem to disgrace and disaster, audiences would be in no mood to pass easy moral judgement. It would make no sense to dismiss Oedipus or Medea, Antigone and Electra with anything approximating the catch-all, infinitely damning modern term for those who do not make it: losers. These great fictional characters belonged to a far nobler, more dignified and more humane category which tragedy helped to map: that of the tragic failure, the person who loses without thereby forfeiting the right to sympathy and mercy.

Tragedy is the sympathetic, morally complex account of how good people can end up in disaster. It attempts to teach us that goodness is seldom fairly rewarded or error paid for in commensurate ways. The most shocking events can befall the more or less innocent or the only averagely muddled and weak. We do not inhabit a properly moral universe: disaster at points befalls those who could not have expected it to be a fair outcome, given what they did. The Greeks were the originators of a remarkable, appalling and still-too-seldom-accepted possibility that failure is not reserved simply for the evil.

We are used to according automatic respect to the central figures of great tragic works, but there is nothing inherently noble about the personalities of Hamlet or Madame Bovary, Jude the Obscure or Anna Karenina. That we accord them dignity has to do with the way their stories have been told to us; if we had left the task to the media, they would have been indistinguishable from the usual objects of popular ridicule and loathing.

The real purpose of tragedy is not to teach us to be kind to fictional creations, it is to encourage us to apply a complex lens to the travails of all those around us and, crucially at points, to ourselves. Without having any of the dramatic talent of a Sophocles or Shakespeare, we need to tell our own stories of loss and error with some of the same generosity that they employed, thereby holding on to what can often feel, especially at our lowest points, like a hugely improbable idea: that though we have failed, however stupid our mistakes, we remain deserving of that gracious and grand epithet, a gift from the Greeks to all humankind: a 'tragic failure'.

THE WEAKNESS OF STRENGTH

We may sometimes wonder how certain irritating people have come into our lives. After spending time around them, what dominates our awareness of them is their flaws: how rigid they can be, how muddled, self-righteous, vague or proud. We grow into experts in their deficiencies of character.

We should in our most impatient and intemperate moments strive to hold on to the concept of the weakness of strength. This dictates that we should interpret people's weaknesses as the inevitable downside of certain merits that drew us to them, and from which we will benefit at other points (even if none of these benefits are apparent right now). What we're seeing are not their faults, pure and simple, but rather the shadow side of things that are genuinely good about them. If we were to write down a list of strengths and then of weaknesses, we'd find that almost everything on the positive side of the ledger could be connected up with something on the negative. The theory urges us to search a little more assiduously than is normal for the strength to which a maddening characteristic must be twinned. We can see easily enough that someone is pedantic and uncompromising; we tend to forget, at moments of crisis, their thoroughness and honesty. We know so much about a person's messiness, we have forgotten their uncommon degree of creative enthusiasm. The very same character trait that we approve of will be inseparable from tendencies we end up regretting. This isn't bad luck or the case with one or two people, it's a law of nature. There can, perplexingly, be no such thing as a person with only strengths.

In the 1870s, when he was living in Paris, the American novelist Henry James became a friend of the celebrated Russian novelist Ivan Turgenev, who was also living in the city at that time. James was particularly taken with the unhurried, tranquil style of the Russian writer's storytelling: he spent a long time on every sentence, weighing different options, changing, polishing, until – at last – everything was perfect. It was a hugely ambitious, inspiring approach to literature.

But in personal and social life, these same virtues could make Turgenev an aggravating companion. He was almost impossible to pin down for an appointment, writing florid, nuanced letters of apology for his delays and changes of plan. James would invite him for lunch for 1 p.m., Turgenev would agree, then suddenly change his mind twenty minutes before, sending a note to say that he'd had to leave town on an urgent trip. Eventually he'd make an appointment that seemed to work, but would show up an hour and a half late.

James might have been tempted to end the friendship forthwith, but he had the wisdom not to interpret Turgenev's disastrous timekeeping as an isolated part of his personality but rather to see it as an emanation of the very same side of his character that enabled him to produce some of the greatest literary works of the age. The same trait might generate *Fathers and Sons* and, around appointments, six cancelled meetings. Musing in a letter about Turgenev's greatness as a writer and his trickiness as a friend, James remarked that the Russian novelist had thoroughly exhibited the 'weakness of his strength'.

The theory of the weakness of strength invites us to be calm and forensic about the most irritating aspects of those we live around. There is no comfort in being told that these aspects are not real or significant. The consolation comes in not viewing them in isolation, in remembering the accompanying trait that redeems them and explains the friendship, in recalling that a lack of time management might have its atonement in creativity or that dogmatism might be the offshoot of precision.

It is always an option to move away and find people who will have new kinds of strengths, but – as time will reveal – they will also have new, fascinating and associated kinds of weaknesses.

Kindness is built out of a constantly renewed and gently resigned awareness that weakness-free people do not exist.

MOTIVES

One of the fundamental paths to sympathy is the power to hold on, in the most challenging situations, to a distinction between a person's overt unpleasant actions and the more pitiable motives that may underlie them. Pure evil is seldom at work. Almost all our worst moments can be traced back to an unexotic, bathetic, temptingly neglected ingredient: pain.

A traditional folk tale known as 'Androcles and the Lion', originally recounted by the ancient Roman philosopher Aulus Gellius, tells of a Barbary lion – nine feet long with a splendid dark mane – who lived in the forested foothills of the Atlas Mountains (in what is today Algeria). Usually he kept far from human settlements, but one year, in spring, he started approaching the villages at night, roaring and snarling menacingly in the darkness. The villagers were terrified. They put extra guards on the gates and sent out heavily armed hunting parties to try to slaughter the beast.

It happened around this time that a shepherd boy named Androcles followed his sheep far into the high mountain pastures. One evening, he sought shelter in a cave. He had just lit a candle and was setting out his blanket when he saw the ferocious animal glaring at him from a corner. At first he was terrified. It seemed as if the angry lion might be about to pounce and rip him to pieces. But then Androcles noticed something: there was a thorn deeply embedded in one of the lion's front paws and a huge tear was running down his noble face. The creature wasn't murderous, he was in agony. So instead of trying to flee or defend himself with his dagger, the boy's fear turned to pity. Androcles approached the lion, stroked his mane and gently, reassuringly extracted the thorn from the paw, wrapping it in a strip of cloth torn from his own blanket. The lion licked the boy's hand and became his friend for life.

The story is a reminder of what kindness demands. We resent others with unhelpful speed when we lack the will to consider the origins of their behaviour. The lion is in terrible pain, but has no capacity to understand what is hurting him and what he might need from others. The lion is all of us when we lack insight into our own distress. The thorn is a troubling, maddening element of our inner lives – a fear, a biting worry, a regret, a sense of guilt, a feeling of humiliation, a strained hope or an agonized disappointment that rumbles away powerfully but just out of range of our standard view of ourselves. The art of living is to a large measure dependent on an ability to understand our thorns and explain them with a modicum of grace to others – and, when we are on the other side of the equation, to imagine the thorns of others, even those whose precise locations or dimensions we will never know for certain.

WHAT TO THINK OF OUR ENEMIES

People are bad, always, because they are in difficulty. They slander, gossip, denigrate and growl because they are not in a good place. Though they may seem strong, though their attacks can place them in an apparently dominant role, their ill intentions are all the proof we require to know as a certainty that they are not well. Contented people have no need to hurt others.

The theory should help us to reverse some of the humiliation that comes from being attacked. It is only too easy to imagine that those who have hurt us are somehow invulnerable and noble; we readily remember reasons to be ashamed of ourselves. However, to hold on to the idea that hurt generates meanness casts our opponent in the subservient role. It isn't us who must be pitiful but our attacker who feels such a need to crush us. One has to feel very small in order to belittle.

The theory helps to restore a kind of justice that we may not ourselves directly be able to administer. The explanation of the origins of nastiness changes how we assess our opponent. No longer are they necessarily strong and impervious. We have not been able to punish them, but the universe has in a sense, and the clearest evidence for the sentence lies in the unhappiness that is powering their attacks. They have not got away with injuring us; their punishment lies in the pain they must be enduring in order to have such an urgent need to lash out. We, who have no wish to hurt, are in fact the stronger party; we, who have no wish to diminish others, are truly powerful. We can move from helpless victims to imaginative witnesses of justice.

This may sound overly convenient; but it is also plainly true. We are not beyond improvement, of course, but people simply never need to harm others if they are not first tormented themselves.

The logic of the argument points to how we might, when our short-term irritation has worn off, deal with those who have injured us. The temptation is to grow strict and inflict punishment back. But with a better understanding of the insecurity and sadness that power ill temper in the first place, there is only one plausible, though extremely challenging, way forward: a response of love.

POLITENESS

For most of history, the idea of being 'polite' has been central to our sense of what is required to count as a kind and civilized person. But more recently, politeness has come under suspicion. While we may not reject it outright, it's not a word we now instinctively reach for when we want to explain why we like or admire someone. Politeness can seem to carry almost the opposite of its traditional connotations, suggesting an offensive or insolent degree of insincerity. A polite person can be judged as a bit of a fake and, in their own way, really rather rude.

The rise in our collective suspicion of politeness has a history. In the late eighteenth century, an ideal of Romantic anti-politeness emerged, largely driven forward by the Swiss philosopher Jean-Jacques Rousseau, who powerfully redescribed politeness in terms of inauthenticity, servility and deceit. What was important for Rousseau was never to hide or moderate emotions and thoughts, but to remain – at all times – fundamentally true to oneself.

Rousseau's writings generated highly influential attitudes to which we remain heirs. What ultimately separates the polite from the frank person isn't really a knowledge of etiquette. The difference doesn't hang upon considerations of which knife to use at a formal dinner, when to say please or thank you, or how to word a wedding invitation. It comes down to a contrasting set of beliefs about human nature. The polite person and the frank person behave differently chiefly because they see the world in highly divergent ways. The following are some of the key ideological issues that separate them.

Original Goodness vs. Natural Sin

Frank people believe in the importance of expressing themselves honestly principally because they trust that what they happen to think and feel will always prove fundamentally acceptable to the world. Their true sentiments and opinions may, when voiced, be bracing of course, but no worse. Frank types assume that what is honestly avowed cannot really ever be vindictive, disgusting, tedious or cruel. In this sense, the frank person sees themselves a little in the way we typically see small children: as blessed by an original and innate goodness.

Tellingly, we don't usually think that the strictures of politeness apply to the very young. We remain interested to hear about whatever may be passing through their minds and stay unalarmed by their awkward moments, infelicities or negative statements. If they say that the pasta is yuck or that the taxi driver has a head like a weird goldfish, it sounds funny rather than wounding. The frank person taps into just this childlike optimism in their uninhibited approach to themselves. Their trust in their basic purity erodes the rationale for editing or self-censorship.

The polite person, by contrast, proceeds under a grave suspicion of themselves and their impulses. They sense that a great deal of what they feel and want really isn't very nice. They are indelibly in touch with their darker desires and can sense their fleeting wishes to hurt or humiliate certain people. They know they are sometimes a bit revolting and cannot forget the extent to which they may come across as offensive and frightening to others. They therefore set out on a deliberate strategy to protect others from what they know is within them. It isn't lying as such; they merely understand that being 'themselves' is a treat that they must take enormous pains to spare everyone else from experiencing – especially anyone they claim to care about.

Paradoxically, the polite person who is pessimistic about their own nature doesn't in fact end up behaving horribly with anyone.

So aware are they of their own dislikeable sides, they nimbly minimize their impact upon the world. It is their extraordinary suspicion of themselves that helps them to be – in everyday life – uncommonly friendly, trustworthy and kind.

The Stranger is Like Me vs. the Stranger is Other

The frank person operates with a charming, unconscious assumption that other people are at heart pretty much like them. This can make them very clubbable and allows them to create some astonishing intimacies across social barriers at high speed. When they like listening to a particular piece of music at high volume, they will take it as obvious that you probably do as well. Because they are very enthusiastic about spicy food, or never want to add salt to a dish, it doesn't cross their mind to ask if you actually like this restaurant or would favour a salt cellar on the table. They are correspondingly undisturbed by the less obvious clues about some of the dissonant feelings that may be unfolding in the minds of other people: if someone is a bit quiet at a meeting, it doesn't occur to the frank person to worry that they might have said something wrong or badly misjudged the situation.

For their part, the polite person starts from the assumption that others are highly likely to be in quite different places internally, whatever the outward signs. Their behaviour is therefore tentative, wary and filled with enquiries. They will explicitly check with others to take a measure of their experiences and outlook: if they feel cold, they are very alive to the possibility that you may be feeling perfectly warm and so will take trouble to ask if you'd mind if they went over and closed the window. They are aware that you might be annoyed by a joke that they find funny or that you might very sincerely hold political opinions quite at odds with their own. They don't take what is going on for them as a guide to what is probably going on for you. Their manners are grounded in an acute sense of the gulf that can separate humans from one another.

Robustness vs. Vulnerability

The frank person works with an underlying sense that other people are internally for the most part extremely robust. Those around them are not felt to be forever on the verge of self-doubt and self-hatred. Their egos are not assumed to be gossamer thin and at perpetual risk of deflating. There is therefore understood to be no need to broadcast constant small signals of reassurance and affirmation. When you go to someone's house, the fact that the meal was tasty will be obvious to everyone, not least the person who spent the day preparing it. There is no need to keep stressing the point in a variety of discreet ways. When one meets an artist, there's no need to mention that their last work was noticed and appreciated; they'll know this well enough. And the office junior must have a pretty clear sense that they are making the grade without any need to stop and spell it out. The frank person assumes that everyone's ego is already at least as big and strong as it should be. They are even likely to suspect that if you praise someone for the little things, you'll only inflate their self-regard to undue and dangerous proportions.

The polite person starts from a contrary assumption that all of us are permanently only millimetres away from inner despair and self-hatred. However confident we may look, we are very vulnerable – despite even great outward plaudits and recognition – to a sense of being disliked and taken for granted. Every piece of neglect, every silence or slightly harsh or off-the-cuff word has a profound capacity to hurt. All of us are walking around without a skin. The cook, the artist and the office junior will inevitably share in a craving for evidence that what they do and are is OK. Accordingly, the polite person will be drawn to spending a lot of time noticing and commenting positively on the most apparently minor facets of others' achievements: they will say that the watercress soup was the best they've had for years (and that they'd forgotten how much they liked it); they'll mention that the ending of the writer's new novel made them cry and that work on the Mexico deal was particularly helpful to, and noticed by, the whole company. They will know that everyone we come across has a huge capacity to be hurt by what we sometimes refer to as 'small things'.

There's likely to be an associated underlying difference in attitudes to money and love in the context of work. For the frank person, money is the crucial ingredient we want from other people in our professional lives. They therefore don't feel any great need – in service situations, for example – to express gratitude or take particular pains to create a semblance of equality with an employee. The waiter or the person at the car-hire desk has, they feel, no special need of kindness on top of the money they will already be securing through the transaction.

Yet the polite person knows that we take a lot of ourselves into our jobs and need to find respect and a form of love from them as much as we need cash. So they will be conscious of an additional need to contribute smiles and a pleasant word or two to the person stamping their passport or changing the bedclothes in the hotel. These people are doing their jobs for the money of course, but payment never invalidates an equally strong emotional hunger for a sense of having been useful and appreciated by another person, however brief and functional the encounter may have seemed.

Grand vs. Small Gestures

The frank person is often very kind but in a bold way. They are interested in enormous acts of generosity and kindness towards major sections of humanity: perhaps the rescue of the whole continent of Africa or a plan to give every child in the country an equally good start in life. But a consequence of their enthusiasm can be a certain impatience with smaller gestures, which they may view as a distraction from larger causes. There is really no point, they may feel, in spending time and money sending people flowers, writing notes after a dinner or remembering birthdays when a fundamental transformation of the human condition is at hand.

The polite person also cares passionately about spreading kindness, love and goodness on a mass scale, but they are cautious about the chances of doing so on any realistic time horizon. Yet their belief that perhaps one can't improve things enormously for a huge number of people in the coming decades makes them feel that it is still very much a worthy goal to try to effect modest, minor improvements in the lives of the few humans one does have direct contact with in the here and now. They may never be able to transform another person's prospects entirely or rescue the species from its agony, but they can smile and stop for a brief conversation with a neighbour. Their modesty around what is possible makes them acutely sensitive to the worth of the little things that can be done to attenuate the bitterness of existence. Far more than their frank counterpart, they'll often find time for a chat.

Self-Certainty vs. Self-Doubt

The frank person has a high degree of confidence as to their ability to judge relatively quickly and for the long term what is right and wrong about a given situation. They feel they can tell who has behaved well or badly or what the appropriate course of action should be around a dilemma. This is what gives them the confidence to get angry with what strikes them (immediately) as rank stupidity, or to blow up bridges with people they've become vexed with, or to state a disagreement emphatically and to call another person stupid, monstrous or a liar to their face. Once they have said something, they know they can't take it back but they don't really want to. Part of their frankness is based on the notion that they can understand at speed the merits of any situation, the characters of others and the true nature of their own commitments.

The polite person is much more unsure on all these fronts. They are conscious that what they feel strongly about today might not be what they end up thinking next week. They recognize that ideas that sound very strange or misguided to them can be attempts to state – in garbled forms – concepts that are genuinely important to other people and that they themselves may come round to with time. They see their own minds as having great capacities for error and as being subject to imperceptible moods which will mislead them, and so are keen not to make statements that can't be taken back or to make enemies of people they might decide are in fact worthy of respect further down the line.

The polite person will be drawn to deploying softening, tentative language and holding back on criticism wherever possible. They will suggest that an idea might not be quite right. They will say that a project is attractive but that it could be interesting to look at alternatives as well. They will concede that an intellectual opponent may well have a point. They aren't just lying or dodging tough decisions. Their behaviour is symptomatic of a nuanced and intelligent belief that few ideas are totally without merit, no proposals are 100 per cent wrong and almost no one is entirely foolish. They work with a conception of reality in which good and bad are deviously entangled and in which bits of the truth are always showing up in unfamiliar guises in unexpected people. Their politeness is a logical, careful response to the complexity they identify in themselves and in the world.

Both the frank person and the polite person have important lessons to teach us. But it may be that at this point in history it is the distinctive wisdom of the polite person that is most ripe for rediscovery and articulation, and that may have the most effective power to take the edge off some of the more brutal and counterproductive consequences of the reigning ideology of frankness.

DIPLOMACY

Diplomacy is an art that evolved initially to deal with problems in the relationships between countries. The leaders of neighbouring states might be touchy on points of personal pride and quickly roused to anger; if they met head on they might be liable to infuriate each other and start a war. Instead, they learned to send emissaries, people who could state things in less inflammatory ways, who wouldn't take the issues so personally, who could be more patient and emollient. Diplomacy was a way of avoiding the dangers that come from decisions taken in the heat of the moment. In their own palaces, two kings might be thumping the table and calling their rivals by abusive names; but in the quiet negotiating halls, the diplomat would say, 'My master is slightly disconcerted that . . .'

We still associate the term diplomacy with embassies, international relations and high politics, but it refers in essence to a set of skills that matter in many areas of daily life, especially at the office and on the landing, outside the slammed doors of loved ones' bedrooms.

Diplomacy is the art of advancing an idea or a cause without unnecessarily inflaming passions or unleashing a catastrophe. It involves an understanding of the many facets of human nature that can undermine agreement and stoke conflict, and a commitment to unpicking these with foresight and grace.

The diplomat remembers, first and foremost, that some of the vehemence with which we can insist on having our own way draws energy from an overall sense of not being respected or heard. We will fight with particular tenacity and apparent meanness over a so-called small point when we have a sense that another has failed to honour our wider need for appreciation and esteem.

Knowing the intensity of the craving for respect, diplomats – though they may not always be able to agree with others – take the trouble to show that they have bothered to see how things look through foreign eyes. They recognize that it is almost as important to people to feel heard as to win their case. We can put up with a lot once someone has demonstrated that they at least know how it is for us. Diplomats put extraordinary effort into securing the health of the overall relationship so that smaller points can be conceded along the way without attracting feelings of untenable humiliation. They know how much – beneath pitched fights over money or entitlements, schedules or procedures – a demand for esteem can stir. They are careful to trade generously in emotional currency, so as not always to have to pay excessively in other, more practical denominations.

Frequently, what is at stake within a negotiation with someone is a request that they change in some way: that they learn to be more punctual, or take more trouble on a task, or be less defensive or more open-minded. The diplomat knows how futile it is to state these wishes too directly. They know the vast difference between having a correct diagnosis of how someone needs to grow and a relevant way to help them do so. They know too that what holds people back from evolution is fear and therefore grasp that what we may most need to offer those whom we want to acknowledge difficult things is, above anything else, love and reassurance. It helps greatly to know that those recommending change are not speaking from a position of impregnable perfection but are themselves wrestling with comparable demons in other areas. For a diagnosis not to sound like mere criticism, it helps for it to be delivered by someone with no compunctions to owning up to their own shortcomings. There can be few more successful pedagogic moves than to confess genially from the outset, 'And I am, of course, entirely mad and flawed as well . . .'

In negotiations, the diplomat is not addicted to indiscriminate or heroic truth-telling. They appreciate the legitimate place that minor lies or omissions can occupy in the service of greater truths. They know that if certain local facts are emphasized, then the most important principles in a relationship may be forever undermined. So they will enthusiastically say that the financial report or the home-made cake was really very pleasing and will do so not to deceive but to affirm the truth of their overall attachment, which might be lost were a completely accurate account of their views to be laid out. Diplomats know how a small lie may have to be the guardian of a larger truth.

Another trait of the diplomat is to be serene in the face of obviously bad behaviour: a sudden loss of temper, a wild accusation, a very mean remark. They don't take it personally, even when they may be the target of rage. They reach instinctively for reasonable explanations and have clearly in their minds the better moments of a currently frantic but essentially lovable person. They know themselves well enough to understand that abandonments of perspective are both hugely normal and usually indicative of nothing much beyond passing despair or exhaustion. They do not aggravate a febrile situation through self-righteousness, a symptom of both not knowing oneself too well and a very selective memory. The person who bangs a fist on the table or announces extravagant opinions is most likely to be simply rather worried, frightened, hungry or just very enthusiastic: conditions that should rightly invite sympathy rather than disgust.

At the same time, the diplomat understands that there are moments to sidestep direct engagement. They do not try to teach a lesson whenever it might first or most apply; they wait till it has the best chance of being heard. At points, they disarm difficult people by reacting in unexpected ways. In the face of a tirade, instead of going on the defensive, the diplomatic person might suggest some lunch. When a harshly unfair criticism is launched at them, they might nod in partial agreement and declare that they've often said such things to themselves. They give a lot of ground away and avoid getting cornered in arguments that distract from the deeper issues. They remember the presence of a far better version of the somewhat unfortunate individual currently on display.

The diplomat's tone of reasonableness is built, fundamentally, on a base of deep pessimism. They know what the human animal is; they understand how many problems are going to beset even a very good marriage, business, friendship or society. Their good-humoured way of greeting problems is a symptom of having swallowed a healthy measure of sadness from the outset. They have given up on the ideal, not out of weakness but out of a mature readiness to see compromise as a necessary requirement for getting by in a radically imperfect world.

The diplomat may be polite, but they are not averse to delivering bits of bad news with uncommon frankness. Too often, we seek to preserve our image in the eyes of others by tiptoeing around harsh decisions – and thereby make things far worse than they need to be. We should say that we're leaving them, that they're fired, that their pet project isn't going ahead, but we mutter instead that we're a little preoccupied at the moment, that we're delighted by their performance and that the scheme is being actively discussed by the senior team. We mistake leaving some room for hope for kindness. But true niceness does not mean seeming nice, it means helping the people we are going to disappoint to adjust as best they can to reality. By administering a sharp, clean blow, the diplomatic person kills off the torture of hope, accepting the frustration that is likely to come their way: the diplomat is kind enough to let themselves sometimes be the target of hate.

The diplomat succeeds by being a realist. They know we are inherently flawed, unreasonable, anxious, laughably absurd creatures who scatter blame unfairly, misdiagnose pains and react appallingly to criticism – especially when it is accurate – and yet they are hopeful too of the possibilities of progress when our disturbances have been properly factored in and cushioned with adequate reassurance, accurate interpretation and respect. Diplomacy seeks to teach us how many good things can still be accomplished when we make some necessary accommodations with the crooked, sometimes touching and hugely unreliable material of human nature.

CODA: IN PRAISE OF KINDNESS

Part of what can hold us back from being kind is how unattractive the concept sounds. Taking pride in being kind sounds like something we might settle on only when every other, more robust ambition had been exhausted.

This suspicion too has a long history. For centuries, it was

Christianity that intoned to us about the importance of kindness, co-opting the finest artworks to the task of rendering us more tender and forgiving, charitable and gentle. But it also, rather fatefully, identified a conflict between being successful and being kind – a conflict from which the idea of kindness has yet to recover. The suggestion has been of a choice between kindness and a lowly position, on the one hand, and nastiness and worldly triumph, on the other. It can seem as if kindness might be something of interest chiefly to those who have failed.

The movement known as Romanticism has further cast the kind person into the role of the unexciting bore, identifying drama and allure with the naughty and the 'wicked' (which has become a term of praise) while bathing niceness in an aura of tedium. The choice seems to be between being authentic, spontaneous and a bit cruel or else sweet, gentle and distinctly off-putting.

There's a financial aspect to the dichotomy too. Kind people do not seem well cut out to win in the game of capitalism. Business success appears to demand an ability not to listen to excuses, not to forgive, not to be detained by sentiment. Kind people seem destined to end up either broke or overlooked.

Semi-consciously, kindness also seems incompatible with sexual desirability. Being erotic appears to be connected with a degree of heedless disregard and selfishness. We want our friends to be nice, but appreciate our lovers as a touch dangerous.

The three charges are desperately unfair. Niceness can happily coexist with being successful, interesting and sexual. It's hardly possible to succeed without a deep interest in the welfare of one's colleagues. It's not possible to be uninhibited in bed without a bedrock of trust built on kindness (it's rare to want to be enslaved and punished by someone we don't fundamentally believe is very nice). We can be kind and successful, kind and interesting, kind and sexual.

Kindness is a cardinal virtue awaiting our renewed, unconflicted appreciation.

2 Charm

SHYNESS

Shyness may seem like an ingrained, almost natural disposition, but it is at heart a highly treatable condition provoked by a set of somewhat misfounded ideas about ourselves and our position in the world.

Our shy episodes are rooted in an experience of difference. They, the ones who have sparked our intimidation, are all women or all men, all from the north or all from the south, all rich or all poor, all confident people or all winners. And we are not – and therefore have nothing whatever to say.

To dislodge us from our silence, we can think of ourselves as each possessing two different kinds of identities. Our local identity comprises our age, gender, skin colour, sexuality, social background, wealth, career, religion and personality type. But beyond this, we also have a universal identity, made up of what we have in common with every other member of the species: we all have problematic families, have all been disappointed, have all been idiotic, have all loved, have all had problems around money, all have anxieties – and will all, when we are pricked, start to bleed.

The last line is Shylock's from his famous impassioned outburst in Shakespeare's *The Merchant of Venice*, one of the most beautiful celebrations of universal identity ever delivered: 'I am a Jew. Hath not a Jew eyes? hath not a Jew hands, organs, dimensions, senses, affections, passions? fed with the same food, hurt with the same weapons, subject to the same diseases, healed by the same means, warmed and cooled by the same winter and summer, as a Christian is? If you prick us, do we not bleed? if you tickle us, do we not laugh? if you poison us, do we not die?'

The point is relevant not just for a politically excluded minority; it can serve the shy just as well. In the face of the most daunting foreignness, expressed through accents, jobs, in jokes or age, there must remain a common core. We may come from the land of ugly boys while she is a beautiful woman; we may come from the province of the poor while he is a successful moneymaker; we are almost retired and they are starting their twenties. But we must, with Shylock in mind, look beyond the differences and insist on a universal commonality.

Shakespeare had read and absorbed the writings of the Roman playwright Terence, who is remembered for one very famous declaration: '*Homo sum, humani nil a me alienum puto*' ('I am human, I consider nothing human alien to me'). Shyness is the most modest, kind and unfortunate way of insisting on the specialness of one's particular province.

At the heart of the shy person's self-doubt is a certainty that they must be boring. But, in reality, no one is ever truly boring. We are only in danger of coming across as such when we don't dare (or know how) to communicate our deeper selves to others. The human animal witnessed in its essence, with honesty and without artifice, with all its longings, crazed desires and despair, is always gripping. When we dismiss a person as boring, we are merely pointing to someone who has not had the courage or concentration to tell us what it is like to be them. But we invariably prove compelling when we succeed in detailing some of what we crave, envy, regret, mourn and dream. The interesting person isn't someone to whom obviously and outwardly interesting things have happened, someone who has travelled the world, met important dignitaries or been present at critical geopolitical events. Nor is it someone who speaks in learned terms about the great themes of culture, history or science. They are someone who has grown into an attentive, self-aware listener and a reliable correspondent of their own mind and heart, and who can thereby give us faithful accounts of the pathos, drama and strangeness of being them.

The gift of being interesting is neither exclusive nor reliant on exceptional talent; it requires only honesty and focus. The person we call interesting is in essence someone alive to what we all deeply want from social intercourse: an uncensored glimpse of what life looks like through the eyes of another person and reassurance that we are not entirely alone with all that feels most bewildering, peculiar and frightening in us.

VULNERABILITY

There is a particular way of discussing oneself which, however long it goes on for, never fails to win friends, reassure audiences, comfort couples, bring solace to the single and buy the goodwill of enemies: the confession of vulnerability.

To hear that we have failed, that we are sad, that it was our fault, that our partners don't seem to like us much, that we are lonely, that we have wished it might all be over – there is scarcely anything nicer anyone could learn.

This is often taken to signal a basic nastiness in human nature, but the truth is more poignant. We are not so much crowing when we hear of failure as deeply reassured – reassured to know that we aren't humiliatingly alone with the appalling difficulties of being alive. It is all too easy to suspect that we have been uniquely cursed in the extent of our troubles, of which we seldom find evidence in the lives around us.

We put so much effort into being perfect. But the irony is that it's failure that charms, because others so need to hear external evidence of problems with which we are all too lonely: how un-normal our sex lives are; how arduous our careers are proving; how unsatisfactory our family can be; how worried we are pretty much all the time.

Revealing any of these wounds might, of course, place us in great danger. Others could laugh; the media could have a field day. That's the point. We get close by revealing things that would, in the wrong hands, be capable of inflicting humiliation on us. Friendship is the dividend of gratitude that flows from an acknowledgement that one has offered something very valuable by talking: the key to one's self-esteem and dignity. It's deeply poignant that we should expend so much effort on trying to look strong before the world when, all the while, it's really only ever the revelation of the somewhat embarrassing, sad, melancholy and anxious bits of us that renders us endearing to others and transforms strangers into friends.

WORRYING WHETHER OR NOT THEY LIKE US

One of the most acute questions we ask ourselves in relation to new friends and acquaintances is whether or not they like us. The question feels so significant because, depending on how we answer it in our minds, we will either take steps to deepen the friendship or, as is often the case, immediately make moves to withdraw from it so as to spare ourselves humiliation and embarrassment.

But what is striking and sad is how essentially passive we are in relation to this enquiry. We assume that there is a more or less binary answer, that it is wholly in the remit of the other person to settle it, and that there is nothing much we could do to shift the verdict one way or the other. Either someone wants to be our friend or they don't, and the answer, while it is about us, is essentially disconnected from any of our own initiatives.

We are hereby failing to apply to other people a basic lesson we can appreciate well enough when we study the functioning of our own judgements: we often don't know what we think of other people. Our moods hover and sway. There are days when we can see the point of someone and others when their positive sides elude us entirely. But, and this is the key point, what usually helps us to decide what someone means to us is our sense of what we mean to them.

The possibility of friendship between people therefore frequently hangs in the balance because both sides are, privately, waiting for a sign from the other as to whether or not they are liked before they dare to show (or even register) any enthusiasm of their own. Both sides proceed under the tacit assumption that there is some a priori verdict about their value that the other person will be developing in their mind that has no connection to how they themselves behave and is impervious to anything they could say or do.

Under pressure, we forget the fundamental malleability within the question of whether someone wants to be friends with us or not. Most of it depends on how we behave to them. If we have a little courage and can keep our deep suspicions of ourselves and our terror of their rejection of us at bay, we have every opportunity to turn the situation in our direction. We can dare to persuade them to see us in a positive light, chiefly by showing a great deal of evidence that we see them in a positive light. We can apply the full range of techniques of charm: we can remember small things about them, display an interest in what they have been up to, laugh at their witty moments and sympathize with them around their sorrows.

Though our instinct is to be close to superstitious in our understanding of why people like us, we have to be extremely unlucky to land on people who genuinely show no interest in a friendship with us once we have carried out a full set of charming manoeuvres with any level of sincerity and basic tact.

Friendships cannot develop until one side takes a risk and shows they are ready to like even when there's as yet no evidence that they are liked back. We have to realize that whether or not the other person likes us is going to depend on what we do, not – mystically – what we by nature 'are', and that we have the agency to do rather a lot of things. Even though we may initially get very few signs of their interest (they might be looking a little distracted and behaving in an offhand way), we should assume that this is only a legacy of a restraint that springs from fear that they are not able to please – and that so long as we keep showing them warmth and encouragement to appease their self-suspicion, the barriers will eventually come down.

It is sad enough when two people dislike each other. It is even sadder when two people fail to connect because both parties defensively but falsely guess that the other doesn't like them – and yet, out of low self-worth, takes no risk whatever to alter the situation. We should stop worrying quite so much whether or not people like us, and make that far more interesting and socially useful move: concentrate on showing that we like them.

WARMTH

There is a kind of host who follows every rule of etiquette and outward sign of civility yet who may nevertheless come across as 'coldly polite', leaving guests bored and without any wish to return for more.

What separates a cold from a warm person are not intentions. Both warm and cold characters may be equally full of goodwill and ache with an inward desire for closeness. At stake is a guess about what is going on in another person. From a touching modesty, the coldly polite believe in appearances. They trust that the outward respectability, composure and self-possession of those they encounter must be more or less the whole truth about them. They believe that people are as much in need, and as sane, as they indicate they are on the surface: that is, they believe that they are fine. Their way of hosting others is therefore guided by a sense of the inherent invulnerability and high-mindedness of their guests: they assume that these figures must wish to speak only of serious topics, especially cultural and political ones, that they will want to sit formally and eat a prescribed number of courses, that they would have no interest in small signs of reassurance, that they won't wish to give expression to wayward and absurd sides of themselves, that they won't have any awkward bodily urges or needs, and that their minds will be resolute and well-lit places. In other words, the coldly polite do not apply the knowledge they have of themselves to their interactions with others.

The warm, on the other hand, make a well-founded guess that

those they encounter, despite the observable initial evidence, are not what they seem. They may look adult and composed, but the truth will be reassuringly more complicated. They will, beneath the surface, be intensely confused about many things, in great need of comforting and play, filled with regrets, embarrassed about their bodies, troubled by peculiar urges and beset by a sense of failure. The warm know themselves well enough to walk past the surface presentation and assume that their own stranger selves will have echoes in the lives of others. That is why they might suggest that we get down from the table and have some toasted sandwiches on the sofa, or might want to dance to some songs popular long ago, or might need an extra cushion for our back, or might need to spend quite a long time in the bathroom and might want a magazine while inside. The warm know how sad an illness can leave us feeling and so will remember to ask if our ears are still giving us trouble; they'll recall that we've had trouble sleeping recently; they'll understand if we want to take another look at an attractive person they noticed that we spotted in a restaurant. When we spill something, they'll exclaim that they're so glad it's us because this sort of thing happens to them all the time. The warmly polite person knows that beneath the competent surface everyone is clumsy, frightened, desirous and fascinatingly unbalanced – and they bring this knowledge to bear in every encounter, whatever its outwardly forbidding nature.

This knowledge prevents the warm person from being, at points, overfriendly or cheerful. They do not equate friendliness with a relentlessly upbeat tone. They know how much is sad and anxious in everyone. They don't want to flatter in us ways that could raise the cost of revealing anything more despairing or confused. They leave the door open for a possible need to admit at pretty much any point to something highly shameful. They seem permanently ready to travel with us to the darker, more panicked sides of our minds.

They are in this sense the opposite of the voices we so frequently hear in commercial contexts that ask us if we're having a great day today and that wish us a perfect afternoon in a city we've just touched down in. The warm don't sidestep the knowledge that we may feel like crying even in front of a beautiful entrée or that the thought of returning home after a business trip may be quietly horrific. They don't insist on treating us like cheerful Martians encountering broken, complex humans for the first time.

It can seem like an act of extreme respect to imagine that others are not as troubled or perturbed as we are. Much of our childhood experience subtly reinforces the belief that there are categories of grown-ups, starting with teachers, that share in none of the child's fears. We may, at a certain age, need such an illusion to make the world feel stable enough. But we pay a high price in loneliness for this faith in the face value of figures of authority. True adulthood begins with a firmer hold on the notion that the solid and dignified person will, behind the scenes, almost certainly be craving something quite ordinary – something as unelevated and as human as a hug, a cry or a glass of milk.

TEASING

We are so used to thinking of teasing in its cruel, mocking forms and hating it as such that it can sound initially implausible to think that there could be such a thing as good, affectionate teasing, a kind that we might long for and feel honoured to receive.

The origins of our need to be teased lie in the way that we have all ended up, in one form or another, unbalanced and boxed in by our excesses. Perhaps we have grown too serious and committed to scholarship and mental activity. Or we are too cynical and unready to admit to any need for innocence and spontaneous joy. Or we have invested too much in being refined and luxurious in our way of life.

The person who teases us, and attracts our gratitude for doing so, recognizes the imbalance and appeals, behind the back of our dominant selves, to an unrepresented subordinate side of us: the one that isn't merely intellectual, or that would love a chance sometimes to smile and try out naivety, or that would be reassured by an invitation to mop the floor or go camping. The good teaser aims to reform us, not through lectures, but by encouraging finely administered tart jokes at our surface selves. They consider our ponderousness and nickname us 'Hamlet', they note our commitment to the dark side of existence and ask us if there are any rules against *Weltschmerz* smiling, they hand us the dishcloth and wonder if Sir or Madam might like to scrub the lasagne dish.

And when this happens, we don't hate them for it. It feels like being nicely tickled and we want more, admiring their insights into our imbalances and the frank accuracy with which they are attempting to bolster certain sides of us. They know that we are not merely academic or world-weary or grand, and sense how much we are longing to find a way out. The English critic Cyril Connolly captured the phenomenon in relation to weight: 'Imprisoned in every fat man, a thin man is wildly signalling to be let out.' The image is ripe for extension: inside every bitter cynic, a bruised optimist is looking for an opening. Inside the rule-bound, precise, formal person, a playful, silly self is hoping for release. Inside the important person admired for their status is a child who wants to be liked for themselves.

In Alan Hollinghurst's novel *The Line of Beauty*, there is a moment when the narrator, Nick, ends up at a large party attended by the then British prime minister Mrs Thatcher. Pop music is playing loudly. Daringly, Nick goes up and introduces himself to the political leader and asks if she might like to dance. Like every good teaser, he can guess that there is someone struggling to be let out. There is a moment of acute hesitation and what looks almost like pain on the prime minister's face, but then a large smile breaks out and she replies, 'You know, I'd like that *very* much.'

It is gratifying to be warmly teased because it is a sign that the teaser has bothered to study a struggle within ourselves and perceptively taken the side of the under-represented party. They have not been intimidated, as so many others are, by a front we don't ourselves wholly identify with or like. They know it cannot be the whole story and have made a kindly, accurate guess as to what the reality might be. We are being taught a lesson, in the very nicest way, without sternness or admonition. Our smile isn't just a sign that we have found something funny, but an admission of how much we ourselves would like to change – and how much we are relying on our friends to help us do so.

One of the largest questions we can ask ourselves, one which directly points us to the areas of our nature we should like to reform, is: what would I like to be teased about?

THE GOOD LISTENER

Being a good listener is one of the most important and enchanting life skills anyone can have. Yet few of us know how to do it, not because we are evil but because no one has taught us how and – a related point – few have listened sufficiently well to us. So we come to social life greedy to speak rather than listen, hungry to meet others but reluctant to hear them. Friendship degenerates into a socialized egoism.

Like most things, the answer lies in education. Our civilization is full of great books on how to speak – Cicero's *On the Orator* and Aristotle's *Rhetoric* were two of the greatest in the ancient world – but sadly no one has ever written a book called *The Listener*. There are a range of things that the good listener is doing that make it so nice to spend time in their company. Without necessarily quite realizing it, we're often propelled into conversation by something that feels both urgent and somehow undefined. We're bothered at work; we're toying with more ambitious career moves; we're not sure if so-and-so is right for us; a relationship is in difficulties; we're fretting about something or feeling a bit low about life in general (without being able to put a finger on exactly what's wrong); or perhaps we're very excited and enthusiastic about something, though the reasons for our passion are tricky to pin down.

At heart, all these are issues in search of elucidation. The good listener knows that we'd ideally move – via conversation with another person – from a confused, agitated state of mind to one that was more focused and (hopefully) more serene. Together with them, we'd work out what was really at stake. But in reality this tends not to happen, because there isn't enough of an awareness of the desire and need for clarification within conversation. There aren't enough good listeners. So people tend to assert rather than analyse. They restate in many different ways the fact that they are worried, excited, sad or hopeful, and their interlocutor listens but doesn't assist them to discover more. Good listeners fight against this with a range of conversational gambits.

They hover as the other speaks: they offer encouraging little remarks of support, they make gentle positive gestures – a sigh of sympathy, a nod of encouragement, a strategic 'hmm' of interest. All the time they are egging the other to go deeper into issues. They love saying, 'Tell me more about . . .'; 'I was fascinated when you said . . .'; 'Why did that happen, do you think?' or 'How did you feel about that?' The good listener takes it for granted that they will encounter vagueness in the conversation of others. But they don't condemn, rush or get impatient, because they see vagueness as a universal and highly significant trouble of the mind that it is the task of a true friend to help with. Often, we're in the vicinity of something but we can't quite close in on what's really bothering or exciting us. The good listener knows we benefit hugely from encouragement to elaborate, to go into greater detail, to push a little further. We need someone who, rather than launch forth, will simply say two rare, magic words: 'Go on.' We mention a sibling and they want to know a bit more. What was the relationship like in childhood? How has it changed over time? They're curious about where our concerns and excitements come from. They ask things like, 'Why did that particularly bother you?' 'Why was that such a big thing for you?' They keep our histories in mind; they might refer back to something we said before and we feel they're building up a deeper base of engagement.

It's fatally easy to say vague things: we simply mention that something is lovely or terrible, nice or annoying. But we don't really explore why we feel this way. The good listener has a productive, friendly suspicion of some of our own first statements and is after the deeper attitudes that are lurking in the background. They take things we say like, 'I'm fed up with my job' or 'My partner and I are having a lot of rows . . .' and help us to concentrate on what it really is about the job we don't like or what the squabbles might deep down be about. They're bringing to listening an ambition to clear up underlying issues.

A key move of the good listener is not always to follow every byway or subplot introduced by the speaker, for they may be getting lost and further from their own point than they would wish. The good listener is always looking to take the speaker back to their last reasonable idea – saying, 'Yes, yes, but you were saying just a moment ago . . .' or 'So, ultimately, what do you think it was about?' The good listener is, paradoxically, a skilled interrupter. But they don't, as most people do, interrupt to intrude their own ideas; they interrupt to help the other get back to their original, more sincere yet elusive concerns.

The good listener doesn't moralize. They know their own minds well enough not to be surprised or frightened by strangeness. They give the impression that they recognize and accept human folly; they don't flinch when we mention our terrors and desires. They reassure us they're not going to shred our dignity. Saying one feels like a failure or a pervert could mean being dropped. The good listener signals early and clearly that they don't see us in these terms. Our vulnerability is something they warm to rather than being appalled by. It is only too easy to end up experiencing ourselves as strangely cursed and exceptionally deviant or uniquely incapable. But the good listener makes their own strategic confessions, so as to set the record straight about the meaning of being a normal (that is, very muddled and radically imperfect) human being. They confess not so much to unburden themselves as to help others accept their own nature and see that being a bad parent, a poor lover or a confused worker is not a malignant act of wickedness but an ordinary feature of being alive that others have unfairly edited out of their public profiles.

When we're in the company of people who listen well, we experience a very powerful pleasure, but too often we don't really realize what it is about what this person is doing that is so welcome. By paying strategic attention to our feelings of satisfaction, we should learn to magnify these pleasures and offer them to others, who will notice, heal and then repay the favour in turn. Listening deserves discovery as one of the keys to good meals, late evenings – and good societies more broadly.

SOCIAL CATASTROPHE

We try so hard to do it right: we are polite, we apologize, we write thank-you letters, we ask how someone's day was, we bring cake. And yet, despite our efforts, nothing will spare us occasional involvement in the sort of outright social calamity that we know, even as it unfolds, is going to sear itself into the memory and be written in indelible ink across our lives.

We might be at a drinks party where we mention how much we enjoyed reading a very funny, very scathing review of a new book. Then someone whispers to us that one of the people we are addressing is the book's author.

Or we were instrumental in having a particular colleague fired – and now they are at the next table in the little restaurant and have looked up and noticed us.

Or our partner left their devastated spouse for us a year ago and now this spouse is next to us in line at the airport, waiting to board the same flight.

Or we notice a heavily pregnant woman standing near us on a train and offer her our seat. And she thanks us and, with a wan smile, specifies that she isn't pregnant at all.

We have not set out to be evil or idiotic – the book really was very badly written, our colleague was truly not suited for the role, our partner is much happier with us, the passenger did legitimately look close to a due date – and yet we have unleashed what is without question a disaster.

One way of reacting is to apologize profusely, then to try to explain, in a lot of detail perhaps, why things are in fact OK. We strive to restore a good impression of ourselves in the other's mind and to repair the violently torn social fabric. We give reasons why we might be being misunderstood or have made a slip. We rehearse the failings of the book but add that in many ways it was lovely too, especially in the later chapters; we explain that there was nothing personal in the sacking, it was a collective decision based purely on objective considerations; we evolve a theory of relationships in which there is no ownership of partners; we start to describe how the cut of their overcoat in that particular position reasonably suggested the outline of a growing infant . . .

But there might be another, better way, one in which we accept – with immensely dignified, stoic pessimism and a sense of dark and gigantic responsibility – that there is simply nothing we can do other than fall silent and absorb our failure and the mismatch between who we are and the direction of the universe. We recognize that any shred of politeness will now lie on the side of leaving things broken, that anything else will be sentimentality and self-serving blather. We give up our pretence of being a wholly kind or ethical person and reckon with our awesome powers to inflict wrong. Our name will always be a byword for insensitivity and idiocy in certain circles and we will have to carry the pain in our hearts until the end. We will be wincing decades from now at the irredeemable proof of a stubborn strain of cowardice and foolishness within us.

Oddly, this kind of clear-eyed self-criticism is not without its uses. It is the necessary foundation for a less blithe and presumptuous, more ethical and more careful future. We will henceforth better understand how easily we can damage other people, how unwittingly we can inflict pain, how tragic the mismatch can be between intentions and effect – and from such an awareness will spring ever greater efforts to be, wherever possible, a bit more gentle, tolerant, forgiving, darkly funny and uncomplaining, a bit less self-righteous. Our moments of social catastrophe will reinforce our always fragile but deeply necessary commitment to a life of self-examination, kindness and good manners.

3 Calm

PESSIMISM

A pessimist is someone who calmly assumes from the outset, and with a great deal of justification, that things tend to turn out very badly in almost all areas of existence. Strange though it can sound, pessimism is one of the greatest sources of serenity and contentment.

The reasons are legion. Relationships are rarely if ever the blissful marriage of two minds and hearts that Romanticism teaches us to expect; sex is invariably an area of tension and longing; creative endeavour is pretty much always painful, compromised and slow; any job – however appealing on paper – will be irksome in many of its details; children will always resent their parents, however well intentioned and kindly the adults may try to be. Politics is evidently a process of muddle and dispiriting compromise.

Our degree of satisfaction is critically dependent on our expectations. The greater our hopes, the greater the risks of rage, bitterness, disappointment and a sense of persecution. We are not always humiliated by failing at things; we are humiliated only if we first invested our pride and sense of worth in a given achievement and then did not reach it. Our expectations determine what we will interpret as a triumph and what must count as a failure. 'With no attempt there can be no failure; with no failure no humiliation. So our self-esteem in this world depends entirely on what we *back* ourselves to be and do,' wrote the psychologist William James. 'It is determined by the ratio of our actualities to our supposed potentialities . . . thus:

$$\text{Self-esteem} \quad = \quad \frac{\text{Success}}{\text{Expectations}}.\text{'}$$

The problem with our world is that it does not stop emphasizing that success, calm, happiness and fulfilment could, somehow, one day be ours. And in this way it never ceases to torture us.

As with optimists, pessimists would like things to go well. But by recognizing that many things can – and probably will – go wrong, the pessimist is adroitly placed to secure the good outcome both parties ultimately seek. It is the pessimist who, having never expected anything to go right, ends up with one or two things to smile about.

RAGE

However illogical rage can look, it is never right to dismiss it as merely beyond understanding or control. It operates according to a universal underlying rationale: we shout because we are hopeful.

How badly we react to frustration is ultimately determined by what we think of as normal. We may be irritated that it is raining, but our pessimistic accommodation to the likelihood of its doing so means we are unlikely ever to respond to a downpour by screaming. Our annoyance is tempered by what we understand can be expected of existence. We aren't overwhelmed by anger whenever we are frustrated; only when we first believed ourselves entitled to a particular satisfaction and then did not receive it. Our furies spring from events which violate a background sense of the rules of existence.

And yet we too often have the wrong rules. We shout when we lose the house keys because we somehow believe in a world in which belongings never go astray. We lose our temper at being misunderstood by our partner because something has convinced us that we are not irredeemably alone.

So we must learn to disappoint ourselves at leisure before events take us by surprise. We must be systematically inducted into the darkest realities – the stupidities of others, the ineluctable failings of technology, the eventual destruction of all that we cherish – while we are still capable of a relative measure of rational control.

ANXIETY

Anxiety is not a sign of sickness, a weakness of the mind or an error for which we should always seek a medical solution. It is mostly a hugely reasonable and sensitive response to the genuine strangeness, terror, uncertainty and riskiness of existence.

Anxiety is our fundamental state for well-founded reasons: because we are intensely vulnerable physical beings, a complicated network of fragile organs all biding their time before eventually letting us down catastrophically at a moment of their own choosing; because we have insufficient information upon which to make most major life decisions; because we can imagine so much more than we have and live in ambitious mediatized societies where envy and restlessness are a constant; because we are the descendants of the great worriers of the species, the others having been trampled and torn apart by wild animals; because we still carry in our bones – into the calm of the suburbs – the terrors of the savannah; because the trajectories of our careers and of our finances are plotted within the tough-minded, competitive, destructive, random workings of an uncontained economic engine; because we rely for our self-esteem and sense of comfort on the love of people we cannot control and whose needs and hopes will never align seamlessly with our own.

In her great novel *Middlemarch*, the nineteenth-century English writer George Eliot, a deeply self-aware but also painfully anxious figure, reflected on what it would be like if we were truly sensitive, open to the world and felt the implications of everything: 'If we had a keen vision and feeling of all ordinary human life, it would be like hearing the grass grow and the squirrel's heart beat, and we should die of that roar which lies on the other side of silence. As it is, the quickest of us walk about well wadded with stupidity.'

Eliot's lines offer us a way to reinterpret our anxiety with greater benevolence. It emerges from a dose of clarity that is (currently) too powerful for us to cope with, but isn't for that matter wrong. We panic because we rightly feel how thin the veneer of civilization is, how mysterious other people are, how improbable it is that we exist at all, how everything that seems to matter now will eventually be annihilated, how random many of the turnings of our lives are, how much we are prey to accident.

Anxiety is simply insight that we haven't yet found a productive use for, that hasn't yet made its way into art or philosophy.

Which is not to say that there aren't better and worse ways to approach our condition. The single most important move is acceptance. There is no need – on top of everything else – to be anxious that we are anxious. The mood is no sign that our lives have gone wrong, merely that we are alive. We should also be more careful when pursuing things we imagine will spare us anxiety. We can head for them by all means, but for other reasons than fantasies of calm, and with a little less vigour and a little more scepticism. We will still be anxious when we finally have the house, the relationship and the right income.

We should at all points spare ourselves the burden of loneliness. We are far from the only ones to be suffering. Everyone is more anxious than they are inclined to tell us. Even the tycoon and the couple in love are in pain. We have collectively failed to admit to ourselves how much anxiety is our default state.

We must, when possible, learn to laugh about our anxieties, laughter being the exuberant expression of relief when a hitherto private agony is given a well-crafted social formulation in a joke. We may have to suffer alone, but we can at least hold out our arms to our similarly tortured, fractured and, above all else, anxious neighbours, as if to say, in the kindest way possible, 'I know . . .'

Anxiety deserves greater dignity. It is not a sign of degeneracy, rather a kind of masterpiece of insight: a justifiable expression of our mysterious participation in a disordered, uncertain world.

THE NEED TO BE ALONE

Because our culture places such a high value on sociability, it can be deeply awkward to have to explain how much, at certain points, we need to be alone.

We may try to pass off our desire as something work-related – people generally understand a need to finish a project. But, in truth, a far less respectable and more profound desire may be driving us on: unless we are alone, we are at risk of forgetting who we are.

We, the ones who are asphyxiated without periods by ourselves, take other people very seriously – perhaps more seriously than those in the uncomplicated ranks of the endlessly gregarious. We listen closely to stories, we give ourselves to others, we respond with emotion and empathy. But as a result we cannot keep swimming in company indefinitely.

At a certain point, we have had enough of conversations that take us away from our own thought processes, enough of external demands that stop us heeding our inner tremors, enough of the pressure for superficial cheerfulness that denies the legitimacy of our latent melancholy – and enough of robust common sense that flattens our peculiarities and less well-charted ideas.

We need to be alone because life among other people unfolds too quickly. The pace is relentless: the jokes, the insights, the excitements. There can sometimes be enough in five minutes of social life to take up an hour of analysis. It is a quirk of our minds that not every emotion that impacts us is at once fully acknowledged, understood or even – as it were – truly felt. After time among others, there are myriad sensations that exist in an 'unprocessed' form within us. Perhaps an idea that someone raised made us anxious, prompting inchoate impulses for changes in our lives. Perhaps an anecdote sparked off an envious ambition that is worth decoding and listening to in order to grow. Maybe someone subtly fired an aggressive dart at us and we haven't had the chance to realize we are hurt. We need quiet to console ourselves by formulating an explanation of where the nastiness might have come from. We are more vulnerable and tender-skinned than we're encouraged to imagine.

By retreating into ourselves, it looks as if we are the enemies of others, but our solitary moments are in reality a homage to the richness of social existence. Unless we've had time alone, we can't be who we would like to be around our fellow humans. We won't have original opinions. We won't have lively and authentic perspectives. We'll be – in the wrong way – a bit like everyone else.

We're drawn to solitude not because we despise humanity but because we are properly responsive to what the company of others entails. Extensive stretches of being alone may in reality be a precondition for knowing how to be a better friend and a properly attentive companion.

THE IMPORTANCE OF STARING OUT OF THE WINDOW

We tend to reproach ourselves for staring out of the window. Most of the time, we are supposed to be working, or studying, or ticking things off a to-do list. It can seem almost the definition of wasted time. It appears to produce nothing, to serve no purpose. We equate it with boredom, distraction, futility. The act of cupping our chin in our hands near a pane of glass and letting our eyes drift in the middle distance does not enjoy high prestige. We don't go around saying, 'I had a great day today. The high point was staring out of the window.' But maybe, in a better society, this is exactly what people would quietly say to one another.

The point of staring out of a window is, paradoxically, not to find out what is going on outside. It is, rather, an exercise in discovering the contents of our own minds. It is easy to imagine we know what we think, what we feel and what's going on in our heads. But we rarely do entirely. There's a huge amount of what makes us who we are that circulates unexplored and unused. Its potential lies untapped. It is shy and doesn't emerge under the pressure of direct questioning. If we do it right, staring out of the window offers a way for us to be alert to the quieter suggestions and perspectives of our deeper selves. Plato suggested a metaphor for the mind: our ideas are like birds fluttering around in the aviary of our brains. But in order for the birds to settle, Plato understood that we need periods of purpose-free calm. Staring out of the window offers such an opportunity. We see the world going on: a patch of weeds is holding its own against the wind; a grey tower block looms through the drizzle. But we don't need to respond, we have no overarching intentions, and so the more tentative parts of ourselves have a chance to be heard, like the sound of church bells in the city once the traffic has died down at night.

The potential of daydreaming isn't recognized by societies obsessed with productivity. But some of our greatest insights come when we stop trying to be purposeful and instead respect the creative potential of reverie. Window daydreaming is a strategic rebellion against the excessive demands of immediate, but in the end insignificant, pressures in favour of the diffuse, but very serious, search for the wisdom of the unexplored deep self.

NATURE

Nature corrects our erroneous, and ultimately very painful, sense that we are essentially free. The idea that we have the freedom to fashion our own destinies as we please has become central to the contemporary world view: we are encouraged to imagine that we can, with time, create exactly the lives we desire, around our relationships, our work and existence more generally. This hopeful scenario has been the source of extraordinary and unnecessary suffering.

There are many things we want desperately to avoid, which we will spend huge parts of our lives worrying about and which we will then bitterly resent when they force themselves upon us nevertheless.

The idea of inevitability is central to the natural world: the deciduous tree has to shed it leaves when the temperature dips in autumn; the river must erode its banks; the cold front will deposit its rain; the tide has to rise and fall. The laws of nature are governed by forces nobody has chosen, no one can resist and which brook no exception.

When we contemplate nature (a forest in the autumn, for example, or the reproductive cycle of the salmon), we are thinking about rules that in their broad, irresistible structure apply to ourselves as well. We too must mature, seek to reproduce, age, fall ill and die. We face a litany of other burdens too: we will never be fully understood by others; we will always be burdened by primordial anxiety; we will never fully know what it is like to be someone else; we will invariably fantasize about more than we can have; we will realize we cannot – in key ways – be who we would wish.

What we most fear can happen irrespective of our desires. But when we see frustration as a law of nature, we drain it of some of its sting and bitterness. We recognize that limitations are not in any way unique to us. In awesome, majestic scenes (the life of an elephant; the eruption of a volcano), nature moves us away from our habitual tendency to personalize and rail against our lot.

Sometimes we respond quite negatively to encounters with things that are much larger and more powerful than ourselves. It's a feeling that can strike us when we are alone in a new city, trying to negotiate a vast railway terminus or the huge underground system at rush hour, and we sense that no one knows anything about us or cares in the least for our confusion. The scale of the place forces upon us the unwelcome fact that we don't matter in the greater scheme of things and that what is of great concern to us doesn't figure at all in the minds of others. It's a crushing, lonely experience that intensifies anxiety and agitation.

But there's another way an encounter with the large-scale can affect us – and calm us down – that philosophers have called 'the sublime'. Heading back to the airport after a series of frustrating meetings, we notice the sun setting behind the mountains. Tiers of clouds are bathed in gold and purple, while huge slanting beams of light cut across the urban landscape. To record the feeling without implying anything mystical, it seems as if one's attention is being drawn up into the radiant gap between the clouds and the summits, and that one is for a moment merging with the cosmos. Normally the sky isn't a major focus of attention, but now it's mesmerizing. For a while it doesn't seem to matter so much what happened in the office or that the contract will – maddeningly – have to be renegotiated by the legal team.

At this moment, nature seems to be sending us a humbling message: the incidents of our lives are not terribly important. And yet, strangely, rather than being distressing, this sensation can be a source of immeasurable solace and calm.

Things that have up to now been looming large in our minds (something has gone wrong with the Singapore discussion, a colleague has behaved coldly, there's been disagreement about patio furniture) are cut down in size. The sublime drags us away from the minor details which normally – and inevitably – occupy our attention and makes us concentrate on what is truly major. The encounter with the sublime undercuts the gradations of human status and makes everyone – at least for a time – look relatively unimpressive. Next to the mighty canyon or the vast ocean, even the celebrity or the CEO does not seem so mighty.

Deserts offer particular respite in this context. Year by year little changes: a few more stones will crumble from the mesa; a few plants will eke out an existence; the same pattern of light and shadow will be endlessly repeated. Caring about having a larger office or being worried that one's car has a small scratch over the left rear wheel or that the sofa is looking a bit moth-eaten doesn't make much sense against the enormity of time and space. Differences in accomplishments, standing and possessions that torment us in the cities don't feel especially exciting or impressive when considered from the emotional state that a desert induces. Things happen on the scale of centuries. Today and tomorrow are essentially the same. Your existence is a small, temporary thing. You will die and it will be as if you had never been.

It could sound demeaning. But these are generous sentiments when we otherwise so easily suffer by exaggerating our own importance. We are truly minute and entirely dispensable. The sublime does not humble us by exalting others; it gives a sense of the lesser status of all of wretched humanity.

In the late eighteenth century, the German philosopher Immanuel Kant thought 'the starry heavens above' were the most sublime spectacle in nature and that contemplation of this transcendent sight could hugely assist us in coping with our travails. Although Kant was interested in the developing science of astronomy, he saw the field as primarily serving a major psychological purpose. Unfortunately, since then, the advances in astrophysics have become increasingly embarrassed around this aspect of the stars. It would seem deeply odd today if in a science class there were a special section not on the fact that Aldebaran is an orange-red giant star of spectral and luminosity type $K5+III$ and that it is currently losing mass at a rate of $(1-1.6) \times 10^{-11} M_\odot \text{ yr}^{-1}$ with a velocity of 30 km s^{-1} but rather on the ways in which the sight of stars can help us manage our emotional lives and relations with our families – even though knowing how to cope better with anxiety is in most lives a more urgent and important task than steering one's rocket around the galaxies. Although we've made vast scientific progress since Kant's time, we haven't properly explored the potential of space as a source of wisdom, as opposed to a puzzle for astrophysicists to unpick.

On an evening walk you look up and see the planets Venus and Jupiter shining in the darkening sky. As the dusk deepens you might see Andromeda and Aries. It's a hint of the unimaginable extensions of space across the solar system, the galaxy, the cosmos. They were there, quietly revolving, their light streaming down, as spotted hyenas warily eyed a Stone Age settlement; and as Julius Caesar's triremes set out after midnight to cross the Channel and reach the cliffs of England's south coast at dawn. The sight has a calming effect because none of our troubles, disappointments or hopes have any relevance. Whatever happens to us, whatever we do, is of no consequence from the point of view of the universe.

And though we know that the moon is a lifeless accumulation of galactic debris, we might make a point of watching it emerge – as a representative of an entirely different perspective within which our own concerns are mercifully irrelevant.

A central task of culture should be to remind us that the laws of nature apply to us as well as to trees, clouds and cliff faces. Our goal is to get clearer about where our own tantalizingly powerful yet always limited agency stops: where we will be left with no option but to bow to forces infinitely greater than our own.

ACCEPTANCE

The more calm matters to us, the more we will be aware of all the very many times when we have been less calm than we should. We'll be sensitive to our own painfully frequent bouts of irritation and upset. It can feel laughably hypocritical. Surely a genuine devotion to calm would mean ongoing serenity? But this isn't a fair judgement, because being calm all the time isn't ever a viable option. What counts is the commitment one is making to the idea of being a little calmer than last year. We can legitimately count as lovers of calm when we ardently seek to grow calmer, not when we succeed at being calm on all occasions. However frequent the lapses, it is the devotion that matters.

Furthermore, it is a psychological law that those who are most attracted to calm will almost certainly also be especially irritable and by nature prone to particularly high levels of anxiety. We have a mistaken picture of what lovers of calm look like if we assume them to be among the most tranquil of the species.

Typically, lovers of something are not the people who already possess it but those who are hugely aware of how much they lack it – and are therefore especially humble before, and committed to, the task of securing it.

III : Relationships

1 *Getting Together*

BEYOND ROMANTICISM

To fall in love with someone is such a personal and spontaneous process, it can seem hugely implausible to imagine that something else (call it society or culture) might be playing a covert, critical role in governing our relationships in their most intimate moments.

Yet the history of humanity shows us so many varied approaches to love, so many different assumptions about how couples are supposed to get together and so many distinctive ways of interpreting our feelings, we should accept with a degree of grace that the way we go about our relationships must in practice owe rather a lot to the prevailing environment beyond our bedrooms. Our loves unfold against a cultural backdrop that creates a powerful sense of what is 'normal' in love: it subtly directs us as to where we should place our emotional emphases, it teaches us what to value, how to approach conflicts, what to get excited about, when to tolerate and what we can legitimately be incensed by. Love has a history and we ride, sometimes rather helplessly, its currents.

Since around 1750, we have been living in the age of Romanticism, an ideology that began in the minds of poets and artists and has now conquered the world, powerfully (yet always quietly) determining how a shopkeeper's son in Yokohama will approach a first date, how a scriptwriter in Hollywood will shape the ending of a film, or when a middle-aged woman in Buenos Aires might decide to call it a day with her civil servant husband of twenty years.

No single relationship ever follows the Romantic template exactly, but its broad outlines are frequently present nevertheless and might be summed up as follows:

- Romanticism is deeply hopeful about marriage. It tells us that marriage could combine all the excitement of a love affair with all the advantages of a settled and practical union. Romanticism makes the remarkable claim that it may be possible to feel, after twenty years, a bustling household and a number of children, almost all the longings that previous ages had restricted to a lover at the time of the first embrace.

- Along the way, Romanticism has conceptually united love and sex. It has elevated sex to the supreme expression of admiration and respect for another person. Frequent, mutually satisfying sex is assumed to be not just pleasurable but the expected bellwether of the health of a relationship. Romanticism has thereby turned infrequent sex and adultery from the problems they always were into the catastrophes they now are.

- Romanticism has proposed that true love must mean an end to all loneliness. The right partner will, it promises us, understand us entirely, possibly without our needing to speak very much; they will intuit our souls.

- Romanticism believes that choosing a partner is a matter of surrendering to feelings rather than evaluating practical considerations. For most of recorded history, people had fallen into relationships and married for dynastic, status or financial reasons. It was certainly not expected that, on top of everything else, one should love one's partner. But for Romanticism, a sound couple should be pulled together by an overwhelming instinct and will know in their hearts – after a few pleasant weeks and some extraordinary sensations in bed – that they have found their destiny.

- Romanticism manifests a powerful disdain for practicalities and money. It has taught us to feel that it is cold – or un-Romantic – to say that we know we are with the right person because they make an excellent financial fit or because we gel over bathroom etiquette and attitudes to punctuality. People, we have learned to think, only turn to practical considerations when all else has failed ('I couldn't find love, I had to settle for convenience') or because they are extraordinarily sinister (the gold-digger, the social climber).

- Romanticism believes that true love should involve delighting in a lover's every facet, that it is synonymous with accepting everything about someone. The idea that one's partner (or oneself) might need to evolve and mature is taken to be a sign that a relationship is on the rocks: 'You're going to have to change' is a last-ditch threat and 'Love me for who I am' the most noble of cries.

This template of love is a historical creation. It is hugely beautiful and often enjoyable – for a while. The Romantics were brilliantly perceptive about some dimensions of emotional life and were extremely talented about expressing their hopes and longings. Many of the feelings they celebrated had existed before, but the Romantics elevated them, turning them from passing fancies into serious concepts with the power to determine the course of relationships over a lifetime.

We can also state at this point that Romanticism has been a disaster for love. It is an intellectual and spiritual movement which has had a devastating impact on the ability of ordinary people to lead successful emotional lives. Our strongest cultural voices have, to our huge cost, given us a very unhelpful script to apply to a hugely tricky task. We have been told, among other things, that:

- we should meet a person of extraordinary inner and outer beauty and immediately feel a special attraction to them, and they to us;

- we should have highly satisfying sex, not only at the start, but for evermore;

- we should never be attracted to anyone else;

- we should understand one another intuitively;

- we don't need an education in love (we may need to train to become a pilot or a brain surgeon, but not a lover – we will pick that up along the way, by following our feelings);

- we should have no secrets and spend constant time together (work shouldn't get in the way);

- we should raise a family without any loss of sexual or emotional intensity;

- our lover must be our soulmate, best friend, co-parent, co-chauffeur, accountant, household manager and spiritual guide.

Reflecting on the history of Romanticism should be consoling because it suggests that quite a lot of the troubles we have with relationships don't stem (as we normally, guiltily, end up thinking) from our ineptitude, our inadequacy or our regrettable choice of partners. Knowing the history invites another, more useful idea: we were set an incredibly hard task by our culture, which then had the temerity to present it as easy.

It seems crucial systematically to question the assumptions of the Romantic view of love – not in order to destroy love, but to save it. We need to piece together a post-Romantic theory of couples, because in order to make a relationship last we will almost certainly have to be disloyal to most of the Romantic emotions that edged us into it in the first place. The idea of being post-Romantic shouldn't imply cynicism; that one has abandoned the hope of relationships ever working out well. The post-Romantic attitude is just as ambitious about good relationships, but it has a very different sense of how hope can be honoured.

We need to replace the Romantic template with a psychologically mature vision of love we might call Classical, which encourages in us a range of unfamiliar but hopefully effective attitudes:

- that it is normal that love and sex do not always belong together;

- that discussing money early on, up front, in a serious way is not a betrayal of love;

- that realizing that we are rather flawed, and our partner is too, is of huge benefit to a couple in increasing the amount of tolerance and generosity in circulation;

- that we will never find everything in another person, nor they in us, not because of some unique incapacity, but because of the basic operations of human nature;

- that we need to make immense and often rather artificial-sounding efforts to understand one another because intuition will never be enough;

- that practicalities matter – so, for example, there is special dignity around the topics of laundry and domestic management.

Such attitudes and many more belong to the new, more hopeful future of love.

CHOOSING A PARTNER

Our modern understanding of love is built on the principle of freedom of choice. We have been unshackled from extraneous inhibiting forces – economic, familial, religious – in order to enjoy the freedom to form relationships with exactly whom we like.

But we have, along the way, made a painful discovery: that the greatest inhibitor of our freedom to choose partners as we would wish comes from within. It turns out that we are never exactly free to love in accordance with wisdom or our aspirations for happiness.

The originators of the idea of free choice in love certainly imagined that their bold suggestion would bring to an end the sort of unhappy relationships previously brokered by parents and society. But our obedience to our instincts has, very often, proved to be its own disaster. Respecting the special feelings we get around certain people in nightclubs and at train stations, at parties and on websites appears not to have made us any happier in our unions than a medieval couple shackled in marriage by two royal courts keen to preserve the sovereignty of a slice of ancestral land. 'Instinct' has been little better than 'calculation' in underwriting the quality of our love stories.

This is because we don't fall in love first and foremost with those who care for us best and most devotedly; we fall in love with those who care for us in ways that we expect. Adult love emerges from a template of how we should be loved that was created in childhood and is likely to be connected to a range of problematic compulsions that militate in key ways against our chances of growth.

Far more than happiness, what motivates us in relationships is a search for familiarity – and what is familiar is not restricted to comfort, reassurance and tenderness; it may include feelings of abandonment, humiliation and neglect, which can form part of the list of paradoxical ingredients we need to refind in adult love. We might reject healthy, calm and nurturing candidates simply on the basis that they feel too right, too eerie in their unfamiliar kindness, and nowhere near as satisfying as a bully or an ingrate, who will torture us in just the way we need in order to feel we are in love.

To get at the peculiar instincts which circulate powerfully in the less noticed corners of our brains, we might try to finish stub sentences that invite us to share what might charm or repel us in others:

If someone shows me huge kindness and consideration, I . . .

If someone isn't entirely convinced by me, I . . .

When someone tells me they really need me, I . . .

Our honest reactions are legacies that reveal our underlying assumptions about the kind of love it feels we are allowed, and are perhaps not an especially good guide to personal or mutual happiness.

It is common to advise people who are drawn to tricky candidates simply to leave them for more wholesome options. This is theoretically appealing yet often practically impossible. We cannot magically redirect the wellsprings of attraction. Rather than aim for a transformation in the types of people we are drawn to, it may be wiser to try to adjust how we respond and behave around the difficult characters whom our past mandates that we will find interesting.

Our problems are often generated because we continue to respond to compelling people in the way we learned to behave as children around their templates. For instance, maybe we had a rather irate parent who often raised their voice. We loved them, but reacted by feeling that when they were angry we must be guilty. We got timid and humble. Now if a partner (to whom we are magnetically drawn) gets cross, we respond as squashed, browbeaten children: we sulk, we assume it's our fault, we feel got at and yet deserving of criticism.

But rather than seek radically to re-engineer our instincts, we can try to learn to react to our lovers not as we did as children but in the more mature and constructive manner of a rational adult. There is an enormous opportunity to move ourselves from childlike to more adult patterns of response in relation to the difficulties we are attracted to.

Many of us are highly likely to end up with somebody with a particularly knotty set of issues which trigger our desires as well as our childlike defensive responses. The answer isn't usually to shut down the relationship, but to strive to deal with the compelling challenges it throws up with some of the wisdom we weren't capable of when we first encountered these in a parent or caregiver.

It probably isn't in our remit to locate a wholly grown-up person to love; but it is always in our remit to behave in more grown-up ways around a partner's less mature sides.

A: Partner's tricky behaviour	B: Childlike response on our part	C: More adult response we should aim for
Raising voice	'It's all my fault…'	'This is their issue. I don't have to feel bad.'
Patronizing	'I'm stupid.'	'There are lots of kinds of intelligence. Mine is fine.'
Morose	'I have to fix you.'	'I'll do my best, but I'm not ultimately responsible for your mindset – and this doesn't have to impact on my self-esteem…'
Overbearing	'I deserve this.'	'I'm not intimidated by you.'
Distracted, preoccupied	Attention-seeking: 'Notice me.'	'You're busy, I'm busy, that's OK…'

THAT WE ARE A HELLISH PROPOSITION

The idea that one is in many ways an extremely difficult person to live around sounds, at first, improbable and even offensive. Yet fully understanding and readily and graciously admitting this possibility may be the surest way of making certain that one proves a somewhat endurable proposition. There are few people more deeply insufferable than those who don't, at regular intervals, suspect they might be so.

We are, all of us, hellish. We don't need to be thinking of anyone in particular to know this is true for everyone. We have all – in one way or another – been inadequately parented, have a panoply of unfortunate psychological traits, are beset by bad habits, are anxious, jealous, ill-tempered and vain. We are necessarily going to bring an awesome amount of trouble into someone else's life.

We tend to be shielded from this unwelcome news through a mixture of sentimentality and neglect. Our parents may have loved us too much to outline the drawbacks; our friends may not have had the will. And our exes are liable to have been too keen to escape to bother with our re-education.

Furthermore, it is impossible, on one's own, to notice the extent of one's power to madden. Our eccentric hours and reliance on work to ward off feelings of vulnerability can pass without comment when we fall singly into bed past one in the morning. Our peculiar eating habits lack reality without another pair of eyes to register our dismaying combinations.

Eventually, a partner will call us out. It will feel like a horrible personal attack that a nicer person would not have put us through. But it is merely an inevitable response to failings anyone exposed to us would have eventually needed to bring up. We would all do well to have a detailed response to the suggestion, best raised early on, that we might be a trial to be with.

Everyone, seen close up, has an appalling amount wrong with

them. The specifics vary hugely but the essential point is shared. It isn't that a partner is too critical or unusually demanding. They are simply the bearer of inevitably awkward news. Asking anyone to be with us is in the end a peculiar request to make of someone we claim to care intensely about.

THE HELLISHNESS OF OTHERS

In an analogous move, to evolve a clear-eyed and unpanicked view of the grave failings of one's partner is among the most generous actions we are capable of in love. This is because the success or failure of a relationship doesn't hinge on whether the other is deeply flawed – they are. What matters is how we interpret their failings; how we understand the reasons why they have previously been and will again in the future be very difficult to be with.

The crux is whether we can move from interpreting behaviour as a sign of meanness to viewing it as a symptom of pain and anxiety. We will have learned to love when our default response to unfortunate moments is not to feel aggrieved but to wonder what damaged aspects of a partner's rocky past have been engaged.

Annoying characteristics almost always have their roots in childhood, long before our arrival. They are, for the most part, strategies that were developed for coping with stresses that could not correctly be processed by an immature mind. An overcritical, demanding parent might have made them feel as if being disorganized and untidy was a necessary rebellion, a crucial assertion of independence against a threatening demand for compliance. A watchfulness around social status might have been the outcome of a succession of bankruptcies in a father's business during adolescence. An avoidant personality might have resulted from an early unbearable disappointment.

We are ready for relationships not when we have encountered perfection, but when we have grown willing to give flaws the charitable interpretations they deserve.

Our partners aren't uniquely damaged. We just know them a lot better than the exciting stranger. Our partner suffers from the disadvantages of incumbency: of having been in our lives for so long that we have had the opportunity to be patiently introduced to the full range of their inadequacies. Our certainty that we might be happier with another person is founded on ignorance, the result of having been shielded from the worst and crazier dimensions of a new character's personality – which we must accept are sure to be there, not because we know them in any detail, but because we know the human race.

A charitable mindset doesn't make it lovely to be confronted by the other's troubles. But it strengthens our capacity to stick with them, because we see that their failings don't make them unworthy of love, rather all the more urgently in need of it.

THE LONGING FOR REASSURANCE

There are sweet moments, early on in relationships, when one person can't quite work up the courage to let another know just how much they like them. They'd love to touch the other's hand and find a place in their life; but their fear of rejection is so intense they hesitate and falter. Our culture has a lot of sympathy for this awkward and intensely vulnerable stage of love. We're taught to be patient about the way people might grow somewhat flustered or tongue-tied. Or they might act sarcastically or coldly, not from indifference, but as a way of disguising a disturbingly powerful enthusiasm. However, the assumption is that the terror of rejection will be limited in scope and focused on one particular stage of a relationship: its beginning. Once a partner is finally accepted and the union gets under way, the assumption is that the fear must come to an end.

But one of the odder features of relationships is that, in truth, the fear of rejection never ends. It continues, even in quite sane people, on a daily basis, with frequently difficult consequences – chiefly because we refuse to pay it sufficient attention and aren't trained to spot its counter-intuitive symptoms in others. We haven't found a winning way to keep admitting just how much reassurance we need.

Acceptance is never a given; reciprocity is never assured. There can always be new threats, real or perceived, to love's integrity. The trigger to insecurity can be apparently minuscule. Perhaps the other has been away at work for unusual amounts of time; or they were pretty animated talking to a stranger at a party; or it's been a while since sex took place. Perhaps they weren't very warm to us when we walked into the kitchen. Or they've been rather silent for the last half an hour.

Instead of requesting reassurance endearingly and laying out our longing with charm, we have tendencies to mask our needs beneath some tricky behaviours guaranteed to frustrate our ultimate aims. Within established relationships, when the fear of rejection is denied, two major symptoms tend to show up.

First, we may become distant – or what psychotherapists call 'avoidant'. We want to get close to our partners but feel so anxious that we may be unwanted, we freeze them out: we say we're busy, pretend our thoughts are elsewhere. We could get involved with a third person, the ultimate defensive attempt to be distant – and often a perverse attempt to assert that we don't require a love we feel too vulnerable to ask for.

We grow into avoidant patterns when – in childhood – attempts at closeness ended in degrees of rejection, humiliation, uncertainty or shame that we were ill-equipped to deal with. We became, without consciously realizing it, determined that such levels of exposure would never happen again. At an early sign of being disappointed, we therefore now understand the need to close ourselves off from pain. We are too scarred to know how to stay around and mention that we are hurt.

Or else we become controlling – or what psychotherapists calls 'anxious'. We grow suspicious, frantic and easily furious in the face of the ambiguous moments of love; catastrophe never feels too far away. A slightly distant mood must, we feel, be a harbinger of rejection; a somewhat non-reassuring moment is an almost certain prelude to the end. Our concern is touching, but our way of expressing it often less so, for it emerges indirectly as an attack rather than a plea. In the face of the other's swiftly assumed unreliability, we complain administratively and try to control procedurally. We demand that they be back by a certain hour, we berate them for looking away from us for a moment, we force them to show us their commitment by putting them through an obstacle course of administrative chores. We get very angry rather than admit, with serenity, that we're worried. We ward off our vulnerability by denigrating the person who eludes us. We pick up on their weaknesses and complain about their shortcomings. Anything rather than ask the question which so much disturbs us: do you still care? And yet, if this harsh, graceless behaviour could be truly understood for what it is, it would be revealed not as rejection or indifference, but as a strangely distorted – yet very real – plea for tenderness.

A central solution to these patterns is to normalize a new and more accurate picture of emotional functioning: to make it clear just how predictable it is to be in need of reassurance – and at the same time, how understandable it is to be reluctant to reveal one's dependence. We should create room for regular moments, perhaps as often as every few hours, when we can feel unembarrassed and legitimate about asking for confirmation. 'I really need you. Do you still want me?' should be the most normal of enquiries. We should uncouple the admission of need from any associations with the unfortunate and punitive term 'neediness'. We must get better at seeing the love and longing that lurk behind some of our and our partner's most cold, stern or managerial moments.

PARTNER-AS-CHILD

Small children sometimes behave in stunningly unfair and shocking ways: they scream at the person who is looking after them, angrily push away a bowl of animal pasta, immediately discard something you have just fetched for them. But we rarely feel personally agitated or wounded by their behaviour. And the reason is that we don't readily assign negative motives or mean intentions to very small people. We reach around for the most benevolent interpretations. We don't think they are doing it in order to upset us. We probably think that they are getting a bit tired, or their gums are sore, or they are upset by the arrival of a younger sibling. We've got a large repertoire of alternative explanations which defend us from panic or agitation.

This is the reverse of what tends to happen around adults in general and our lovers in particular. Here we imagine that others have deliberately got us in their sights. If the partner is late for our mother's birthday because of 'work', we may assume it's an excuse. If they promised to buy us some extra toothpaste but then 'forgot', we'll imagine a deliberate slight. They probably relish the thought of causing us a little distress.

But if we employed the infant model of interpretation, our first assumption would be quite different: maybe they didn't sleep well last night and are too exhausted to think straight; maybe they've got a sore knee; maybe they are doing the equivalent of testing the boundaries of parental tolerance. Seen from such a point of view, the lover's adult behaviour doesn't magically become nice or acceptable. But the level of agitation is kept safely low. It's very touching that we live in a world where we have learned to be so kind to children; it would be even nicer if we learned to be a little more generous towards the childlike parts of one another.

It sounds strange at first – and even condescending or despairing – to keep in mind that in crucial ways one's partner always remains a child. On the outside they're obviously a functioning adult. But the partner-as-child theory urges us to recognize that parts of the psyche always remain tethered to how they were at the early stages of life. This way of seeing the person one is with may be a helpful strategy for managing times when they are very difficult to cope with: when there are outbursts of deeply unreasonable petulance, sulkiness or flashes of aggression. When they fall far short of what we ideally expect from grown-up behaviour and we dismissively label such attitudes as 'childish', we are – without quite realizing it – approaching a hugely constructive idea, but then (understandably though unfortunately) seeing it as simply an accusation, rather than what it truly is: recognition of an ordinary feature of the human condition.

The therapeutic benefit is the observation that we are generally very good at loving children. Our ability to continue to keep calm around children is founded on the fact that we take it for granted that they are not able to explain what is really bothering them. We deduce the real cause of their sorrow from amid the external symptoms of rage, because we grasp that little children have very limited abilities to diagnose and communicate their own problems.

A central premise of the partner-as-child theory is that it's not an aberration or unique failing of one's partner that they retain a childish dimension. It's a normal, inevitable feature of all adult existence. You are not desperately unlucky to have hitched yourself to someone who is still infantile in many ways. Adulthood simply isn't a complete state; what we call childhood lasts (in a submerged but significant way) all our lives. Therefore some of the responses we reflexively offer to children must forever continue to be relevant when we're dealing with another grown-up.

Being benevolent to one's partner's inner child doesn't mean infantilizing them. This is no call to draw up a chart detailing when they are allowed screen time or to award stars for getting dressed on their own. It means being charitable in translating things they say in terms of their deeper meaning: 'You're a bastard' might actually be a way of trying to say, 'I feel under siege at work and I'm trying to tell myself I'm stronger and more independent than I really feel'; or 'You just don't get it, do you?' might mean, 'I'm terrified and frustrated and I don't really know why. Please be strong.'

Of course, it's much harder being grown up around another adult whose inner child is on display than it is being with an actual child. That's because we can see how little and undeveloped a toddler or a five-year-old is, so sympathy comes naturally. We know, and are visually reminded, that it would be a disaster to suddenly turn on the child and try to hold them fully responsible for every moment of their conduct. Psychology has been warning us for half a century or more that this isn't the right route.

However, we don't yet have this cultural back-up fully in force to assist us in coping with a partner's childish sides. The problem with adults is that they look misleadingly adult – so the need for an accurate, corrective reimagining of their inner lives is more unexpected. We need to force ourselves to picture the turmoil, disappointment, worry and sheer confusion in people who may outwardly appear merely aggressive. Our lover may be tall and able to chair meetings at work, but their behaviour may still sometimes be dramatically connected with their early years. We're so keen never to seem patronizing by treating someone as younger than they are that we overlook the need occasionally to ignore the outward, adult sides of our partner in order to perceive, sympathize with and assuage the angry, confused infant lurking inside.

LOVE AND EDUCATION

The idea of wanting to change our partners sounds deeply disturbing because, collectively, we have been heavily influenced by a particular aspect of the Romantic conception of love. This states that the principal marker of true affection is the capacity to accept another person in their totality, in all their good and bad sides – and in a sense, particularly their bad sides. To love someone is, according to Romantic philosophy, quite simply to love them as they are, without any wish to alter them. We must embrace the whole person to be worthy of the emotion we claim to feel.

At certain moments of love, it does feel particularly poignant and moving to be loved for things that others have condemned us for or not seen the point of. It can seem the ultimate proof of love that our trickier sides can arouse interest, charity and even desire. When a partner finds you shy at parties, they don't laugh – they are sweet and take your tongue-tied state as a sign of sincerity. They're not embarrassed by your slightly unfashionable clothes because, for them, it's about honesty and the strength to ignore public opinion. When you have a hangover, they don't say it was your own fault for drinking too much; they rub your neck, bring you tea and keep the curtains closed.

But we draw the wrong conclusion from such sweet moments: the idea that loving someone must always mean accepting them in every area, that love is in essence unconditional approval. Any desire for change must, according to this ideology, arouse upset, annoyance and deep resistance. It seems proof that there can't be love, that something has gone terribly wrong . . .

But there is another, more workable and mature philosophy of love available, one that's traceable back to the ancient Greeks. This states that love is an admiration for the good sides, the perfections, of a person. The Greeks took the view that love is not an obscure emotion. Loving someone is not an odd chemical phenomenon indescribable in words. It just means being awed by another for all the sorts of things about them that truly are right and accomplished.

So, what do we do with what we perceive as their weaknesses, the problems and regrettable aspects? The Greek idea of love turns to a notion to which we desperately need to rehabilitate ourselves: education. For the Greeks, given the scale of our imperfections, part of what it means to deepen love is to want to teach – and to be ready to be taught. Two people should see a relationship as a constant opportunity to improve and be improved. When lovers teach each other uncomfortable truths, they are not abandoning the spirit of love. They are trying to do something very true to genuine love, which is to make their partners more worthy of admiration.

We should stop feeling guilty for simply wanting to change our partners and we should never resent our partners for simply wanting to change us. Both these projects are, in theory, highly legitimate, even necessary. The desire to put one's lover right is, in fact, utterly loyal to the essential task of love.

Unfortunately, under the sway of Romantic ideology, most of us end up being terrible teachers and equally terrible students. That's because we rebel against the effort necessary to translate criticism into sensible-sounding lessons and the humility required to hear these lessons as caring attempts to address the more troublesome aspects of our personalities.

Instead, in the student role, at the first sign that the other is adopting a pedagogical tone, we tend to assume that we are being attacked and betrayed, and therefore close our ears to the instruction, reacting with sarcasm and aggression to our 'teacher'.

Correspondingly, when there is something we would like to teach, so unsure are we that we're going to be heard (we develop experience of how these things usually go) or that we have the right to speak, our lessons tend to be expressed in a tone of hysterical annoyance. What might have been an opportunity for a thoughtful lesson will emerge – under the panicky, scared, 'classroom' conditions of the average relationship – as a series of shouted, belittling insults met with rebellion and fury.

It's a paradox of the field that our teaching efforts tend to succeed the less we care that they do so. A sense that everything is at stake and the world is ending – easy enough impressions to reach in relationships when it is late at night and the irritation is large – guarantees to turn us into catastrophic pedagogues.

The good teacher knows that timing is critical to successful instruction. We tend automatically to try to teach a lesson the moment the problem arises, rather than when it is most likely to be attended to (which might be several days later). And so we typically end up addressing the most delicate and complex teaching tasks just at the point when we feel most scared and distressed and our student is most exhausted and nervous. We should learn to proceed like a wily general who knows how to wait for just the right conditions to make a move. We should develop a cult of optimal timing in addressing tricky matters, passing down from generation to generation stories of how, after years of getting nowhere with impulse-driven frontal assaults, a great teacher stood patiently by the dishwasher early in the morning, when everyone was well rested, until their partner had put down the newspaper, reflected on the upcoming holidays and then carefully advanced a long-prepared point, and eventually won a decisive teaching victory.

The defensive have no trust in the benevolence of teachers. There is in their deep minds no distinction between a comment on their behaviour and a criticism of their right to exist. Defensiveness raises the cost of disagreement – and thereby dialogue – intolerably.

Somewhere in the early years of the defensive person there will have been a sense of grave danger about being in the subordinate position, which would have inspired a flight into claims of hyper-competence. It is the task of all parents to criticize their children and break bad news to them about their wishes and efforts. But there are rather different ways of going about this. The best form of pedagogy leaves the child at once aware of a need to improve and with a sense that they are liked despite their ignorance and flaws. Yet there are also cases where criticism cuts too deep, where the child is left not just corrected but tarred with an impression of utter worthlessness. To recognize – without shame – and understand sympathetically why one has become excessively defensive are key to unwinding habits of self-protection and therefore to opening oneself up to education and improvement. We needed those defences once. Now we can afford to let them go.

When teaching and learning fail, we enter the realm of nagging. Nagging is the dispiriting, unpleasant, counterproductive but wholly understandable and poignant version of the noble ambition to improve a lover. There is always so much we might fairly want to change about our partners. We want them to be more self-aware, punctual, generous, reliable, introspective, resilient, communicative, profound . . . Nagging is, in essence, an attempt at transferring an idea for improvement from one mind to another that has given up hope. It has descended into an attempt to insist rather than invite, to coerce rather than charm.

Lamentably, it doesn't work. Nagging breeds its evil twin, shirking. The other pretends to read the paper, goes upstairs and feels righteous. The shrillness of one's tone gives them all the excuse they need to trust that we have nothing kind or true to tell them.

It seems one can change others only when the desire that they evolve has not yet reached an insistent pitch, when we can still bear that they remain as they are. All of us change only when we have a sense that we are understood for the many reasons why change is so hard for us. We know, of course, that the bins need our attention, that we should strive to get to bed earlier and that we have been a disappointment. But we can't bear to hear these lessons in an unsympathetic tone; we want – tricky children that we are – to be indulged for our ambivalence about becoming better people.

The tragedy of nagging is that its causes are usually so noble and yet it doesn't work. We nag because we feel that our possession of the truth lets us off having to convey it elegantly. It never does. The solution to nagging isn't to give up trying to get others to do what we want. Rather, it is to recognize that persuasion always needs to be couched in terms that make intuitive sense to those we want to alter.

We should at the same time stop judging faulty attempts at instruction so harshly. Rather than reading every grating lesson as an assault on our whole being, we should take it for what it is: an indication, however flawed, that someone can be bothered – even if they aren't yet breaking the news perfectly. We should never feel ashamed of instructing or of needing instruction. The only fault is to reject the opportunity for education if it is offered, however clumsily. Love should be a nurturing attempt by two people to reach their full potential, never just a crucible in which to look for endorsement for the panoply of present failings.

2 *The Importance of Sex*

SEXUAL LIBERATION

We are often given the impression that we live in sexually enlightened times and belong to a liberated age. We ought therefore, by now, to be finding sex a relatively straightforward and untroubling matter. But a narrative of enlightenment ignores the fact that we remain intermittently hugely conflicted, embarrassed, ashamed and indeed odd about sex, only with one added complication: we are meant to find the matter simple.

In reality, none of us approaches sex as we are meant to, with the cheerful, sporting, non-obsessive, clean, loyal, well-adjusted outlook that we convince ourselves is the norm. We are universally eccentric around sex, but only in relation to some highly and cruelly distorted ideals of normality. Most of what we are sexually remains very frightening to communicate to anyone we would want to think well of us. We may choose to die without having had certain conversations.

The dilemma is how simultaneously to appear normal and yet allow ourselves to be known. That we have to endure such a searing division is a direct legacy of Romanticism, for this movement of ideas blithely insisted that sex could be a beautiful, clean and natural force utterly in sympathy with the spirit of love. It might be passionate at points, but at heart it was kindly, tender, sweet and filled with affection for a single person. This sounds charming – and once in a while, for a bit, it is even true. But it woefully neglects some critical components of erotic excitement and can't help but leave us deeply embarrassed about certain sides of what we want.

To start the list, here are just some of the unpalatable truths that stir in our minds:

- it's very rare to maintain sexual interest in only one person, however much one loves them, beyond a certain time;

- it's entirely possible to love one's partner and regularly want to have sex with strangers, frequently types who don't align with our ordinary concerns;

- one can be a kind, respectable and democratic person and at the same time want to inflict or receive very rough treatment;

- it's highly normal to have fantasies about scenarios one would not wish to act out in reality and that might involve illegal, violent, hurtful and unsanitary aspects;

- it may be easier to be excited by someone one dislikes or thinks nothing of than by someone one loves.

These aren't just points of mild curiosity. They are fundamentals of the human sexual personality that stand in shocking contrast to everything that society suggests is true.

Despite our best efforts to cleanse it of its peculiarities, sex can't be *normal* in the ways we might like it to be. True liberation is a challenge that remains before us as we patiently build up the courage to admit to the nature of our desires and learn to talk to our loved ones and ourselves with a pioneering, unfrightened honesty.

THE MEANING OF SEXUAL EXCITEMENT

Sexual desire makes us want, and do, what are, by the standards of ordinary life, highly peculiar things. We seek to put our mouths in unusual places in other people's bodies, penetrate implausible orifices and say surprising and uncommon things.

Throughout the twentieth century the biggest influence on how people thought about sex came from the work of Sigmund Freud. The psychoanalyst moved sex from a marginal topic of discussion to the centre of the cultural conversation. Radically, he insisted that sex might be profoundly connected with almost everything else in our lives. But, problematically and rather unwittingly, he made it sound as if everything else could be degraded or at least made sinister by this connection. One might have thought oneself interested in noble subjects like art or politics, but in truth, Freud seemed from a distance to be suggesting, one was just being rather base in a disguised way. Through a Freudian lens, everything appeared to have been contaminated by a hidden stratum of sexual concern.

Yet, with no disrespect to Freud himself, exactly the reverse might be true. It is not the case that when we look at art or politics we are merely being kinky; rather that when we think we are merely being kinky we are in fact pursuing some very earnest and intelligible goals that are connected with a raft of other, higher aspirations. Our sexual lives are much more in contact with our values than we tend to suppose. What seems incomprehensibly perverse is usually a very logical endeavour to reach a profound and honourable goal by bodily means: we are, via sex, seeking to connect emotionally with, and make ourselves understood by, another person.

Take the practice of jamming our face against someone's vulva or testicles. Oral sex can be hard to explain. Yet as in so many sexual acts, a feeling of being accepted is at the heart of the draw. For most of life, we learn to keep our eyes strictly averted from others' genital areas. We take immense care in changing rooms to deploy towels in strategic ways to ensure that no one will glimpse parts of us that we have learned to refer to, tellingly, as 'private'. The thrill of oral sex is connected to a brief, magnificent reversal of all our internalized taboos. We no longer have to feel ashamed or guilty. The act may be physical, but the ecstasy is in essence an emotional relief that our secret and in subjective ways 'bad' sides have been witnessed and enthusiastically endorsed by another.

Much the same holds for anal sex. The anus is the most proscribed and dangerous part of the body, surrounded by the strictest taboos and most severe dictates on hygiene. But this restriction only directly feeds into the tenderness of being allowed to explore this part of another person and of oneself in the context of a relationship. We're not forgetting that the anus is the locus of disgust; we are, within sex, relishing the fact for symbolizing how much we have, with our partner, created a small, fenced-off utopia in which the normal rules do not apply. Anal play would lose much of its capacity to delight if the anus were no more 'dirty' than a forehead or a shin; the pleasure is dependent on another human letting us do something avowedly filthy with and for them, and upon the implication that this is something they would never do with a person they cared little about. It is exactly the feeling that something is wrong, perverse or obscene that makes the mutual agreement to try it so great a mark of trust.

Similar psychological dynamics apply to degradation within sex. Normally – and with immense justification – we take instinctive offence at the slightest signs of condescension. We are furious or depressed if someone calls us a 'cunt' or a 'fucking bastard' or tells us we're a 'shit' or 'worthless'. These are the terms people use when they most want to hurt or upset another person, when they are desperate to show contempt or hatred. So on the face of it, it is shocking and disturbing to think that we (or our partner) might get erotically excited by using just these sorts of abusive terms in bed.

We would be wise to begin studying the issue through the lens of perhaps the greatest novel of the twentieth century, Marcel Proust's *In Search of Lost Time*. In the first volume, *Swann's Way*, Proust's unnamed narrator, then a young teenager, is taking a walk near his grandmother's house in the French countryside. As he passes a building at the edge of the village, he notices, in an upper bedroom, a woman, Mademoiselle Vinteuil, making love to a female friend. He is mesmerized and climbs a little hill for a better view. There he sees something even more surprising unfolding: Mademoiselle Vinteuil has positioned a photograph of her dead father on the bedside table and is encouraging her lesbian lover to spit on the image as they have sex, this gesture proving extremely exciting to them both. Early readers of Proust's novel were puzzled by and heavily critical of this scene of erotic defilement. What was this revolting episode doing in an otherwise gracious and beautiful love story, filled with tender evocation of riverbanks, trees and domestic life? Proust's editor wanted to cut the scene, but the novelist insisted on retaining it, asking the editor to understand its importance within his overarching philosophy of love.

Proust tried hard to make sure his readers would not judge Mademoiselle Vinteuil harshly, going so far as to suggest that even the woman's father wouldn't ultimately have minded being spat on by her lover, so long as he understood what was really going on: 'I have since reflected that if Monsieur Vinteuil had been able to be present at this scene, he might still, and in spite of everything, have continued to believe in his daughter's soundness of heart.' Proust's argument is that defilement during sex isn't what it seems. Ostensibly, it's about violence, hatred, meanness and a lack of respect. But for Proust, it symbolizes a longing to be properly oneself in the presence of another human being, and to be loved and accepted by them for one's darkest sides rather than just for one's politeness and good manners. Mademoiselle Vinteuil is, in her day-to-day behaviour, an extremely moral and kindly character, and yet this pressure to be always responsible and 'good' also begs moments of release.

Sex in which two people can express their defiling urges is, for Proust, at heart an indication of a quest for complete acceptance. We know we can please others with our goodness, but – suggests Proust – what we really want is also to be endorsed for our more peculiar and dark impulses. The discipline involved in growing up into a good person seeks occasional alleviation, which is what sex can provide in those rare moments when two partners trust one another enough to reveal their otherwise strictly censored desires to dirty and insult. Though defiling sex seems on the surface to be about hurting another person, really it's a quest for intimacy and love – and a delight that, for a time at least, we can be as bad as we like and still turn out to be the object of another's affection.

Defilement therefore has meaning: it is a surprising way of trying to improve a relationship. It's not an act of sabotage or a denial of love. It's a deeply curious but, in its own way, very logical quest for closeness.

We need to embrace a similarly radical understanding of the many aspects of our sexualities that seem very odd at first. We are such complicated and surprising machines; we need to foster the rehabilitation (by which we mean the wise, sympathetic investigation) of parts of ourselves that are otherwise so easy to disown or panic around. Although our erotic enthusiasms may sometimes sound off-putting, they are almost always motivated by a search for the good: a desire to build a connection marked by understanding, sympathy and kindness.

AFFAIRS

An affair is a love – or sexual – story between two people, one of whom (at least) is ostensibly committed to someone else. Most importantly, in our times, an affair is a disaster, pretty much the greatest betrayal that can befall us, a harbinger of untrammelled suffering, frequently the end of the relationship it has violated and almost always an occasion for fierce moralizing and the division of participants into goodies (who have been betrayed) and monsters (who have betrayed).

However, in trying to understand affairs and make sense of their pains as well as their less frequently confessed attractions, we should grasp that the way we interpret affairs today is very particular to our own times. Judged against the long span of human experience, we are remarkably contorted about the whole business. People have always had affairs, but what an affair *means* has been subject to huge changes across societies and eras.

When Does an Affair Begin?

Once an affair has been uncovered, we often ask – in the position of the betrayed, pained party – when it began. Pinpointing the precise moment promises to shed light on its motivations and on possible ways to prevent any further such calamities in the future.

There is, understandably, a hunt for the exact time when the two straying individuals met and physical contact began. We think of how two people had a drink after a business dinner or met online or flirted at a party and agreed to meet up a few days later. We concentrate on details: when their knees touched under the table, when one of them lightly put their arm round the other's waist and when they first lied about where they were going or to whom they were sending a message.

This kind of detective work feels obvious, but it overlooks a complexity: the start of an affair should not be equated with the moment when two straying people meet. Affairs begin long before there is anyone to have an affair with. Their origins lie with certain initially minute fissures that open up within a subtly fracturing couple. The affair pre-dates, possibly by many years, the arrival of any actual lover.

The situation is duplicated in many other areas, the study of history for one. It is common to ask when a cataclysmic event such as, for example, the French Revolution began. A traditional response is to point to the summer of 1789, when some of the deputies at the Estates General took an oath to remain in session until a constitution had been agreed on, or a few days later when a group of Parisians attacked and broke into the Bastille prison. But a more sophisticated and instructive approach locates the beginning significantly earlier: with the bad harvests of the previous ten years, with the loss of royal prestige following military defeats in North America in the 1760s or with the rise of a new philosophy in the middle of the century that stressed the idea of citizens' rights. At the time, these incidents didn't seem particularly decisive; they didn't immediately lead to major social change or reveal their solemn nature. But they slowly and powerfully put the country on course for the upheavals of 1789: they moved the country into a revolution-ready state.

Likewise, affairs begin long before the meeting at the conference or the whispered confidences at the party. It is not key to fixate on the trip to Miami or the login details of the website. The whole notion of who is to blame and for what suddenly starts to look much more complicated and less clear cut. One should be focusing on certain conversations that didn't go well in the kitchen three summers ago or the sulk in the taxi home five years before. The drama began long before anything dramatic unfolded.

This is how some of the minute but real causes might be laid out by a partner who eventually strayed.

Unending busy-ness

It was a Sunday morning. My partner had been taken up for months with a big project and I'd been very understanding. Now it was over and I was looking forward to some closeness and a trip to a cafe. But suddenly there was something new that he needed to look at on his phone. I glanced over at his face, which was lit up by the glow of the screen, and his eyes looked cold, determined and resolutely elsewhere. Or else my partner hatched a sudden firm plan to reorganize the kitchen cupboards just when at last we might have had a quiet time in the park together. That's perhaps when the afternoon of passion in Bordeaux really began: with the need to stop everything in order to swap around the crockery and the glasses.

Neglect

I was away on an exhausting trip and in a break between meetings I fought for the chance to call my partner. She picked up, but the television continued on in the background. She had even forgotten that I'd had to give a speech and it felt a little humiliating to have to remind her and to hear her lacklustre 'great' in response.

Shaming

We were with some new friends, people we didn't know too well and wanted to create a good impression on. My partner was looking to amuse them and, having cast around for options, started to tell everyone a story about how I once showed the wrong slides in a presentation at work. He knows how to tell a good story and there was a lot of laughter.

Ownership

Without discussing it, my partner arranged that we'd both go and have lunch with her parents. It wasn't so much that I minded going, it was the fact that she didn't feel the need to ask if I minded and if the timing was convenient. On another occasion, without even mentioning it, she bought a new kettle and got rid of the old one. It was as if I had no say at all. Sometimes she'd just tell me what to do – 'Take the bins out', 'Pick up some mineral water at the shop', 'Put on different shoes' – without adding 'please' or 'would you mind' or 'it would be lovely if . . .' Just a few words would have made all the difference.

Flirting

I was at a party with my partner and I saw him across the room, bending towards this person, saying something. He was laughing, being charming. He put his hand on the back of her chair. Later he said it had been a very boring conversation.

One too many arguments

It wasn't the basic fact of having disagreements, it was the sheer number of them – and their unending, repetitive nature. One that sticks in the memory was when we were at the seaside and things should have been happy for once. Yet my partner chose again to ramp up the tension about a Thai takeaway that had been ordered. I remember arguing and, at the same time, one part of my mind was disassociating, looking down upon the two of us standing on the pier with cross faces and wondering, 'Why?'

Lack of tenderness

We were walking along the street together near the antiques market and I reached out to hold my partner's hand, but he failed to notice. Another time he was doing something at the kitchen table and I put an arm round his shoulder, but he said sharply, 'Not now.' In bed I'm always the one to turn towards him and kiss him goodnight. He responds but never, ever initiates. This rankles more than it seems normal or possible to say.

Erotic disengagement

There was a sexual idea I'd been getting interested in but I felt awkward about mentioning it to my partner. I tried to give a few hints, but she didn't give the impression she was curious. She didn't encourage me to expand. Instead she gave me the impression that it would be a lot more convenient if I just kept whatever it was that tickled me to myself.

Individually, none of these things may be very dramatic. Some little version of one or other of them may be happening pretty much every day. And it's not all one way: both parties are probably doing some of these things quite regularly, without particularly noticing or meaning to.

Yet a careful historian of infidelity might pinpoint any one of them as the moment at which – in a true sense – an affair began. Long before the party or the conference, the feeling was implanted deep in someone's mind (perhaps beyond the range of their conscious awareness) that there was something important missing in their relationship that another person might, possibly, be able to supply.

It is common, when an affair is discovered, to become an inquisitorial prosecutor: to seize the phone and ask the 'cheat' in detail where they have been; to read through their emails; to parse every receipt. But such assiduousness is a little late, a bit misdirected and rather too self-serving. We should look further back than the moment when a lover came on the scene. The revolution didn't begin with the sexual act or the dirty texts and with the actual storming of our domestic citadel; it began on an innocent sunny afternoon many years before, when there was still a lot of goodwill, when a hand was proffered and when the partner was perhaps fatefully careless about how they received it. That might be a rather more painful account of our relationship and its troubles than either of us is ready to contemplate for now, but it might also be a more accurate and ultimately more useful one.

How to Spot a Couple Who Might be Headed for an Affair

Having arguments does not, in itself, say very much about the likelihood of a relationship disintegrating. What matters is how arguments are interpreted, conducted and resolved. The fragile unions aren't necessarily the ones in which people shout, insist that this is finally it, call the other a ninny and slam the door; they are the ones in which emotional disconnection and rupture are not correctly identified, examined and repaired.

A number of qualities are required to ensure that a couple know how to argue well. There is, first and foremost, the need for each party to be able to pinpoint sources of discomfort in themselves early and accurately: to know how to recognize what they are unhappy about and what they need in order to flourish in the couple. This is not necessarily as obvious as one might imagine. It can take time and psychological insight to know that it was actually the missing phone call or the request to move the date of the holiday that is really the source of anger.

Then there is the equally vital quality of feeling that one has the right to speak, that one isn't duty bound to be 'good' and not cause trouble, that it is acceptable to say when one is miserable and troubled by something – however small it might appear; that it is better to spoil a few evenings than ruin a marriage.

It can help to have a sanguine assessment of how human relationships tend to go: to accept that a bit of disappointment and some friction belong to the necessary ingredients of good enough love, that it isn't a disaster to be cross at points and seemingly convinced that this should be the end.

A subsidiary talent is knowing *how* to speak up. It might not be exactly the moment the problem appears; diplomatic skills matter. One might need to wait until some of the surface tension has dissipated; perhaps the next morning can do just as well. One needs a background confidence not to have to blurt out every objection in a panicked diatribe or shout a wounded feeling across the room when the other is themselves too upset to hear it. One needs to know how to formulate one's complaints into a convincing, perhaps even humorously framed point that has a chance of winning over its target.

It matters in all this that one both feels attached to the partner and at the same time has an active impression that one could walk away from them were matters ever truly to escalate. Feeling that one has options, does not therefore have to cling and deserves good treatment ensures that one's voice can be measured and that the status quo will remain manageable.

These factors tend to be absent in those unfortunate couples who not only argue but lack the gift of arguing well. The following range of inner obstacles prevents them from dealing effectively with their emotional disconnection and anger.

Over-optimism about relationships

Fragile couples tend, paradoxically, to be very hopeful about love. They associate happiness with conflict-free unions. They do not expect, once they have found the person they unwisely see as The One, ever to need to squabble, storm out of a room or feel unhappy for the afternoon. When trouble emerges, as it inevitably does, they do not greet it as a sign that love is progressing as it should but as alarming evidence that their relationship may be illegitimate and fundamentally flawed. Their hopes drain them of the energy needed for the patient tasks of diplomatic negotiation and routine maintenance.

Being out of touch with pain

Fragile couples tend not to be good detectives with regard to their own sufferings. They may be both unhappy and yet unsure as to the actual causes of their dissatisfactions. They know something is wrong in their union, but they can't easily trace the catalyst. They can't zero in on how it was the lack of trust in them around money that rankles or how it was their behaviour towards a demanding youngest child that is hurting. They lash out in vague or inaccurate directions, their attacks either unfairly general or unconvincingly specific.

Shame

A shamed person has fundamental doubts about their right to exist: somewhere in the past, they have been imbued with the impression that they do not matter very much, that their feelings should be ignored, that their happiness is not a priority, that their words do not count. Once they are part of a couple, shamed people hurt like anyone else, but their capacity to turn their hurt into something another person can understand and be touched by is recklessly weak. Shamed people will sulk rather than speak, hide rather than divulge, feel secretly wretched rather than candidly complain. It is frequently very late, far too late, by the time shamed people finally let their lover know more about the nature of their desperation.

Excessive anxiety

Complaining well requires an impression that not everything depends on the complaint being heard perfectly. Were the lesson to go wrong, were the other to prove intransigent, one could survive and take one's love elsewhere. Not everything is at stake in an argument. The other hasn't ruined one's life. One therefore doesn't need to scream, hector, insist or nag. One can deliver a complaint with some of the nonchalance of a calm teacher who wants listeners to learn but can bear it if they don't because the information can always be conveyed tomorrow, or the next day.

Excessive pride

It takes an inner dignity not to mind too much about having to level complaints around things that could sound laughably 'small' or that leave one open to being described as petty or needy. With too much pride and fear, it can become unbearable to admit that one has been upset since lunch because someone didn't take one's hand on a walk or wishes so much that they would be readier for a hug last thing at night. One has to feel quite grown up inside not to be offended by one's own more childlike appetites for reassurance and comfort. It is an achievement to know how to be strong about one's vulnerability. One may have said, rather too many times, from behind a slammed door, in a defensive tone, 'No, nothing is wrong whatsoever. Go away', when secretly longing to be comforted and understood like a weepy, upset child.

Hopelessness about dialogue

Fragile couples often come together with few positive childhood memories of conversations working out: early role models may simply have screamed and then despaired of one another. They may never have witnessed disagreements eventually morphing into mutual understanding and sympathy. They would deeply love to be understood, but they can bring precious few resources to the task of making themselves so.

None of these factors means there will automatically be an affair, but they are generators of emotional disconnection that contributes to an all-important affair-ready state. Outwardly, things can seem good. A couple may have an interesting social life, some lovely children, a new apartment. But a more judicious analysis will reveal an unexpected degree of risk. An affair won't in these circumstances – however it may look later – be just an idle self-indulgence or a momentary lack of self-control. It will be the result of identifiable long-term resentments that a couple, otherwise blessed and committed, lacked the inner resources and courage to investigate.

The Role of Sex in Affairs

When an affair is discovered, it is common to describe the person who strayed as despicably sexually profligate. They are lustful, wanton, dog-like. They have ceded control to their animal selves. But we get a more nuanced view of the role of sex in affairs by asking a deliberately obtuse, philosophical-sounding question: why is sex so nice?

One possible answer, which can sound a little odd, is: because we have advanced tendencies to hate ourselves and find ourselves unacceptable. And sex with a new person has an exceptional capacity to reduce feeling like that.

A long-term relationship can all too easily enforce a sense that we are neither very admirable nor worthy. Management of family life, of cleaning rotas, of finances and of relations with friends and in-laws can contribute to an impression that one is fundamentally troublesome and undeserving of sustained notice. The mood around us is fractious and ungrateful. 'Not you again' may be the implicit message one receives upon entering any room.

Physically, we have strict instructions to keep ourselves to ourselves. There is one person on the planet we are meant to be naked in front of and this figure is unlikely to be particularly impressed by or even vaguely cognizant of our appearance. With everyone else, we are a cautious, swaddled being. We would not dare to come more than thirty centimetres near to most of humanity.

And then, suddenly, in the context of an affair, everything changes. We can be unlaced and carefree. Our tongue, normally carefully shielded and used to form vowel sounds and break down toast or the morning cereal, is given permission to enter another person's mouth. We are no longer just the one who makes problems around the in-laws and doesn't pull their weight around the house or the finances; instead we are someone whose very essence has, via the flesh, been witnessed and endorsed.

What we may be *doing* is slipping off another's top or inviting them to release our trousers, but what all this *means* is that another human has – exceptionally – chosen to find us worthy.

For so-called cheats (who will most likely have to pay a very heavy price indeed for going to bed with another person), sex can have remarkably little to do with 'sex'. It is an activity continuous with a range of non-physical needs for tenderness, acceptance, care and companionship. It is an attempt, negotiated through the body but focused on the satisfactions of the psyche, to make up for a long-standing painfully severed emotional connection with a primary partner.

The crucial, active element in an affair isn't really the physical sex per se: it's the sense of closeness, the warmth, the shared liking for which physical sex provides the occasion.

The thought opens us up to a more defined, perhaps more searing and yet usefully more accurate avenue of pain in relation to our partner. The problem is not that they have been horny, something for which we cannot really be held responsible and which we can therefore safely moralize about. It is that they have been lonely – something which it is a great deal harder to bear and think ourselves wholly innocent about.

How to Reduce the Risk of Affairs

The traditional way to try to reduce the chances of someone having an affair is to focus on controlling their actions and outward movements: not letting them go to social events without us, calling them at random times or reducing their access to social media.

But people don't have affairs because they are able to meet attractive others, they have affairs because they feel emotionally disconnected from their partners. The best way to stop their being tempted to sleep with someone else is not, therefore, to reduce their opportunities for contact; it is to leave them free to wander the world while ensuring that they feel heard by and are reconciled with their partners. It is emotional closeness, not curfews, that guarantees the integrity of couples.

At a practical level, the route to closeness requires us to ensure that the two main sources of distance, resentment and loneliness, are correctly identified and regularly purged. The more we can tell our partners what we are annoyed and disappointed about, what we long for and are made anxious by, and the more we can feel heard for doing so, the less we will bear grudges, keep our distance and seek revenge by stripping naked with someone else. Few things are more properly romantic (in the true sense of the word, meaning conducive to love) than highly honest conversations in which we have an opportunity to lay bare the particular ways in which our partners have disappointed us. Nothing may so endear us to someone as a chance to tell them why they have let us down.

To guide us in our restorative complaints, we might consider the following range of prompts.

I sometimes feel frustrated with you when . . .

It sounds like a nasty theme but, when handled correctly, it is the gateway to great tenderness and closeness. It provides us with an opportunity to do something very rare: level criticism without anger. And it's a chance to hear criticism as more than an attack, to interpret it for what it may truly be: a desire to learn how to live together with less occasion for anger.

I'd love you to realize that you hurt me when . . .

We're carrying around wounds that we have found it, understandably and inevitably, hard to articulate. Perhaps the complaints sounded too petty or humiliating to mention at the time. The problem is that when they fester, the currents of affection start to get blocked and soon we may find that we flinch when our partner tries to touch us. This prompt provides a safe moment in which to reveal a set of – typically entirely unintentional – hurts. Maybe last week there was something around work, or their mother, or the way they responded to a fairly innocent enquiry in the kitchen before a run. It's vital that our partner doesn't step in and deny that the hurt took place. There is no such thing as a hurt that is too small to matter when emotional closeness is at stake.

One of the hardest things for you to understand about me is . . .

We end up lonely because there is something important about who we are that our partner appears not to grasp or, so we can conclude, does not even want to take on board. But this lack of interest is rarely malevolent; it is usually more the case that there hasn't been a proper occasion for exploration. The feeling that one person knows another is the constant enemy of long-term couples. Our partners may understand us well, but we still need patiently and diplomatically to keep explaining things that remain unclear between us. We are changing all the time, we're no longer who we were last month, and we can struggle to explain our own evolutions and needs even to ourselves. We must never be furious with our beloveds for not grasping facets of our identity we haven't yet properly managed to share with them.

What I'd love you to appreciate about me is . . .

We don't want untrammelled praise, merely the odd moment when we can tell our partner what we feel is worthy of appreciation, maybe a little more appreciation than we have until now spontaneously received. We might want to draw attention to our best intentions (even when they didn't entirely work out); to the sweeter aspects of our character; or to the good things about us which have quietly removed conflicts that would otherwise have emerged in the background. We're reminding both of us that there are reasons why we deserve love.

Where I'm unfulfilled in my life . . .

It need not always be the fault of a lover that we are dissatisfied and restless. The longing for an affair can arise from a sense that the world more generally has not heard us, that we have been abandoned with career anxieties or lag behind our peers in terms of achievement and assets. Day to day, we tend not to explain the origins of these distressed moods very well. Our partner is the witness to them but can't easily recognize where the unhappiness is coming from. So they make the next most obvious move and start to assume that we are simply mean or bad-tempered. This is a chance to explain the back-ground existential fear and professional ennui responsible for some of our most acute everyday irritations and withdrawn states; a chance to demonstrate that we are not bad, merely longing for their reassurance and support to battle our impression of insignificance and failure.

We also need, in order to be close and resist the lure of an affair, to be able to speak with unusual candour about our sexual aspirations. Nothing more quickly reduces the need to act out a fantasy than the ability to speak about it – and be heard with sympathy, tolerance and curiosity. Here are some of the prompts that might induce the right sort of conversation about sex:

Something I'm really inhibited about sexually is . . .

I would love it if you could understand that sometimes I want . . .

What I wish I could change about me and sex is . . .

What I wish I could change about you and sex is . . .

None of these prompts can guarantee that an affair will never hap-pen, but they could at least help to diagnose and repair the feelings of resentful distance or erotic loneliness that are the hidden drivers of the desire to wander off with someone else. We should dare to spend less time banning our partners from having lunch with strangers or travelling alone, and more time ensuring that they feel understood for their flaws and confusions – and appreciated for their virtues.

Affairs and High Horses

Whatever its benefits and pains, being involved in an affair should, if nothing else, cure us once and for all of any tendency to moralize – that is, to look harshly and with strict judgement on the misdemeanours and follies of others.

An affair should naturally induct us into the full scale of our mendacity, impatience, weakness, cowardliness, derangement and sentimentality. We should thereafter never be able to feel impervious and superior when hearing of certain insane things that others have done in the name of love or desire. We will have joined the legions of the sexually chastened, who can have no more illusions as to their own purity or steadiness of mind.

And yet we won't be able to give up on ourselves entirely either; we'll have to keep going with life and somehow find a way to forgive ourselves for the days and nights we lost to our madness. At best, we will learn how to laugh darkly at ourselves, to know at all times that, however grand and authoritative some parts of our lives might seem, we are only ever millimetres away from tragedy and lunacy.

Our affairs will force us to dismount from our high horses and do away forever with any sense of superiority – and from there, we will have no option but to go on to be infinitely kind and unendingly generous towards anyone who ever wants to have, or has ever been involved in, those delightful, wretched, tumultuous, destructive and compelling adventures we call affairs.

3 *Dealing with Problems*

ARGUMENTS

An average couple will have between thirty and fifty significant arguments a year, 'significant' meaning an encounter which departs sharply from civilized norms of dialogue, would be uncomfortable to film and show friends, and might involve screaming, rolled eyes, histrionic accusations, slammed doors and liberal uses of terms like 'arsehole' and 'knobhead'.

Given the intensity of the distress that arguments cause us, we could expect modern societies to have learned to devote a great deal of attention and resources to understanding why they happen and how we might more effectively defuse or untangle them. We might expect there to be school and university courses on how to manage arguments successfully and official targets for reducing their incidence.

But there are some strong reasons for our collective neglect. The first is that our Romantic culture sentimentally implies that there might be a necessary connection between true passion and a fiery temper. It can seem as if fighting and hurling insults might be signs, not of immaturity and a woeful incapacity for self-control, but of an admirable intensity of desire and strength of commitment.

Romanticism also conspires to suggest that arguments might be part of the natural weather of relationships and could never therefore be fairly analysed through reason or dismantled with logic. Only a pedant would seek to *think* through an argument – as opposed to letting it run its sometimes troubling and rowdy but ultimately always necessary course.

At a more intimate level, it may be that we cannot quite face what arguments show us about ourselves, presenting an unbearable insult to our self-love. Once the argument is over, the viciousness, self-pity and pettiness on display are repulsive to think about and so we artfully pretend to ourselves and our partner that what happened last night must have been a peculiar aberration, best passed over in silence from the calmer perspective of dawn.

We are further stymied in our investigations because there is so little public evidence that a version of what occurs in our union might unfold in everyone else's as well. Out of shame and a desire to seem normal, we collectively shield each other from the reality of relationships – and then imagine that our behaviour must be uniquely savage and childish and therefore incapable of redemption or analysis. We miss out on a chance to improve because we take ourselves to be the mad exceptions.

None of this needs to be the case. We argue badly and regularly principally because we lack an education in how to teach others who we are. Beneath the surface of almost every argument lies a forlorn attempt by two people to get the other to see, acknowledge and respond to their emotional reality and sense of justice. Beyond the invective is a longing that our partner should witness, understand and endorse some crucial element of our own experience.

The tragedy of every sorry argument is that it is constructed around a horrific mismatch between the *message* we so badly want to send ('I need you to love me, know me, agree with me') and the manner in which we are able to deliver it (with impatient accusations, sulks, put-downs, sarcasm, exaggerated gesticulations and forceful 'fuck you's).

A bad argument is a failed endeavour to communicate, which perversely renders the underlying message we seek to convey ever less visible. It is our very desperation which undermines us and ushers in the unreasonableness that prevents whatever point we lay claim to from making its way across. We argue in an ugly way because, in our times of distress, we lose access to all better methods of explaining our fears, frustrated hopes, needs, concerns, excitements and convictions. And we do this principally because we are so scared that we may have ruined our lives by being in a relationship with someone who cannot fathom the inner movements of our souls. We would do things so much better if only we cared a little less.

We don't, therefore, end up in bitter arguments because we are fundamentally brutish or resolutely demented but because we are at once so invested and yet so incapable. It is the untutored force of our wish to communicate that impedes our steady ability to do so.

And yet, though arguments may be destructive, avoiding points of conflict isn't straightforwardly the answer either. An argument is about something, so its content needs eventually to be faced up to if a relationship is to survive. The priority is not so much to skirt points of contention as to learn to handle them in less counterproductively vindictive and more gently strategic ways.

Some of the reason why we argue so much and so repetitively is that we aren't guided to spot the similarities that run through our arguments; we do not have to hand an easy typology of squabbles that could be to domestic conflict what an encyclopedia of birds is to an ornithologist.

Though fights can from the outside look generic, with similar displays of agitation and aggression, we should come to recognize the very distinct kinds of rows in operation. Each type listed here foregrounds a particular way in which we typically fail to communicate a vital and intense truth to a partner.

By examining them in turn, we may gradually assemble an understanding of some of the obstacles we face, and greet moments of dissent with a little less surprise and rather more tolerance and humorous recognition. We will be reminded – once more – that love is a skill, not an emotion.

The Interminable Argument

One of the hardest to unpick, this type of argument looks, from a distance, as though it is always new and always unique. One day it is about something someone said to a friend, the next about a family reunion. Sometimes it centres around a stain that's appeared on the sofa, sometimes around the bank's approach to the setting of interest rates.

What is hard to imagine is that we may unwittingly – all along – be having the same argument in disguise. The flashpoints of agitation may superficially seem diverse but are in fact all reconfigurations of the same basic conflictual material.

Arguments about whether to take the train or the bus, or about putting out the bins, or about the economic potential of Africa, or about a scratch on a wooden table, or about whether it's OK to be five minutes late for a dental appointment, or about what to give a friend as a wedding present, or about the difference between a serviette and a napkin – all of these may be emerging from the repeated frustrated attempt to transmit a single intimate truth: *I feel you don't respect my intelligence.*

We keep arguing because we never manage to identify and address the key issue we're actually cross about. Irritability is anger that lacks self-knowledge.

Why should it be so hard to trace the origins of our rage? At points because what offends us is so humiliating in structure. It can be shameful for us to realize that the person in whom we have invested so much may not actually desire us physically, or may not fundamentally be kind, or could be exploiting us financially or gravely impeding our professional aspirations. We come under immense internal pressure not to square up to truths that would require us to accept a range of practically difficult and emotionally devastating realizations. We prefer to let our anger seep out in myriad minor conflicts over seemingly not very much rather than have to argue over the direction of our lives.

We may, furthermore, not have grown up with a sense that our dissatisfactions ever deserved expression. Our parents might have been too anxious, too vulnerable or too bullying to allow much room for our early needs. We might have become masters in the art of not complaining and of accepting what we are given as the price of survival and of protection of those we loved. This doesn't now spare us feelings of frustration. It simply makes us incapable of giving them a voice.

We are hence doomed to keep having small or diversionary squabbles so as not to have to touch the fundamental truth at the core of our complaints: *You don't show me enough physical affection. My life is harder than your life. Your family are much worse than you think they are. I'm threatened by your friends. You have the wrong approach to money.*

But naturally, in the course of not having the big discussion, we poison everything else. No day is free of the marks of the conflict that has not been expressed.

We should learn to have the courage of our frustrations – and of our fears. It is always better to touch the ur-argument than for a relationship to die by a thousand squabbles. We will cease to fight so much when we can face up to, and voice, what we're really furious about.

The Defensive Argument

We often operate in romantic life under the mistaken impression – unconsciously imported from law courts and school debating traditions – that the person who is 'right' or has the stronger case should, legitimately, 'win' an argument. But this is fundamentally to misunderstand the point of relationships, which is not so much to defeat an opponent as to help each other evolve into the best versions of ourselves.

There's a kind of argument that erupts when one partner has a largely correct insight into the problems of their partner. With a stern and gleeful tone, they may declare, 'You've been drinking too much', 'You hogged the conversation at the party', 'You're always boasting', 'You don't take enough responsibility', 'You waste too much time online' or 'You never take enough exercise.'

The insights are not wrong; that's what is so tricky. The critic is correct, but they are unable to 'win' because there are no prizes in love for correctly discerning the flaws of our partners – other than self-satisfied loneliness. For paradoxically, by attacking a partner with clinical energy, we reduce our chances of ever reaching the real goal: the evolution of the person we have to live with.

When we're on the receiving end of a difficult insight into our failings, what makes us bristle and deny everything isn't generally the accusation itself (we know our flaws all too well), it's the surrounding atmosphere. We know the other is right, we just can't bear to take their criticism on board, given how severely it has been delivered. We start to deny everything because we are terrified: the light of truth is shining too brightly. The fear is that if we admit our failings, we will be crushed, shown up as worthless, required to attempt an arduous, miserable process of change without sympathy or claim on the affections of the other.

We feel so burdened with shame and guilt already, a lover's further upbraiding is impossible to listen to. There's too much pre-existing fragility in our psyches for us to admit to another difficult insight into what's wrong with us.

Plato once outlined an idea of what he called the 'just lie'. If a crazed person comes to us and asks, 'Where's the axe?' we are entitled to lie and say we don't know – because we understand that if we were to tell the truth they would probably use the tool to do something horrendous to us. That is, we can reasonably tell a lie when our life is in danger. In the same way, our partner might not literally be searching for an axe when they make their accusation, but psychologically this is precisely how we might experience them – which makes it understandable if we say we simply don't know what they are talking about.

It may feel unfair to ask our partner to take our fears on board. But if they want to help the relationship they will need to make it clear that they won't ever use the truth (if it is acknowledged) as a weapon.

What is so sad is how easily we the accused might, if only the circumstances were more sympathetic, confess to everything. We would in fact love to unburden ourselves and admit to what is broken and wounded in us.

People don't change when they are gruffly told what's wrong with them; they change when they feel sufficiently supported to undertake the change they – almost always – already know is due.

The Spoiling Argument

There is a kind of argument that begins when one partner deliberately –and for no immediately obvious reason – attempts to spoil the good mood and high spirits of the other.

The cheerful partner may be making a cake for their visiting nephew or whistling a tune while they rearrange the kitchen. They may be making plans for the weekend or discussing what fun it will be to see an old school friend again soon. Or they may be expressing unusual optimism about their professional future and financial prospects.

Despite our love for them, something about the situation may suddenly grate with us. Within a short time, we may find ourselves saying something unusually harsh or critical: we may point out a flaw in their school friend (they tell very boring anecdotes, they can be pretty snobbish); we may take exception to their rearrangement of the cupboards; we may find fault with the cake; we may bring up an aspect of their work that we know our partner finds dispiriting; we may complain that they haven't properly considered the roadworks when planning the weekend. We do everything to try to induce a mood of anxiety, friction and misery.

On the surface it looks as if we're simply monsters. But if we dig a little deeper a more understandable (though no less regrettable) picture may emerge. We are acting in this way because our partner's buoyant and breezy mood can come across as a forbidding barrier to communication. We fear that their current happiness could prevent them from knowing the shame or melancholy, worry or loneliness that presently possesses us. We are trying to shatter their spirits because we are afraid of being lonely.

We don't make this argument explicitly to ourselves but a dark instinct in our minds experiences our partner's upbeat mood as a warning that our uncheery parts must now be unwelcome. And so we make a crude, wholly immature but psychologically comprehensible assumption that we will never be properly known and loved until our partner can feel as sad and frustrated as we do, a plan for the recalibration of their mood that we put into motion with malicious determination.

But of course that's not how things pan out. We may succeed in making our partner upset but we almost certainly won't thereby secure the imagined benefits of their gloom: they won't – once their mood has been spoilt – emerge with any greater appetite for listening to our messages of distress or for cradling us indulgently in their consoling arms. They will just be furious.

The better move, if only we could manage it, would be to confess to, rather than act out, our impulses. We should admit to our partner that we have been seized by an ugly fear about their happiness, laughingly reveal how much we would ideally love to cause a stink and firmly pledge that we won't. We would all the while remind ourselves that every cheerful person has been sad and that the buoyant among us have by far the best chances of keeping afloat those who remain emotionally at sea.

The spoiling argument is a wholly paradoxical plea for love that leaves one party ever further from the tenderness and shared insight they crave. Knowing how to spot the phenomenon should lead us, when we are the ones cheerily baking or whistling a tune, to remember that the person attempting to ruin our mood isn't perhaps just nasty (though they are a bit of that too); they are, childishly but sincerely, worried that our happiness may come at their expense and are, through their remorseless negativity, in a garbled and maddening way begging us for reassurance.

The Pathologizing Argument

There are arguments in which one person gets so upset that they start to behave in ways that range far beyond the imagined norms of civilized conduct: they speak in a high-pitched voice, they exaggerate, they weep, they beg, their words become almost incoherent, they pull their own hair, they bite their own hand, they roll on the floor.

Unsurprisingly, it can be supremely tempting for their interlocutor to decide that this dramatic behaviour means they have gone mad – and to close them down on this score. To press the point home, the unagitated partner may start to speak in a preternaturally calm way, as if addressing an unruly dog or a red-faced two-year-old. They may assert that, since their partner has grown so unreasonable, there doesn't seem to be any point in continuing the conversation – a conclusion which drives the distressed partner to further paroxysms and convulsions.

It can feel natural to propose that the person who loses their temper in the course of an argument thereby loses any claim to credibility. Whatever point they may be trying to make seems automatically to be invalidated by the fact that they are doing so while in a chaotic state. The only priority seems to be to shift attention to how utterly awful and immature they are being. It is evident: the one who is calm is good; the one who is frothing and spluttering is a cretin.

Unfortunately, both partners end up trapped in an unproductive cycle that benefits neither of them. There's a moment when the calm one may turn and say, 'Since you are mad, there's no point in talking to you.' The awareness – in the raging lover's mind – that, as they rant and flail, they are ineluctably throwing away all possibility of being properly attended to or understood feeds their ever-mounting sense of panic: they become yet more demented and exaggerated, further undermining their credibility in the discussion. Hearing their condition diagnosed as insane by the calm one serves to reinforce a suspicion that perhaps they really are mad, which in turn weakens their capacity not to be so. They lose confidence that there might be any reasonable aspect to their distress which could, theoretically, be explained in a clear way if only they could stop crying.

'I'm not going to listen to you any further if you keep making such a fuss,' the calm partner might go on to say, prompting ever more of precisely this 'fuss'. The frustrated one is gradually turned into a case study fit only for clinical psychology or a straitjacket. They are, as we might put it, 'pathologized', held up as someone who is actually crazy, rather than as an ordinary human who is essentially quite sane but has temporarily lost their self-possession in an extremely difficult situation.

On the other side of the equation, the person who remains calm is automatically cast – by their own imperturbable nature and subtle skills at public relations – as decent and reasonable. But we should bear in mind that it is at least in theory entirely possible to be cruel, dismissive, stubborn, harsh and wrong – and keep one's voice utterly steady. Just as one can, equally well, be red-nosed, whimpering and incoherent – and have a point.

We need to keep hold of a heroically generous attitude: rage and histrionics can be the symptoms of a desperation that sets in when a hugely important intimate truth is being blatantly ignored or denied, with the uncontrolled person being neither evil nor monstrous.

Obviously the method of delivery is drastically unhelpful; obviously it would always be better if we didn't start to cry. But it is not beyond understanding or, hopefully, forgiveness if we were to do so. It's horrible and frightening to witness someone getting intensely worked up, but with the benefit of perspective, their inner condition calls for deep compassion rather than a lecture. We should remember that only someone who internally felt their life was in danger would end up in such a mess.

We should keep this in mind, because sometimes we will be the ones who fall into a deranged state; we won't always be the aggrieved, cooler-headed party. We should all have a little film of ourselves at our very worst moments from which we replay brief highlights and so remember that, while we looked mad, our contortions were only the outer signs of an inner agony at being unable to make ourselves understood on a crucial point by the person we relied on.

We can stay calm with almost everyone in our lives. If we lose our temper with our partners, it is – at best, in part – because we are so invested in them and our joint futures. We shouldn't invariably hold it against someone that they behave in a stricken way; it isn't (probably) a sign that they are mad or horrible. Rather, as we should have the grace to recall, it is just that they love and depend on us very much.

The Absentee Argument

There are so many ways in which the world wounds us. At work, our manager repeatedly humiliates and belittles us. We hear of a party to which we were not invited. A better-looking, wealthier person snubs us at a conference. We develop a skill that turns out not to be much in demand in the world; some people we were with at university set up a hugely successful business.

Our hurt, humiliation and disappointments accumulate – but almost always, we cannot possibly complain about them to anyone. Our managers would sack us if we told them how we felt. Our acquaintances would be horrified by the depth of our insecurities. No one gives a damn about an admirable company that has hurt our feelings through its success. There is no way to take out our distress on geopolitics or economic history or the existential paradox that we are required to make decisions about our lives before we could possibly know what they will entail. We cannot rave at the cosmos or at the accidents of political power. We need, most of the time, simply to politely swallow our hurt and move on.

But there is one exception to this rule: we can rant and moan at a person who is more reliably kind to us than anyone else, a person whom we love more than any other, a blessed being who is waiting for us at home at the end of every new gruelling day . . .

Unfortunately, we don't necessarily always tell our partner that we are causing problems because we are sad about things that have nothing to do with them; we just create arguments to alleviate our distress – we are mean to them because our boss didn't care, the economy wasn't available for a chat and there was no God to implore. We reroute all the humiliation and rage that no one else had time for on to the shoulders of the one person who most cares about our well-being. We tell them that if only they were more supportive, were less intrusive, made more money, were less materialistic, were more imaginative or less naive, less fussy or more demanding, more dynamic or more relaxed, sexier or less obsessed with sex, more intelligent or less wrapped up in the world of books, more adventurous or more settled . . . then we could be happy – our life would be soothed and our errors redeemed. It is, as we imply and occasionally even tell them, *all their fault*.

This is, of course, horrible and largely untrue. But enfolded within our denunciations and absurd criticisms is a strangely loving homage. Behind our accusations is an inarticulate yet large compliment. We complain unfairly as a tribute to the extent of our love and the position the partner has taken in our lives.

We pick a fight with them over nothing much, but what we are in effect saying is: *Save me, redeem me, make sense of my pain, love me even though I have failed*. The fact that we are blaming our partner in ridiculous ways is a heavily disguised but authentic mark of the trust we have in them. We must be civilized and grown up with everyone else, but with one person on the planet, we can at points be maddeningly irrational, utterly demanding and horribly cross – not because they deserve it, but because so much has gone wrong, we are so tired and they are the one person who promises to understand and forgive us. No wonder we love them.

The Argument of Normality

Being in a relationship, even a very good one, requires us constantly to defend our preferences and points of view against the possibility of a partner's objections. We can find ourselves having to argue about what time to go to bed, where to put the sofa, how often to have sex, what to do in a foreign city or what the best colour for a new car might be. In previous eras, the sorts of justifications we wielded were far simpler. The person with more power would simply assert with haughty indifference: *Because I say so . . .* or *Because I want it this way . . .* But we live in a more rational age focused on discussion, where only well-founded and articulated reasons are expected to swing a point.

Because we live in a democratic age too, one of the tools to which warring couples most often have resort when attempting to justify their choices is majority opinion. That is, in the heat of a fight, we remind our opponent that what we want to do, think or feel is *normal.* We suggest that they should agree with us, not only or primarily because of what *we* happen to say, but because they'll find – once they stop to consider the matter with appropriate humility – that all right-thinking people agree with us too. Our position (on travel plans, sexual routines or car colours) isn't mere idiosyncrasy; it is synonymous with that lodestar of contemporary ethics, 'normality'.

As we fight, we bolster our personal and therefore fragile opinion with the supposed impregnable voice of the entire community: *It is not simply that I – one solitary, easily overlooked person – find your attitude very displeasing. All reasonable people – in fact, an electoral majority of the world – are presently with me in condemning your ideas. You are – in your opinion on how to cook pasta, when to call your sister or the merit of the prize-winning novel – utterly alone.*

In a pure sense, what is 'normal' shouldn't matter very much at all. What is widespread in our community is often wrong and what is currently considered odd might actually be quite wise. But however much we know this intellectually, we are profoundly social creatures; millions of years of evolution have shaped our brains so as naturally to give a great deal of weight to the opinions of those around us. In reality, it almost always feels emotionally crucial to try to retain the broad goodwill and acceptance of our community. So the claim to 'normality', however approximately and unfairly it is made, touches on a sensitive spot in our minds – which is precisely why our partner invokes it so deftly.

Nevertheless, we should hold on to the counter-arguments. When it comes to personal life, we have no sound idea of what is normal, because we have no easy access to the intimate truths of others. We don't know what a normal amount of sex really is, or how normal it is to cry, sleep in a different bed or dislike a partner's best friend. There are no reliable polls or witnesses.

In addition, and more importantly, we should cease cynically lauding the idea of the normal when it suits us by acknowledging that almost everything that is beautiful and worth appreciating in our relationship is deeply un-normal. It's very un-normal that some-one should find us attractive, should have agreed to go out with us, should put up with our antics, should have come up with such an endearing nickname for us that alludes to our favourite animal from childhood, should have bothered to spend some of their weekend sewing on buttons for us – and should bother to listen to our anxieties late into the night. We are the beneficiaries of some extremely rare eventualities and it is the height of ingratitude to claim to be a friend of the normal when most of what is good in our lives is the result of awesomely minuscule odds. We should stop badgering our partners with phoney democratic arguments and admit to something far truer and possibly more effective in its honest vulnerability: *We would love something to happen because, and only because, it would make us very happy if it did – and very upset if it didn't.*

The Parental-Resemblance Argument

There is a move many of us make in the heat of an argument with our partner that is at once devastating, accurate and entirely uncalled for. In a particularly contemptuous, sly and yet gleeful tone, partners are inclined to announce, as if a rare truth were being unearthed,

'You're turning into your mother' or 'You're turning into your father.'

The claim is apt to silence us because, however much we may have tried to develop our own independent characters, we can't help but harbour a deep and secret fear that we are prey to an unconscious psychological destiny. In one side of our brains, we are aware of a range of negative qualities we observed in our parents which we sense are intermittently hinted at in our own personalities. And we are terrified.

We catch ourselves rehearsing opinions that once struck us as patently absurd or laughable. At moments of weakness, we find ourselves replaying just the same sarcastic or petty, vain or angry attitudes we once felt sure we would never want to emulate. The accusations of our partner hurt so much because they knock up against a genuine risk.

At the same time, the criticism is deeply underhand. First, because even if we ourselves occasionally share an account of our parents' failings with our partners, the universal rules of filial loyalty mean that we – and only we – are ever allowed to bring these up again in an aggressive tone.

Second, the accusation is unfair because it is attempting to push us into denying something that is invariably partly correct. How could we not be a little like our parents, given the many years we spent around them, the untold genes we share with them and the malleability of the infant mind?

We should never get railroaded into protesting that we are unlike those who put us on the earth; we should undercut the implicit charge by immediately candidly admitting that we are – of course – very much like our parents, as they are akin to theirs. How could we be anything else? Why wouldn't we be? But, in a twist to the normal argument, we should then remind our partners that we chose to be with them precisely in order to attenuate the risks of an unexamined parental destiny. It was and remains their solemn duty not to mock us for being like our parents, but to assist us with kindness to become a little less like them where it counts. By hectoring and accusing us, they aren't identifying a rare truth from which we hide away in shame; they are stating the obvious and then betraying the fundamental contract of adult love. Their task as our partner isn't to bully us into making confessions that we would have been ready to accept from the start, but to help us evolve away from the worst sides of people who have inevitably messed us up a little and yet whom we can't – of course, despite everything – stop loving inordinately.

The Argument from Excessive Logic

It seems odd at first to imagine that we might get angry, even maddened, by a partner because they are, in the course of a discussion, proving to be *too* reasonable and *too* logical. We are used to thinking highly of reason and logic. We are not normally enemies of evidence and rationality. How, then, do these ingredients become problematic in the course of love? But from close up, considered with sufficient imagination, our suspicion can make a lot of sense.

When we are in difficulties, what we may primarily be seeking from our partners is a sense that they understand what we are going through. We are not looking for answers (the problems may be too large for there to be any obvious ones) so much as comfort, reassurance and fellow feeling. In the circumstances, the deployment of an overly logical stance may come across not as an act of kindness, but as a species of disguised impatience.

Let's imagine someone who comes to their partner complaining of vertigo. The fear of heights is usually manifestly unreasonable: the balcony obviously isn't about to collapse, there's a strong iron balustrade between us and the abyss, the building has been repeatedly tested by experts. We may know all this intellectually, but it does nothing to reduce our sickening anxiety in practice. If a partner were patiently to begin to explain the laws of physics to us, we wouldn't be grateful; we would simply feel they had misunderstood us.

Much that troubles us has a structure akin to vertigo: our worry isn't exactly reasonable, but we're unsettled all the same. We can, for example, continue to feel guilty about letting down our parents, no matter how nice to them we've actually been. Or we can feel very worried about money, even if we're objectively economically quite safe. We can feel horrified by our own appearance, even though no one else judges our face or body harshly. Or we can be certain that we're failures who've messed up everything we've ever done, even if, in objective terms, we seem to be doing pretty well. We can obsess that we've forgotten to pack something, even though we've taken a lot of care and can in any case buy almost everything at the other end. Or we may feel that our life will fall apart if we have to make a short speech, even though thousands of people make quite bad speeches every day and their lives continue as normal.

When we recount our worries to our partner, we may receive a set of precisely delivered, unimpassioned logical answers – we have been good to our parents, we have packed enough toothpaste, etc. – answers that are entirely true and yet unhelpful as well, and so in their own way enraging. It feels as if the excessive logic of the other has led them to look down on our concerns. Because, reasonably speaking, we shouldn't have our worries, the implication is that we must be mad for having them.

The one putting forward the 'logical' point of view shouldn't be surprised by the angry response they receive. They are forgetting how weird and beyond the ordinary rules of reason all human minds can be, theirs included. The logic they are applying is really a species of brute common sense that refuses the insights of psychology. Of course our minds are prey to phantasms, illusions, projections and neurotic terrors. Of course we're afraid of many things that don't exist in the so-called real world. But such phenomena are not so much 'illogical' as deserving of the application of a deeper logic. Our sense of whether we're attractive or not isn't a reflection of what we actually look like; it follows a pattern that goes back to childhood and how loved we were made to feel by those we depended on. The fear of public speaking is bound up with long-standing shame and dread of others' judgement.

An excessively logical approach to fears discounts their origins and concentrates instead on why we shouldn't have them – which is maddening when we are in pain. It's not that we actually want our partner to stop being reasonable; we want them to apply their intelligence to the task of sensitive reassurance. We want them to enter into the weirder bits of our own experience by remembering their own. We want to be understood for being the mad animals we are, and then comforted and reassured that it will all be OK anyway.

Then again, it could be that the application of excessive logic isn't an accident or a form of stupidity. It might be an act of revenge. Perhaps our partner is giving brief, logical answers to our worries because their efforts to be sympathetic towards us in the past have gone nowhere. Perhaps we have neglected their needs. If two people were being properly 'logical' in the deepest sense of the word – that is, truly alive to all the complexities of emotional functioning – rather than squabbling around the question 'Why are you being so rational when I'm in pain?', the person on the receiving end of superficial logic would gently change the subject and ask, 'Is it possible I've hurt or been neglecting you?' That would be real logic.

The No-Sex Argument

It could, on the surface, be an argument about almost anything: what time to leave for the airport, who forgot to post the tax form, where to send the children to school . . . But in reality, in disguise, unmentioned and unmentionable, it is typically the very same argument, the no-sex argument, the single greatest argument that ever afflicts committed couples, the argument which has powered more furious oblique exchanges among lovers than any other, the argument that, right now, explains why one person is angrily refusing to speak to another over a bowl of udon noodles in a restaurant in downtown Yokohama and another is screaming in an apartment on an upper floor of a block in the suburbs of Belo Horizonte, why a child has acquired a step-parent and a person is crying over a bottle or at their therapist's office.

The real injury – *you have ceased to want me and I can no longer bear myself or you* – can't be mentioned because it cuts too deep; it threatens too much of our dignity; it is bigger than we are. Late at night in the darkness, time after time, our hand moved towards theirs, tried to coax theirs into a caress and was turned down. They held our fingers limply for a moment and then, as if we were the monster we now take ourselves to be, curled away from us and disappeared into the warren of sleep. We have stopped trying now. It may happen once in a blue moon, a few times a year, but we understand the score well enough: we are not wanted. We feel like outcasts, the only ones to be rejected in this way, the victims of a rare disease. We are nursing an emotional injury far too shaming to mention to others, let alone ourselves, the only ones not to be having sex in a happy, sex-filled world. Our anger aggravates our injury and traps us in cycles of hostility. Perhaps they don't want us in the night because we have been so vile in the day; but so long as our hand goes unwanted, we can never muster the courage to be anything but vindictive in their presence. It hurts more than being single, when at least the neglect was to be expected. This is a sentence without end. We can neither complain nor let the issue go. We feel compelled to fight by proxy about anything we can lay our hands on – the washing powder and the walk to the park, the money for the dentist and the course of the nation's politics – all because we so badly need to be held and to hold, to penetrate or to be penetrated.

It is in a sense deeply strange, even silly, that so much should hang on this issue, that the future of families, the fate of children, the division of assets, the survival of a friendship group should depend on the right sort of frottage of a few centimetres of our upper limbs. It's the tiniest thing and at the same time the very largest. The absence of sex matters so much because sex itself is the supreme conciliator and salve of all conflict, ill feeling, loneliness and lack of interest. It is almost impossible to make love and be sad, indifferent or bitter. Furious perhaps, in a passionate and ardent way. But not – almost never – truly elsewhere or beset by major grievances. The act forces presence, vulnerability, honesty, tenderness, release. It matters inordinately because it is the ultimate proof that everything is, despite everything, still OK.

As ever, so much would change if only we could be helped to find the words to fight our way past our shame and not feel so alone (this should be proof enough that we aren't); if we could point to the problem without fury, without humiliation, without defensiveness; if we could simply name our desperation without becoming desperate; if the one who didn't want sex could explain why in terms that made sense and were bearable and the one who felt cast aside could explain without giving way to vindictiveness or despair.

We would ideally, alongside physics and geography, learn the basics of all this in our last year at high school: learn how to spot and assuage the no-sex argument with an in-depth course and regular refreshments throughout our lives. It is the paradigm of all arguments. Those who can get over it can surmount pretty much any dispute; those who cannot must squabble to the grave.

Were our species to learn how to do this, the world would be suddenly and decisively calmer: there would be infinitely fewer fights, alcoholic outbursts, divorces, affairs, rages, denunciations, recriminations, civil wars, armed conflicts and nuclear conflagrations. At the first signs of no-sex arguments, couples would know how carefully to locate the words that would address their sorrows. There would not always be an answer, but there would always be the right sort of conversation.

PESSIMISM

Whatever disappointing experiences we have lived through in love, we tend to console ourselves with a highly reasonable-sounding thought: that our problems to date have resided not with our expectations, but with the people they were directed towards. It feels profoundly implausible that the difficulties might be structural, might lie with relationships in general, when issues have manifested themselves so distinctly in relation to particular people we were with.

The solution to our agitation lies, strangely, in a philosophy of pessimism: in the expectation of a blunt inevitability that two people will never understand more than a fraction of each other's minds. We are all, in diverse ways, highly arduous propositions. Love begins with the discovery of harmony in very specific areas, but widespread disagreement, misunderstanding, boredom, a certain amount of rage and loneliness are what happens when love finally truly succeeds.

The only people we can think of as profoundly admirable are those we don't yet know very well.

For many of us, love starts rapidly, often at first sight: with an overwhelming impression of the other's loveliness. This phenomenon – the crush – goes to the heart of the modern understanding of love. It could seem like a small incident, a minor planet in the constellation of love, but it is in fact the underlying secret central sun around which our notions of the Romantic revolve. A crush represents in pure and perfect form the essential dynamics of Romanticism: the explosive interaction of limited knowledge, outward obstacles to further discovery and boundless hope.

We wouldn't be able to develop crushes if we weren't so good at allowing a few details about someone to suggest the whole of them. From a few cues only, perhaps a distant look in the eyes, a forthright brow or a generous wit, we rapidly start to anticipate an intense connection and stretches of happiness, buoyed by profound mutual sympathy and understanding.

We cannot be entirely wrong, there are surely genuine virtues to hand, but the primary error of the crush is to ignore the fact that life will in important ways have twisted us all out of shape. No one has come through completely unscathed. The chances of a perfectly admirable human walking the earth are non-existent. Our fears and our frailties play themselves out in a thousand ways – they can make us defensive or aggressive, grandiose or hesitant, clingy or avoidant – but we can be assured that unfortunate tendencies exist in us all and will make everyone much less than perfect and, at moments, extremely hard to live with.

Every human can be guaranteed to frustrate, anger, annoy, madden and disappoint us – and we will (without any malice) do the same to them. There can be no end to our sense of emptiness and incompleteness. This is a truth chiselled indelibly into the script of romantic life. Choosing whom to commit ourselves to is therefore merely a case of identifying a specific kind of dissatisfaction we can bear rather than an occasion to escape from grief altogether.

UNREQUITED LOVE

When love remains unreciprocated for too long, a particular agony can descend. We are haunted by a sense of all that might have been. Epochal happiness seemed tantalizingly close yet is now maddeningly out of reach. We are often kindly counselled to try to forget the beloved and to think of something or someone else. Yet such kindness is misguided. The cure for love does not lie in ceasing to think of the fugitive lover, but in learning to think more intensely and constructively about who they might really be.

What prevents us from loosening our grip on love is simply a lack of knowledge. This is what can make unrequited love so vicious. By denying us the chance to grow close to the beloved, we cannot tire of them in the cathartic and liberating manner that is the gift of requited love. It isn't their charms that are keeping us magnetized; it is our lack of knowledge of their flaws.

The cure for unrequited love is, in structure, therefore very simple. We must get to know them better. The more we learn about them, the less they will ever look like the solution to our uneasy lives.

We will discover the endless small ways in which they are irksome; we'll get to know how stubborn, how critical, how cold and how hurt by things that strike us as meaningless they can be. That is, if we get to know them better, we will realize how much they have in common with everyone else.

Passion can never withstand too much exposure to the full reality of another person. The unbounded admiration on which it is founded is destroyed by the knowledge that a properly shared life inevitably brings.

The cruelty of unrequited love isn't really that we haven't been loved back, rather that our hopes have been aroused by someone who can never disappoint us, someone whom we will have to keep believing in because we lack the knowledge that would set us free.

In a position of longing for a new person when we are constrained within an existing relationship, we must beware too of the 'incumbent problem': the vast but often overlooked and unfair advantage that all new people, and also cities and jobs, have over existing – or, as we put it, incumbent – ones. The beautiful person glimpsed briefly in the street, the city visited for a few days, the job we read about in a couple of tantalizing paragraphs in a magazine all tend to seem immediately and definitively superior to our current partner, our long-established home and our committed workplace and can inspire us to sudden and (in retrospect sometimes) regrettable divorces, relocations and resignations.

When we spot apparent perfection, we tend to blame our spectacular bad luck for the mediocrity of our lives, without realizing that we are mistaking an asymmetry of knowledge for an asymmetry of quality: we are failing to see that our partner, home and job are not especially awful, but rather that we know them especially well.

The corrective to insufficient knowledge is experience. We need to mine the secret reality of other people and places and so learn that, beneath their charms, they will almost invariably be essentially 'normal' in nature: that is, no worse yet no better than the incumbents we already understand.

We should extrapolate what we already know of people and apply it to those we don't yet.

THE LAUNDRY

In the history of Western literature, in hundreds of poems and novels, no Romantic hero or heroine has ever ironed their underpants. This might seem a trivial point, but it is crucial and personally urgent, because it signals that we've taken our cues about what belongs to love from a societal narrative that is radically incomplete and misleading in nature.

Romantic culture takes no interest in the myriad challenges that fall within the realm of the 'domestic', a term that captures all the practicalities of living together, extending across a range of small but vital issues, including who one should visit at the weekend, when to empty the bins, who should clean the oven and how often to have friends over for dinner.

From the Romantic point of view, these things cannot be serious or worth the attention of intelligent people. Relationships are made or broken over grand, dramatic matters: fidelity and betrayal, the courage to face society on one's own terms or the tragedy of being ground down by the demands of convention. The day-to-day minutiae of the domestic sphere seem entirely unimpressive and humiliatingly insignificant by comparison.

Partly as a result of this neglect, we don't go into relationships ready to perceive domestic issues as important potential flashpoints to look out for and devote sustained attention to. We don't acknowledge how much it may end up mattering whether we can maturely resolve issues around how to clean the kitchen floor or the conundrum of whether it is stylish or a touch pretentious to give a cocktail party.

When a problem has high prestige, we are ready to expend energy and time trying to resolve it. This has often happened around

Pieter de Hooch, *Interior with Women beside a Linen Cupboard*, 1663.

large scientific questions. It was entirely understood that mapping the human genome would be enormously difficult, as is the puzzle of artificial intelligence. This respect leads to an unexpected but crucial consequence. We don't panic around the challenges, because we understand the difficulty of what we are attempting to do. We are a lot calmer around prestigious problems. It's problems that feel trivial or silly but nevertheless take up large sections of our lives that drive us to heightened states of agitation. Such agitation is precisely what the Romantic neglect of domestic life has unwittingly encouraged: its legacy is overhasty conversations about the temperature of the bedroom and curt remarks about which news programme to watch, matters which can – over many years – contribute to a critical erosion of our capacities to love.

At certain points in history artists have attempted to correct the distribution of prestige. In the seventeenth century, the Dutch painter Pieter de Hooch specialized in portraying high-status, interesting-looking people engaged in domestic chores. He wanted to show the relevance of such activities to having a good life and to convey that these were not in any way degrading or unworthy tasks. Organizing a linen cupboard was, de Hooch was proposing, no less a task than checking the accounts of a major corporation or making sure that a load-bearing wall was sufficiently strong to support the weight of an attic storey.

Domestic preoccupation isn't really a sign of the death of love. It's what awaits us when love has succeeded. We will only be reconciled to the reality of love when we can accept without rancour the genuine dignity of the ironing board.

IT WAS MEANT TO BE NICER

Often, our partner isn't necessarily being terrible in overt ways, but we feel a growing sadness about the character of our relationship: they're not as focused on us as we'd hoped; there are often times when they don't understand us properly; they're often busy and pre-occupied; they can be a bit offhand or abrupt; they're not hugely interested in the details of our day; they call their friends rather than talk with us. We feel disenchanted and let down. Love was supposed to be lovely. But, without any one huge thing having gone wrong, it doesn't much feel that way day to day.

This sorrow has a paradoxical source: we're upset now because at some point in the past we were really rather fortunate. We're sad because we've been lucky. To explain the seeming paradox we need to have a look at the intimate origins of love.

Our idea of what a good, loving relationship should be like (and what it feels like to be loved) doesn't ever come from what we've seen in adulthood; it arises from a stranger, more powerful source. The idea of happy coupledom taps into a fundamental picture of comfort, deep security, wordless communication and our needs being effort-lessly understood that comes from early childhood. Some of the most popular pictures in the world show a mother very tenderly holding a small child, with an expression of complete devotion on her face. Officially, these are pictures of one specific and very unusual child and one very holy and good mother. But the religious background to the Mother and Child images isn't the key to their appeal. We're moved because we recognize a paradisiacal moment in our own personal story; because we're being brought into semi-conscious contact with a delightful memory of how we were once cared for.

At the best moments of childhood (if things went reasonably well) loving parents offered us extraordinary satisfaction. They knew when we were hungry or tired, even though we couldn't explain. We did not need to strive. They made us feel completely safe. We were held peacefully. We were entertained and indulged. And even if we don't recall the explicit details, the experience of being cherished has made a profound impression on us; it has planted itself in our deep minds as the ideal template of what love should be.

As adults, without really noticing, we continue to be in thrall to this notion of being loved, projecting the best experiences of our

Leonardo da Vinci, *The Madonna Litta*, mid-1490s.

early years into our present relationships and finding them sorely wanting as a result – a comparison that is profoundly corrosive and unfair.

The love we received from a parent can't ever be a workable model for our later, adult, experience of love. The reason is fundamental: we were a baby then, we are an adult now – a dichotomy with several key ramifications.

For a start, our needs were so much simpler. We needed to be washed, amused, put to bed. But we didn't need someone to trawl intelligently through the troubled corners of our minds. We didn't need a caregiver to understand why we prefer the first series of a television show to the second, why it is necessary to see our aunt on Sunday or why it matters to us that the curtains harmonize with the sofa covers or bread must be cut with a proper bread knife. The parent knew absolutely what was required in relation to basic physical and emotional requirements. Our partner is stumbling in the dark around needs that are immensely subtle, far from obvious and very complicated to fulfil.

Secondly, none of it was reciprocal. Our parents were intensely focused on caring for us, but they knew and wholly accepted that we wouldn't engage with their needs. They didn't for a minute imagine that they could take their troubles to us or expect us to nurture them. They didn't need us to ask them about their day. Our responsibility was blissfully simple: all we had to do to please them was to exist. Our most ordinary actions – rolling over on our tummy, grasping a biscuit in our tiny hand – enchanted them with ease. We were loved and didn't have to love – a distinction between kinds of love which language normally artfully blurs, shielding us from the difference between being the privileged customer of love or its more exhausted and long-suffering provider.

Furthermore, our parents were probably kind enough to shield us from the burden that looking after us imposed on them. They maintained a reasonably sunny facade until they retired to their own bedroom, at which point the true toll of their efforts could be witnessed (but by then we were asleep). This was immensely kind, but did us one lasting disservice: it may unwittingly have created an expectation of what it would mean for someone to love us which was never true in the first place. We might in later life end up with lovers who are tetchy with us, who are too tired to talk at the end of the day, who don't marvel at our every antic, who can't even be bothered to listen to what we're saying – and we might feel (with some bitterness) that this is not how our parents were. The irony, which has its redeeming side, is that in truth this is exactly how our parents were, they simply saved it until their bedroom, when we were asleep and realized nothing.

The source of our present sorrow is not, therefore, a special failing on the part of our adult lovers. They are not tragically inept or uniquely selfish. It's rather that we're judging our adult experiences against a very different kind of childhood love. We are sorrowful not because we have landed up with the wrong person but because we have – sadly – been forced to grow up.

SECRETS

Many relationships begin with a deeply misleading but beguiling sense that we can tell a partner everything. At last, there is no more need for the usual hypocrisies. We can come clean about so much that we had previously needed to keep to ourselves: our reservations about our friends, our irritation over small but wounding remarks by colleagues, our interest in less often-mentioned sexual practices. Love can seem founded on the idea of an absence of secrecy.

Then, gradually, we become aware of so much we cannot say. It might be around sex: on a work trip, there was a flirtation; late one evening, we discovered a porn site that beautifully targeted a special quirk of our erotic imagination; we find their brother (or sister) very alluring. Or the secret thoughts can be more broad-ranging: the blog they wrote for work, about their experience in client care, was very boring to read; the dark green scarf they so love wearing is hideous; their best friend from school, to whom they are still very loyal, is excessively silly and dull; in the wedding photo of their parents (lovingly displayed in a silver frame in the living room) their mother looks unbearably smug.

Love begins with a hope of – at last – being able to tell someone else everything about who we are and what we feel. The relief of honesty is at the heart of the feeling of being in love. But this sharing of secrets sets up in our minds, and in our collective culture, a powerful and potentially problematic ideal: that if two people love one another, then they must always tell each other the truth about everything.

The idea of honesty is sublime. It presents a deeply moving vision of how two people can be together and it is a constant presence in the early months. But in order to be kind, and in order to sustain love, it ultimately becomes necessary to keep a great many thoughts out of sight.

Keeping secrets can seem like a betrayal of the relationship. At the same time, the complete truth eventually appears to place the union in mortal danger.

Much of what we'd ideally like to have recognized and confirmed is going to be genuinely disturbing even to someone who is fond of us. We face a choice between honesty and acceptability and – for reasons that deserve a great deal of sympathy – mostly we choose the latter.

We are perhaps too conscious of the bad reasons for hiding something; we haven't paid enough attention to the noble reasons why, from time to time, true loyalty may lead us to say very much less than the whole truth. We are so impressed by honesty, we have forgotten the virtues of politeness, this word defined not as a cynical withholding of important information for the sake of harm, but as a dedication to not rubbing someone else up against the true, hurtful aspects of our nature.

It is ultimately no great sign of kindness to insist on showing someone our entire selves at all times. A dedication to maintaining boundaries and editing our pronouncements belongs to love as much as a capacity to show ourselves as we really are. The lover who does not tolerate secrets, who in the name of 'being honest' divulges information so wounding it cannot be forgotten, is no friend of love. Just as no parent should ever tell a child the whole truth, so we should accept the ongoing need to edit our full reality.

And if one suspects (and one should, rather regularly, if the relationship is a good one) that one's partner might be lying too (about what they are thinking about, about how they judge one's work, about where they were last night . . .), it is perhaps best not to take up arms and lay into them like a sharp, relentless inquisitor, however intensely one yearns to do just that. It may be kinder, wiser and perhaps more in the true spirit of love to pretend one simply didn't notice.

THE WISDOM OF COMPROMISE

We reserve some of our deepest scorn for couples who stay together out of compromise; those who are making a show of unanimity, but who we know are, deep down, not fully happy. Maybe they're primarily together because of the children; maybe they're sticking around because they're scared of being lonely; or maybe they're just worried that anyone else they found wouldn't be much better.

These seem like disgraceful motives to be with anyone – disgraceful on account of a background belief that circulates powerfully through the collective modern psyche: the idea that anyone who puts their mind and will sufficiently to it doesn't have to compromise in love; that there are pain-free, profoundly fulfilling options available for all of us – and the only things that could stand in the way of discovering them would be laziness and cowardice, flaws of character that deserve no particular sympathy or forgiveness. Our high romantic expectations have made us notably impatient around and censorious about those who can't attain them.

But imagine if we were to tweak the premise of the argument a little and for a moment explore the notion that there really might be a pain-free and entirely fulfilling option available for all of us at all times. What if our choices were, in many contexts, in fact often rather more limited than Romanticism proposes? Maybe there aren't as many admirable unattached people in our vicinity as there might be. Maybe we lack the charm, the personality, the career, the confidence or the looks ever to attract the ones who do exist. Maybe time is running out. Or maybe our children really would take it extremely badly if we abandoned the family for the sake of better sex and greater cheer elsewhere.

At the same time, maybe the current situation – while clearly a compromise – is not without its virtues. A partner may be only half-right, quite often maddening and properly disappointing in certain areas, but – humblingly – still more satisfying than being alone. Having children to bring up together may be worth it even with a co-parent about whom one has a long, only semi-private list of reservations. A few cuddles and occasional moments of cosiness may retain a small but decisive edge over a life alone interspersed with humiliating dates.

The capacity to compromise is not always the weakness it is described as being. It can involve a mature, realistic admission that there may – in certain situations – simply be no ideal options. And, conversely, an inability to compromise does not always have to be the courageous and visionary position it is held to be by our impatient and perfectionist ideology. It may just be a slightly rigid, proud and cruel delusion.

Mocking people who compromise is, of course, emotionally very handy. It localizes a problem that it's normal to want to disavow. It pins to a few scapegoat couples what we are all terrified about in our relationships: that a degree of sadness may just be an intrinsic and unavoidable part of them.

Wiser societies would be careful never to stigmatize the act of compromise. It is painful enough to have to do it; it is even more painful to have to hate oneself for having done so. We should rehabilitate and honour the ability to put up with a flawed fellow human being, to nurse our sadness without falling into rage or despair, to reconcile ourselves to our damaged appearance and character and to accept that there may be no better way for us to live but partly in pain and longing, given who we are and what the world can provide. Couples who compromise may in reality not be the enemies of love; they may be at the vanguard of understanding what lasting relationships truly demand.

THE CONSOLATIONS OF FRIENDSHIP

One of the most subtly hurtful and quietly damning of all remarks, perhaps softly and sweetly delivered on the doorstep at the end of a long evening, with the taxi still hovering somewhere just out of sight, is the suggestion that we should in the end probably remain 'just good friends'.

We know exactly what to understand by this. The path towards a tender future is being gently but firmly closed off. We are, with a smile, being shunted into the category of the failed, the ignored and the lightly despised. The other must in some way have worked out the despicable truths about us – all the ones that we tried so hard to disguise and even to believe didn't exist – and has logically decided to take their leave. We return crushed to an apartment which we had left with butterflies and elevated hopes only a few hours before.

We hear the offer of friendship as something synonymous with insult because our Romantic culture has, from our youth, continuously made one thing clear: love is the purpose of existence; friendship is the paltry, depleted consolation prize.

Though this seems like unsurprising common sense, what should detain us and encourage us to probe a little at the claims made on love's behalf is one basic source of evidence: the behaviour, level of satisfaction and state of mind of those who engage in it.

If we were to judge love chiefly by its impact, by the extent of the tears, the depths of the frustrations, the viciousness of the insults that unfold in its name, we would not continue to rate it as we do and might indeed mistake it for a form of illness or aberration of the mind. The scenes that typically unfold between lovers would scarcely be considered imaginable outside conditions of open hostility. Those we love, we honour with our worst moods, our most unfair accusations, our most wounding insults. It is to our lovers that we direct blame for everything that has gone wrong in our lives; we expect them to know everything we mean without bothering to explain it; their minor errors and misunderstandings occasion our sulks and rage.

By comparison, in friendship – the supposedly worthless and inferior state whose mention should crush us at the end of a date – we bring our highest and noblest virtues. Here we are patient, encouraging, tolerant, funny and, most of all, kind. We expect a little less and therefore, by extension, forgive infinitely more. We do not presume that we will be fully understood and so treat failings lightly and humanely. We don't imagine that our friends should admire us without reserve, sticking by us whatever we do, and so we put in effort and behave, pleasing ourselves as well as our companions along the way. We are, in the company of our friends, our best selves.

Paradoxically, it is friendship that often offers us the real route to the pleasures that Romanticism associates with love. That this sounds surprising is only a reflection of how underdeveloped our day-to-day vision of friendship has become. We associate it with a casual acquaintance we see only once in a while to exchange inconsequential and shallow banter. But real friendship is something altogether more profound and worthy of exultation. It is an arena in which two people can get a sense of each other's vulnerabilities, appreciate each other's follies without recrimination, reassure each other as to their value and greet the sorrows and tragedies of existence with wit and warmth.

Culturally and collectively, we have made a momentous mistake which has left us both lonelier and more disappointed than we ever needed to be. In a better world, our most serious goal would be not to locate one special lover with whom to replace all other humans but to put our intelligence and energy into identifying and nurturing a circle of true friends. At the end of an evening, we would learn to say to certain prospective companions, with an embarrassed smile as we invited them inside – knowing that this would come across as a properly painful rejection – 'I'm so sorry, couldn't we just be . . . lovers?'

A MODEST ARGUMENT FOR MARRIAGE

It has become, for many of us, ever harder to know what the point of marriage might be. The drawbacks are evident and well charted. Marriage is a state-sanctioned legal construct, fundamentally linked to matters of property, progeny and pension entitlements – a construct which aims to restrict and control how two people might feel towards one another over fifty or more years. It places a cold, unhelpful, expensive and entirely emotionally alien frame around what is always going to be a private matter of the heart. We don't need a marriage certificate to show affection and admiration. And indeed, forcing commitment only increases the danger of eventual inauthenticity and dishonesty. If love doesn't work out, being married simply makes it much harder to disentangle two lives and prolongs the agony of a dysfunctional union. Love either works or it doesn't – and marriage doesn't help matters one iota either way. It is completely reasonable to suppose that the mature, modern and logical move is to sidestep marriage entirely, along with the obvious nonsense of a wedding.

It would be hopeless to try to defend marriage on the grounds of its convenience. It is clearly cumbersome, expensive and risky, as well as arguably at junctures wholly archaic. But that is the point.

The whole rationale of marriage is to function as a prison that it is very hard and very embarrassing for two people to get out of.

The essence of marriage is to tie our hands, to frustrate our wills, to put high and costly obstacles in the way of splitting up and sometimes to force two unhappy people to stay in each other's company for longer than either of them would wish. Why do we do this?

Originally, we told ourselves that God wanted us to stay married. But even now, when God looms less large in the argument, we continue to ensure that marriage is rather hard to undo. For one thing, we carefully invite everyone we know to watch us proclaim that we'll stick together. We deliberately invite an elderly aunt or uncle whom we don't even like so much to fly around the world to be there. We are willingly creating a huge layer of embarrassment were we ever to turn round and admit it might have been a mistake. Furthermore, even though we could keep things separate, marriage tends to mean deep economic and legal entanglements. We know it is going to take the work of a phalanx of accountants and lawyers to prise us apart. It can be done, of course, but it may be ruinous.

It is as if we somewhere recognize that there might be some quite good, though strange-sounding, reasons to make it harder than it should be to get out of a public lifelong commitment to someone else.

One: Impulse is Dangerous

The Marshmallow Test was a celebrated experiment in the history of psychology designed to measure children's ability to delay gratification, and track the consequences of being able to think long-term. Some three-year-old children were offered a marshmallow, but told they would get two if they held off from eating the first one for five minutes. It turned out that a lot of children just couldn't make it through this period. The immediate benefit of gobbling the marshmallow in front of them was stronger than the strategy of waiting. Crucially, it was observed that these children went on to have lives blighted by a lack of impulse control, faring much worse than the children who were best at subordinating immediate fun for long-term benefit.

Relationships are no different. Here too many things feel very urgent. Not eating marshmallows, but escaping, finding freedom, running away, possibly with the new office recruit . . . Sometimes we're angry and want to get out very badly. We're excited by a stranger and feel like abandoning our present partner at once. And yet as we look around for the exit, every way seems blocked. It would cost a fortune, it would be so embarrassing, it would take an age . . .

Marriage is a giant inhibitor of impulse set up by our conscience to keep our libidinous, naive, desiring selves in check. What we are essentially buying into by submitting to its dictates is the insight that we are (as individuals) likely to make very poor choices under the sway of strong short-term impulses. To marry is to recognize that we require structure to insulate us from our urges. It is to lock ourselves up willingly, because we acknowledge the benefits of the long-term – the wisdom of the morning after the storm.

Marriage proceeds without constant reference to the moods of its protagonists. It isn't about feeling. It is a declaration that it's crucially impervious to our day-to-day desires. It is a very unusual marriage in which the couple don't spend a notable amount of time fantasizing that they aren't in fact married. But the point of marriage is to make these feelings not matter very much. It is an arrangement that protects us from what we desire and yet know, in our more reasonable moments, that we don't truly need or want.

Two: We Grow and Develop Gradually

At their best, relationships involve us in attempts to develop, mature and become 'whole'. We often get drawn to people precisely because they promise to edge us in the right direction.

But the process of our maturation can be agonizingly slow and complicated. We spend long periods (decades perhaps) blaming the other person for problems which arise from our own weaknesses.

We resist attempts at being changed, naively asking to be loved 'for who we are'.

It can take years of supportive interest, many tearful moments of anxiety, much frustration, until genuine progress can be made. With time, after maybe 120 arguments on a single topic, both parties may begin to see it from the other's point of view. Slowly we start to get insights into our own madness. We find labels for our issues, we give each other maps of our difficult areas, we become a little easier to live with.

Unfortunately, the lessons that are most important for us – the lessons that contribute most to our increasing wisdom and rounded completeness as people – are almost always the most painful to learn. They involve confronting our fears, dismantling our defensive armour, feeling properly guilty for our capacity to hurt another person, being genuinely sorry for our faults and learning to put up with the imperfections of someone else.

It is too easy to seem kind and normal when we keep starting new relationships. The truth about us, on the basis of which self-improvement can begin, only becomes clear over time. Chances of development can increase hugely when we stay put and don't succumb to the temptation to run away to people who will falsely reassure us that there's nothing too wrong with us.

Three: Investment Requires Security

Many of the most worthwhile projects require immense sacrifices from both parties and it's in the nature of such sacrifices that we're most likely to make them for people who are also making them for us.

Marriage is a means by which people can specialize – perhaps in making money or in running a home. This can be hugely constructive. But it carries a risk. Each person (especially if one stays at home) needs to be assured that they will not later be disadvantaged by their devotion.

Marriage sets up the conditions in which we can take valuable decisions about what to do with our lives that would be too risky outside its guarantees.

Over time, the argument for marriage has shifted. It's no longer about external forces having power over us: religions, the state, the legal idea of legitimacy, the social idea of being respectable . . .

What we are correctly now focused on is the psychological point of making it hard to throw in the towel. It turns out that we benefit greatly (though at a price) from having to stick with certain commitments, because some of our key needs have a long-term structure.

For the last fifty years, the burden of intelligent effort has been on attempting to make separation easier. The challenge now lies in another direction: in trying to remind ourselves why immediate flight doesn't always make sense; in trying to see the point of holding out for the second marshmallow.

Tethering ourselves to our partner, via the public institution of marriage, makes our unavoidable fluctuations of feeling have less power to destroy a relationship, one that we know, in calmer moments, is supremely important to us. The point of marriage is to be usefully unpleasant – at least at crucial times. Together we embrace a set of limitations on one kind of freedom, the freedom to run away, so as to protect and strengthen another kind, the shared ability to mature and create something of lasting value, the pains of which are aligned to our better selves.

IV : Work

THE DANGERS OF THE GOOD CHILD

Good children do their homework on time; their writing is neat; they keep their bedroom tidy; they are often a little shy; they want to help their parents; they use their brakes when cycling down a hill.

Because they don't pose many immediate problems, we tend to assume that all is well with good children. They aren't the target of particular concern; that goes to the kids who are graffitiing the underpass. People imagine the good children must be fine, on the basis that they do everything that is expected of them.

And that, of course, is precisely the problem. The secret sorrows – and future difficulties – of the good boy or girl begin with their inner need for excessive compliance. The good child isn't good because, by a quirk of nature, they simply have no inclination to be anything else. They are good because they have been granted no other option, because the more transgressive part of what they are cannot be tolerated. Their goodness springs from necessity rather than choice.

Good children may be good out of love for a depressed parent who makes it clear that they just couldn't cope with any more complications or difficulties. Or maybe they are very good to soothe a violently angry parent who could become catastrophically frightening at any sign of less than perfect conduct.

This repression of more challenging emotions, though it generates short-term cordiality, stores up an immense amount of difficulty for later life. Practised educators and parents will spot signs of exaggerated politeness and treat it as the danger it is.

Good children become the keepers of too many secrets and the appalling communicators of unpopular but important things. They say lovely words, they are experts in satisfying the expectations of their audiences, but their real thoughts and feelings are buried, then seep out as psychosomatic symptoms, twitches, sudden outbursts, sulphurous bitterness and an underlying feeling of unreality.

The good child has been deprived of one of the central ingredients of a properly privileged upbringing: the experience of other people witnessing and surviving their mischief.

Grown up, the good child typically has particular problems around sex. They might once have been praised for their purity. Sex, in its necessary extremes and ecstasies, lies at the opposite end of the spectrum. They may in response disavow their desires and detach themselves from their bodies, or perhaps give in to their longings only in a furtive, addictive, disproportionate or destructive way that leaves them feeling disgusted and distinctly frightened.

At work, the good adult also faces problems. As a child, it was enough to follow the rules, never to make trouble and to avoid provoking the merest frustration. But a cautious approach cannot tide one satisfactorily across an adult life. Almost everything interesting, worth doing or important will meet with a degree of opposition. The greatest plan will necessarily irritate or disappoint certain people – while remaining eminently valuable. Every noble ambition has to skirt disaster and ignominy. In their timid inability to brook the dangers of hostility, the good child risks being condemned to career mediocrity and sterile people-pleasing.

Being properly mature involves a frank, unfrightened relationship with one's own darkness, complexity and ambition. It involves accepting that not everything that makes us happy will please others or be honoured as especially 'nice', but it can be important to explore and hold on to it nevertheless.

The desire to be good is one of the loveliest things in the world, but in order to have a genuinely good life, we may sometimes need to be (by the standards of the good child) fruitfully and bravely bad.

CONFIDENCE AND THE INNER IDIOT

In well-meaning attempts to boost our confidence ahead of challenging moments, we are often encouraged to pay attention to our strengths: our intelligence, our competence, our experience.

But this can – curiously – have awkward consequences. There's a type of under-confidence that arises specifically when we grow too attached to our own dignity and become anxious around situations that seem in some way to threaten it. We hold back from challenges in which there is any risk of ending up looking ridiculous, but these of course comprise many of the most interesting options.

In a foreign city, we grow reluctant to ask anyone to guide us, because they might think us an ignorant, pitiable lost tourist. We might long to be close to someone, but never let on out of a fear that they might have caught sight of our absurd inner self. Or at work we don't apply for a promotion, in case this reminds the senior management of their underlying wish to fire us. In a concerted bid never to look foolish, we don't venture very far from our lair; and thereby – from time to time, at least – miss out on the best opportunities of our lives.

At the heart of our under-confidence is a skewed picture of how dignified a normal person can be. We imagine that it might be possible to place ourselves permanently beyond mockery. We trust that it is an option to lead a good life without regularly making a whole-hearted idiot of ourselves.

One of the most charming books written in early modern Europe is *In Praise of Folly* (1511) by the Dutch scholar and philosopher Erasmus. Erasmus advances a liberating argument. In a warm tone, he reminds us that everyone, however important and learned they might be, is a fool. No one is spared, not even the author. However well schooled he himself was, Erasmus remained – he insists – as much of a nitwit as anyone else: his judgement is faulty, his passions get the better of him, he is prey to superstition and irrational fear, he is shy whenever he has to meet new people, he drops things at elegant dinners. This is deeply cheering, for it means that our own repeated idiocies do not have to exclude us from the best company. Looking like a prick, making blunders and doing bizarre things in the night don't render us unfit for society; they just make us a bit more like the greatest scholar of the Northern European Renaissance.

There's a similarly uplifting message to be taken from the work of Pieter Bruegel. His central work, *Dutch Proverbs*, presents a comically disenchanted view of human nature. Everyone, he suggests, is pretty much deranged: here's a man throwing his money into the river; there's a soldier squatting on the fire and burning his trousers; someone is intently bashing his head against a brick wall, while another is biting a pillar. Importantly, the painting is not an attack on just a few unusually awful people: it's a picture of parts of all of us.

The works of Bruegel and Erasmus propose that the way to greater confidence isn't to reassure ourselves of our own dignity; it's to live at peace with the inevitable nature of our ridiculousness. We are idiots now, we have been idiots in the past and we will be idiots again in the future – and that is OK. There aren't any other available options for human beings.

We grow timid when we allow ourselves to be overexposed to the respectable sides of others. Such are the pains people take to appear normal, we collectively create a phantasm – problematic for everyone – which suggests that reasonableness and respectability might be realistic possibilities.

But once we learn to see ourselves as already, and by nature, foolish, it really doesn't matter so much if we do one more thing that might threaten us with a verdict of idiocy. The person we try to love could indeed think us ridiculous. The individual we asked directions from in a foreign city might regard us with contempt. But if these people did so, it wouldn't be news to us; they would only be confirming what we had already gracefully accepted in our hearts long ago: that we, like them – and every other person on the earth – are on

Pieter Bruegel, *Dutch Proverbs*, 1559.

frequent occasions a nitwit. The risk of trying and failing would have its sting substantially removed. The fear of humiliation would no longer stalk us in the shadows of our minds. We would become free to give things a go by accepting that failure and idiocy were the norm. And every so often, amid the endless rebuffs we'd have factored in from the outset, it would work: we'd get a hug, we'd make a friend, we'd get a pay rise.

The road to greater confidence begins with a ritual of telling oneself solemnly every morning, before embarking on the challenges of the day, that one is a muttonhead, a cretin, a dumb-bell and an imbecile. One or two more acts of folly should, thereafter, not feel so catastrophic after all.

IMPOSTOR SYNDROME

Faced with hurdles, we often leave the possibility of success to others, because we don't seem to ourselves to be anything like the sorts of people who win. When we approach the idea of acquiring responsibility or prestige, we quickly become convinced that we are simply – as we see it – 'impostors', like an actor in the role of a pilot, wearing the uniform and delivering authoritative cabin announcements while being incapable of starting the engines.

The root cause of impostor syndrome is an unhelpful picture of what people at the top of society are really like. We feel like impostors not because we are uniquely flawed, but because we can't imagine how equally flawed the elite must necessarily also be underneath their polished surfaces.

Impostor syndrome has its roots far back in childhood – specifically in the powerful sense children have that their parents are really very different from them. To a four-year-old, it is incomprehensible that their mother was once their age and unable to drive a car, call the plumber, decide other people's bedtimes and go on trips with colleagues. The gulf in status appears absolute and unbridgeable. The child's passionate loves – bouncing on the sofa, Pingu, Toblerone . . . – have nothing to do with those of adults, who like to sit at a table talking for hours (when they could be rushing about outside) and drink beer (which tastes of rusty metal). We start out in life with a very strong impression that competent and admirable people are really not like us at all.

This childhood experience dovetails with a basic feature of the human condition. We know ourselves from the inside, but others only from the outside. We're constantly aware of all our anxieties and doubts from within, yet all we know of others is what they happen to do and tell us, a far narrower and more edited source of information. We are very often left to conclude that we must be at the more freakish, revolting end of human nature.

But really we're just failing to imagine that others are every bit as fragile and strange as we are. Without knowing what it is that troubles or racks outwardly impressive people, we can be sure that it will be something. We might not know exactly what they regret, but they will have agonizing feelings of some kind. We won't be able to say exactly what kind of unusual kink obsesses them, but there will be one. And we can know this because vulnerabilities and compulsions cannot be curses that have just descended upon us uniquely; they are universal features of the human mental condition.

The solution to the impostor syndrome lies in making a leap of faith and trusting that others' minds work basically in much the same way as our own. Everyone is probably as anxious, uncertain and wayward as we are.

Traditionally, being a member of the aristocracy provided a fast-track to confidence-giving knowledge about the true characters of the elite. In eighteenth-century England, an admiral of the fleet would have looked deeply impressive to outsiders (meaning more or less everyone), with his splendid uniform (cockaded hat, abundant gold) and hundreds of subordinates to do his bidding. But to a young earl or marquess who had moved in the same social circles all his life, the admiral would appear in a very different light. He would have seen the admiral losing money at cards in their club the night before; he would know that the admiral's pet name in the nursery was 'Sticky' because of his inept way of eating; his aunt would still tell the story of the ridiculous way the admiral tried to proposition her sister in the yew walk; he would know that the admiral was in debt to his grandfather, who regarded him as pretty dim. Through acquaintance, the aristocrat would have reached a wise awareness that being an admiral was not an elevated position reserved for gods; it was the sort of thing Sticky could do.

The other traditional release from under-confidence of this type came from the opposite end of the social spectrum: being a servant. 'No man is a hero to his valet,' remarked the sixteenth-century essayist Montaigne – a lack of respect which may at points prove deeply encouraging, given how much our awe can sap our will to rival or match our heroes. Great public figures aren't ever so impressive to those who look after them, who see them drunk in the early hours, examine the stains on their underpants, hear their secret misgivings about matters on which they publicly hold firm views and witness them weeping with shame over strategic blunders they officially deny.

The valet and the aristocrat reasonably and automatically grasp the limitations of the authority of the elite. Fortunately, we don't have to be either of them to liberate ourselves from inhibiting degrees of respect for the powerful; imagination will serve just as well. One of the tasks that works of art should ideally accomplish is to take us more reliably into the minds of people we are intimidated by and show us the more average, muddled and fretful experiences unfolding inside.

At another point in his *Essays*, Montaigne playfully informed his readers in plain French that 'Kings and philosophers shit and so do ladies.'

Montaigne's thesis is that for all the evidence that exists about this shitting, we might not guess that grand people ever had to squat over a toilet. We never see distinguished types doing this – while, of course, we are immensely well informed about our own digestive activities. And therefore we build up a sense that because we have crude and sometimes rather desperate bodies, we can't be philosophers, kings or ladies; and that if we were to set ourselves up in these roles, we'd just be impostors.

With Montaigne's guidance, we are invited to take on a saner sense of what powerful people are actually like. But the real target isn't just an under-confidence about bodily functions; it is psychological timidity. Montaigne might have said that kings, philosophers and ladies are racked by self-doubt and feelings of inadequacy, sometimes bump into doors and have odd-sounding thoughts about members of their own families. Furthermore, instead of considering only the big figures of sixteenth-century France, we could update the example and refer to CEOs, corporate lawyers, news presenters and successful start-up entrepreneurs. They too can't cope, feel they might buckle under pressure and look back on certain decisions with shame and regret. No less than shitting, such feelings belong to us all. Our inner frailties don't cut us off from doing what they do. If we were in their roles, we'd not be impostors, we'd simply be normal.

Making a leap of faith around what other people are like helps to humanize the world. Whenever we encounter a stranger we're not really encountering such a person, we're encountering someone who is – in spite of surface evidence to the contrary – in basic ways very much like us, and therefore nothing fundamental stands between us and the possibility of responsibility, success and fulfilment.

FAME

Fame seems to offer very significant benefits. The fantasy unfolds like this: when you are famous, wherever you go, your good reputation will precede you. People will think well of you, because your merits have been impressively explained in advance. You will receive warm smiles from admiring strangers. You won't need to make your own case laboriously on each occasion. When you are famous, you will be safe from rejection. You won't have to win over every new person. Fame means that other people will be flattered and delighted even if you are only slightly interested in them. They will be amazed to see you in the flesh. They'll ask to take a photo with you. They'll sometimes laugh nervously with excitement. Furthermore, no one will be able to afford to upset you. When you're not pleased with something, it will become a big problem for others. If you say your hotel room isn't up to scratch, the management will panic. Your complaints will be taken very seriously. Your happiness will become the focus of everyone's efforts. You will make or break other people's reputations. You'll be boss.

The desire for fame has its roots in the experience of neglect and injury. No one would want to be famous who hadn't also, somewhere in the past, been made to feel extremely insignificant. We sense the need for a great deal of admiring attention when we have been painfully overexposed to deprivation. Perhaps our parents were hard to impress. They never noticed us much, as they were so busy with other things, focusing on other famous people, unable to have or express kind feelings, or just working too hard. There were no bedtime stories and our school reports weren't the subject of praise and admiration. That's why we dream that one day the world will pay attention. When we're famous, our parents will have to admire us too (which throws up an insight into one of the great signs of good parenting: that a child has no desire to be famous).

But even if our parents were warm and full of praise, there might still be a problem. It might be that it was the buffeting and indifference of the wider world (starting in the school playground) that were intolerable after all the early years of adulation at home. We might have emerged from familial warmth and been mortally hurt that strangers were not as kind and understanding as we had come to expect. The crushing experience of humiliation might even have been vicarious: our mother being rudely dismissed by a waiter; our father standing awkwardly alone.

What is common to all dreams of fame is that being known to strangers will often be the solution to a hurt. It presents itself as the answer to a deep need to be appreciated and treated decently by other people.

And yet fame cannot, in truth, accomplish what is being asked of it. It does have advantages, which are evident. But it also introduces a new set of very serious disadvantages, which the modern world refuses to view as structural rather than incidental. Every new famous person who disintegrates, breaks down in public or loses their mind is judged in isolation, rather than being interpreted as a victim of an inevitable pattern within the pathology of fame.

One wants to be famous out of a desire for kindness. But the world isn't generally kind to the famous for very long. The reason is basic: the success of any one person involves humiliation for lots of others. The celebrity of a few people will always contrast painfully with the obscurity of the many. Witnessing the famous upsets people. For a time, the resentment can be kept under control, but it is never somnolent for very long. When we imagine fame, we forget that it is inextricably connected to being too visible in the eyes of some, to bugging them unduly, to coming to be seen as the plausible cause of their humiliation: a symbol of how the world has treated *them* unfairly.

So, soon enough, the world will start to go through the old pronouncements of the famous, it will comment negatively on their appearance, it will pore over their setbacks, it will judge their relationships, it will mock their new ventures.

Fame makes people more, not less, vulnerable, because it leaves them open to unlimited judgement. Everyone is wounded by a cruel assessment of their character or merit. But the famous have an added challenge in store. The assessments will flood in from legions of people who would never dare to say to their faces what they can now express from the safety of the newspaper office or screen. We know from our own lives that a nasty remark can take a day or two to recover from.

Psychologically, the famous are of course the very last people on earth to be well equipped to deal with what they're going through. After all, they only became famous because they were wounded, because they had thin skin; because they were in some respects mentally unwell. And now, far from compensating them adequately for their disease, fame aggravates it exponentially. Strangers will voice their negative opinions in detail, unable or simply unwilling to imagine that famous people bleed far more quickly than anyone else. They might even think that the famous aren't listening (though one wouldn't become famous if one didn't suffer from a compulsion to listen too much).

Every worst fear about themselves (that they are stupid, ugly, not worthy of existence) will daily be actively confirmed by strangers. They will be exposed to the fact that people they have never met, people for whom they have nothing but goodwill, actively loathe them. They will learn that detestation of their personality is – in some quarters – a badge of honour. Sometimes the attacks will be horribly insightful. At other times they'll make no sense to anyone who really knows the situation. But the criticisms will lodge in people's minds nevertheless, and no lawyer, court case or magician will ever be able to delete them.

Needless to say, a hurt celebrity won't be eligible for sympathy. The very concept of a deserving celebrity is a joke, about as moving for the average person as the sadness of a tyrant.

To sum up, fame really just means that someone gets noticed a great deal, not that they are more intensely understood, appreciated or loved.

At an individual level, the only mature strategy is to give up on fame. The aim that lay behind the desire for fame remains important. One does still want to be appreciated and understood. But the wise person accepts that celebrity does not actually provide these things. Appreciation and understanding are only available through individuals one knows and cares about, not via groups of a thousand or a million strangers. There is no short cut to friendship – which is what the famous person is in effect seeking.

For those who are already famous, the only way to retain a hold on a measure of sanity is to stop listening to what the wider world is saying. This applies to the good things as much as to the bad. It is best not to know. The wise person knows that their products require attention. But they make a clear distinction between the purely practical needs of marketing and advocacy and the intimate desire to be liked and treated with justice and kindness by people they don't know.

At a collective, political level we should pay great attention to the fact that so many people (particularly young ones) today want to be famous – and even see fame as a necessary condition for a successful life. Rather than dismiss this wish, we should grasp its underlying and worrying meaning: they want to be famous because they do not feel respected, because citizens have forgotten how to accord one another the degree of civility, appreciation and decency that everyone craves and deserves. The desire for fame is a sign that an ordinary life has ceased to be good enough.

The solution is not to encourage ever more people to become famous, but to put greater efforts into encouraging a higher level of politeness and consideration for everyone, in families and communities, in workplaces, in politics, in the media, at all income levels, especially modest ones. A healthy society will give up on the understandable but erroneous belief that fame might guarantee that truly valuable goal: the kindness of strangers.

SPECIALIZATION

One of the greatest sorrows of work stems from a sense that only a small portion of our talents is taken up and engaged by the job we are paid to do every day. We are likely to be so much more than our labour allows us to be. The title on our business card is only one of thousands of titles we theoretically possess.

In his 'Song of Myself', published in 1855, the American poet

Walt Whitman gave our multiplicity memorable expression: 'I am large, I contain multitudes.' By this he meant that there are always so many interesting, attractive and viable versions of oneself, so many good ways one could potentially live and work, and yet very few of these ever get properly enacted in the course of the single life we have. No wonder that we're quietly and painfully conscious of our unfulfilled destinies, and at times recognize with a legitimate sense of agony that we really could well have been something and someone else.

The big economic reason why we can't explore our potential as we might is that it is hugely more productive for us not to do so. In *The Wealth of Nations* (1776), the Scottish economist and philosopher Adam Smith first explained how what he termed the 'division of labour' was at the heart of the increased productivity of capitalism. Smith zeroed in on the dazzling efficiency that could be achieved in pin manufacturing, if everyone focused on one narrow task (and stopped, as it were, exploring their Whitman-esque 'multitudes'):

One man draws out the wire, another straights it, a third cuts it, a fourth points it, a fifth grinds it at the top for receiving the head; to make the head requires two or three distinct operations; to put it on is a peculiar business; to whiten the pins is another; it is even a trade by itself to put them into the paper; and the important business of making a pin is, in this manner, divided into about eighteen distinct operations, all performed by distinct hands. I have seen a small manufactory where they could make upwards of forty-eight thousand pins in a day. But if they had all wrought separately and independently, and without any of them having been educated to this peculiar business, they could have made perhaps not one pin in a day.

Adam Smith was astonishingly prescient. Doing one job, preferably for most of one's life, makes perfect economic sense. It is a tribute to the world Smith foresaw – and helped to bring into being – that we have all ended up doing such specific jobs and carry such puzzling titles as Senior Packaging & Branding Designer, Intake and Triage Clinician, Research Centre Manager, Risk and Internal Audit

Controller and Transport Policy Consultant. We have become tiny, relatively wealthy cogs in giant, efficient machines. And yet, in our quiet moments, we reverberate with private longings to give our multitudinous selves expression.

One of Adam Smith's most intelligent and penetrating readers was the German economist Karl Marx. Marx agreed entirely with Smith's analysis: specialization had indeed transformed the world and possessed a revolutionary power to enrich individuals and nations. But where he differed from Smith was in his assessment of how desirable this development might be. We would certainly make ourselves wealthier by specializing, but we would also, as Marx pointed out, dull our lives and cauterize our talents. In describing his utopian communist society, Marx placed enormous emphasis on the idea of everyone having many different jobs. There were to be no specialists here. In a pointed dig at Smith in *The German Ideology* (1846), Marx wrote:

In communist society . . . nobody has one exclusive sphere of activity but each can become accomplished in any branch he wishes . . . thus it is possible for me to do one thing today and another tomorrow, to hunt in the morning, to fish in the afternoon, rear cattle in the evening, criticize after dinner . . . without ever becoming a hunter, fisherman, shepherd or critic.

Part of the reason why the job we do, as well as the jobs we don't get to do, matters so much is that our occupation decisively shapes who we are. How exactly our characters are marked by work is often hard for us to notice – our outlooks just feel natural to us – but we can observe the identity-defining nature of work well enough in the presence of practitioners from different fields. The primary school teacher treats even the middle-aged a little as if they were in need of careful shepherding; the psychoanalyst has a studied way of listening and seeming not to judge while exuding a pensive, reflective air; the politician lapses into speeches at intimate dinner parties. Every occupation weakens or reinforces aspects of our nature. There are jobs that keep us constantly tethered to the immediate moment (A&E

nurse, news editor); others that focus our attention on the outlying fringes of the time horizon (futurist, urban planner, reforester). Certain jobs daily sharpen our suspicions of our fellow humans, suggesting that the real agenda must always be far from what is overtly being said (journalist, antiques dealer); others intersect with people at the candid, intimate moments of their lives (anaesthetist, hairdresser, funeral director). In some jobs, it is clear what you have to do to move forward and how promotion occurs (civil servant, lawyer, surgeon), a dynamic that lends calm and steadiness to the soul, and diminishes tendencies to plot and manoeuvre; in others (television producer, politician), the rules are muddied and seem bound up with accidents of friendship and fortuitous alliances, encouraging tendencies to anxiety, distrust and shiftiness.

The psychology inculcated by work doesn't neatly stay at work; it colours the whole of who we end up being. We start to behave across our whole lives like the people work has required us to be in our productive hours. Along the way, this narrows character. When certain ways of thinking become called for daily, others start to feel peculiar or threatening. By giving a large part of one's life over to a specific occupation, one necessarily has to perform an injustice to other areas of latent potential. Whatever enlargements it offers our personalities, work also possesses a powerful capacity to trammel our spirits.

We can ask ourselves the poignant autobiographical question: what sort of person might I have been had I had the opportunity to do something else? There will be parts of us that we've had to kill (perhaps rather brutally) or that lie in shadow, twitching occasionally on late Sunday afternoons. Contained within other career paths are other plausible versions of ourselves which, when we dare to contemplate them, reveal important, but undeveloped or sacrificed, options.

We are meant to be monogamous about our work and yet truly have talents for many more jobs than we will ever have the opportunity to explore. We can understand the origins of our restlessness when we look back at our childhoods. As children, in a single Saturday morning, we might put on an extra jumper and imagine being an Arctic explorer, then have brief stints as an architect making a Lego house, a rock star making up an anthem about cornflakes and an inventor working out how to speed up colouring in by gluing four felt-tip pens together. We might then put in a few minutes as a member of an emergency rescue team before trying out being a pilot brilliantly landing a cargo plane on the rug in the corridor; we'd perform a life-saving operation on a knitted rabbit and finally we'd find employment as a sous-chef helping make a ham and cheese sandwich for lunch. Each one of these 'games' might have been the beginning of a career. And yet we had to settle on only a single option, pursued unremittingly for half a century.

Compared to the play of childhood, we're all leading fatally restricted lives. There is no easy cure. As Adam Smith argued, the causes don't lie in some personal error we're making. It's a limitation forced upon us by the greater logic of a competitive market economy. But we can allow ourselves to mourn that there will always be large aspects of our character that won't be satisfied. We're not being silly or ungrateful. We're simply registering the clash between the demands of the employment market and the free, wide-ranging potential of every human life. There's a touch of sadness to this insight. But it is also a reminder that this sense of being unfulfilled will accompany us in whatever job we choose: we can't overcome it by switching jobs. No one job can ever be enough.

There's a parallel here – as so often – between our experience at work and what happens in relationships. There's no doubt that we could (without any blame attaching to a current partner) have successful relationships with dozens, even hundreds of different people. Each would bring to the fore different sides of our personality, please us (and upset us) in different ways and introduce us to new excitements. Yet, as with work, specialization brings advantages: it means we can focus, bring up children in stable environments and learn the disciplines of compromise. In love and work, life requires us to be specialists even though we are by nature equally suited for wide-ranging exploration. And so we will necessarily carry about within us, in embryonic form, many alluring versions of ourselves which will never be given the proper chance to live. It's a sombre thought but a consoling one too. Our suffering is painful but, in its commonality, has a curious dignity to it as well, for it applies as much to the CEO as to the intern, to the artist as to the accountant. Everyone could have found so many versions of happiness that will elude them. In suffering in this way, we are participating in the common human lot. We may with a certain melancholic pride remove the job search engine from our bookmarks and cancel our subscription to a dating site in due recognition of the fact that – whatever we do – parts of our potential will have to go undeveloped and have to die without ever having had the chance to come to full maturity – for the sake of the benefits of focus and specialization.

ARTISTS AND SUPERMARKET TYCOONS

Shanghai-based Xu Zhen is one of the most celebrated Chinese artists of the age. He operates in a variety of media, including video, sculpture and fine art. His work displays a deep interest in business; he appears at once charmed and horrified by commercial life. In recent years, he has become especially fascinated by supermarkets. He's interested, in part, in how lovely they can be. He likes the alluring packaging, the abundance (the feel of lifting something off a shelf and seeing multiple versions of it waiting just behind) and the exquisite precision with which items are displayed. He particularly likes the claim of comprehensiveness that supermarkets implicitly make: the suggestion that they can, within their cavernous interiors, provide us with everything we could possibly need to thrive.

At the same time, Xu Zhen feels there's something very wrong with real supermarkets, and commercial life in general. The actual products they sell often aren't the things we genuinely need. Despite

Xu Zhen, *Supermarket*, 2007/2015.

the enormous choice, what we require to thrive isn't on offer. Meanwhile, the backstories of the brightly coloured things on sale are often exploitative and dark. Everything has been carefully calculated to get us to spend more than we mean to. Cynicism permeates the whole system.

In response, the Chinese artist mocks supermarkets repeatedly. His work involves recreating, at a very large scale, entire supermarkets in galleries and museums. The products in these supermarkets look real, you're invited to pick them up, but then you find out they are empty, as physically empty as Xu Zhen feels they are spiritually incomplete. His checkouts are similarly deceptive. They seem genuine: you scan your products at a high-tech counter, but you then get a receipt which turns out to be a fake; you've bought 'nothing' of value.

The supermarket installation takes us on a journey. At first it is getting us to share the artist's excitement around supermarkets and then it's puncturing the illusion: it's a gigantic, deliberate let-down. It's highly significant that Xu Zhen's critique of supermarkets is ironic. We tend to become ironic around things that we feel disappointed by but don't think we'll ever be able to change. It's a manoeuvre of disappointment stoically handled. A lot of art is ironic in its critiques of capitalism; we've come to expect this. It mocks all that is wrong but has no alternatives to put forward. A kind of hollow laughter seems the only fitting response to the compromises of commercial life.

Xu Zhen is trapped in the paradigm of what an artist does. A real artist, we have come to suppose – and the current ideology of the art world insists – couldn't be enthusiastic about improving a supermarket. He or she could only mock from the sidelines. Nowadays, fortunately, we've loosened old highly restrictive definitions of what a 'real' man or a 'real' woman might be like, but there remain comparably strict social taboos hemming in the idea of what a 'real' artist is allowed to get up to. They can be as experimental and surprising as they like . . . unless they want to run a food shop or an airline or

Xu Zhen, *Supermarket*, 2007/2014.

an energy corporation, at which point they cross a decisive bound-
ary, fall from grace, lose their special status as artists and become
the supposed polar opposites: mere business people.

We should take Xu Zhen seriously, perhaps more seriously than
he takes himself. Beneath the irony, Xu Zhen has the ambition to
discover what an ideal supermarket might be like, how it might be a
successful business and how capitalism could be reformed. Somewhere within his project, he carries a hope: that a corporation like a
supermarket could be brought into line with the best values of art
and assume psychological and spiritual importance inside the frame-
work of commerce.

Thousands of miles away from Shanghai, in the flatlands of East
Anglia, lies an elegant modern building completed in 1978 by the
architect Norman Foster. The Sainsbury Centre for the Visual Arts
is filled with some of the greatest works of contemporary art. Here
we find masterpieces by Henry Moore, Giacometti and Francis
Bacon. The collection is made possible thanks to the enormous
wealth of the Sainsbury family, who own and run Britain's second-
largest supermarket chain. Discounted shoulders of lamb, white
bread and special two-for-one offers on satsumas have led to exquisite display cases containing Giacometti's elongated, haunting figures
and Barbara Hepworth's hollowed-out ovaloids. The gallery seems
guided by values that are light years from any actual supermarket.
It is intent on feeding the soul and the patrons and curators are deeply
ambitious about the emotional and educational benefit of the experience: they want you to come out cleansed and improved.

From a very different direction, the Sainsbury family arrived at
a strikingly similar conclusion to Xu Zhen. Art and supermarkets
are essentially opposed. And like Xu Zhen, they are caught in an
identity trap, though this is a very different one: the identity trap of
the philanthropist. The philanthropist has been imagined as a person
who makes a lot of money in the brutish world of commerce, with
all the normal expectations of maximizing returns, squeezing wages
and focusing on obvious opportunities, and then makes a clean

From sell-by dates to enduring art: The Sainsbury Centre for the
Visual Arts at the University of East Anglia, designed by
Norman Foster and Wendy Cheesman, 1978.

The Sainsbury Centre, interior.

break. In their spare hours, they can devote their wealth to projects that are profoundly non-commercial: the patient collection of Roman coins, Islamic vases or modern sculptures. But philanthropists know that if they ever took an art-loving attitude to their businesses these might suffer economic collapse. Instead of making big things happen in the real world, they would become mere artists who make little interesting things in the sheltered, subsidized world of the gallery.

The situation is strangely tantalizing. The artist finds a little that is lovable and much that's wrong around supermarkets, but can't imagine running or bringing the ideals of art into action in one. The supermarket owners love art, but can't imagine bringing their psychologically and aesthetically ambitious sides into focus in their business. These two parties are both like pioneers, at the edge of unexplored territory. There is a huge idea they are both circling round. The goal is a synthesis of business and art: a supermarket that is truly guided by the ideals of art, a capitalism that is compatible with the higher values of humanity.

Up to now, we have collectively learned to admire the values of the arts (which can be summed up as a devotion to truth, beauty and goodness) in the special arena of galleries. But their more important application is in the general, daily fabric of our lives – the area that's currently dominated by an often depleted vision of commerce. It's a tragic polarization: we encounter the values we need, but only in a rarefied setting, while we regard these values as alien to the circumstances in which we most need to meet them. For most of history, artists have laboured to render a few square inches of canvas utterly perfect or to chisel a single block of stone into its most expressive form. Traditionally, the most common size for a work of art was between three and six feet across. And while artists have articulated their visions across such expanses, the large-scale projects have been given over wholesale to businesses and governments, which have generally operated with much lower ambitions. We're so familiar with this polarization, we regard it as if it were an inevitable fact of nature, rather than what it really is: a cultural and commercial failing.

Ideally artists should absorb the best qualities of business and vice versa. Rather than seeing such qualities as opposed to what they stand for as artists or business people, they should see them as great enabling capacities which help them fulfil their missions to the world. Xu Zhen will probably never get to build an airport, a marina, an old people's home or a supermarket, but the ideal next version of him will. We should want to simultaneously raise and combine the ambitions of artists (to make the noblest concepts powerful in our lives) and of business (to serve us in a deep sense successfully).

CONSUMER SOCIETY

Since time immemorial, the overwhelming majority of the earth's inhabitants have owned more or less nothing: the clothes they stood up in, some bowls, a pot and a pan, perhaps a broom and, if things were going well, a few farming implements. Nations and peoples remained consistently poor, with global GDP not growing at all from year to year. The world was in aggregate as hard up in 1800 as it had been at the beginning of time. Then, starting in the early eighteenth century, in the countries of north-western Europe, a remarkable phenomenon occurred: economies began to expand and wages to rise. Families who had never before had any money beyond what they needed to survive found they could go shopping for small luxuries: a comb or a mirror, a spare set of underwear, a pillow, some thicker boots or a towel. Their expenditure created a virtuous economic circle: the more they spent, the more businesses grew, the more wages rose. By the mid-eighteenth century, observers recognized that they were living through a period of epochal change that historians have since described as the world's first 'consumer revolution'. In Britain, where the changes were most marked, enormous new industries sprang up to cater for the widespread demand for

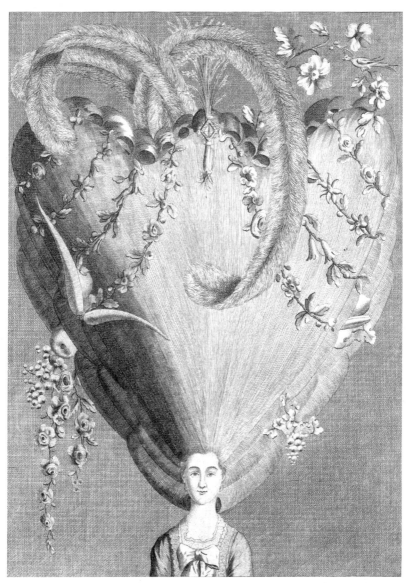

Fripperies, the motor of a sound economy: Matthew Darly,
The Extravaganza, or The Mountain Head Dress, 1776.

goods that had once been the preserve of the very rich alone. In the cities, it was possible to buy furniture made by Chippendale, Hepplewhite and Sheraton, porcelain made by Wedgwood and Crown Derby, and cutlery from the manufacturers of Sheffield, while hats, shoes and dresses featured in bestselling journals such as *The Gallery of Fashion* and *The Lady's Magazine*. Styles for clothes and hair, which had formerly gone unchanged for decades, now altered every year, often in extremely theatrical and impractical directions. In the early 1770s, there was a craze for decorated wigs so tall that their tops could be accessed only by standing on a chair. It was fun for the cartoonists. So vivid and numerous were the consumer novelties that the austere Dr Johnson wryly wondered whether prisoners were soon 'to be hanged in a new way' too.

The Christian Church also looked on and did not approve. Up and down the country, clergymen delivered bitter sermons against the new materialism. Sons and daughters were to be kept away from shops; God would not look kindly on those who paid more attention to household decoration than to the state of their souls.

But along with the consumer revolution there now emerged an intellectual revolution that sharply altered the understanding of the role of 'vanities' in an economy. In 1705, a London physician called Bernard Mandeville published an economic tract (unusually but charmingly written in verse) entitled *The Fable of the Bees*, which proposed that – contrary to centuries of religious and moral thinking – what made countries rich (and therefore safe, honest, generous-spirited and strong) was a very minor, unelevated and apparently undignified activity: shopping for pleasure. It was the consumption of what Mandeville called 'fripperies' – hats, bonnets, gloves, butter dishes, soup tureens, shoehorns and hair clips – that provided the engine for national prosperity and allowed the government to do in practice what the Church only knew how to sermonize about in theory: make a genuine difference to the lives of the weak and the poor. The one way to generate wealth, argued Mandeville, was to ensure high demand for absurd and unnecessary things. Of course, no one *needed* embroidered handbags, silk-lined slippers or ice creams, but it was a blessing that they could be prompted by fashion to *want* them, for on the back of demand for such trifles workshops could be built, apprentices trained and hospitals funded. Rather than condemn recreational expenditure, as Christian moralists had done, Mandeville celebrated them for their consequences. As his subtitle put it, it was a case of 'Private Vices, Public Benefits':

It is the sensual courtier who sets no limit to his luxury, the fickle strumpet who invents new fashions every week and the profuse rake and the lavish heir who most effectively help the poor. He that gives most trouble to thousands of his neighbours and invents the most operose manufactures is, right or wrong, the greatest friend to society. Mercers, upholsterers, tailors and many others would be starved in half a year's time if *pride* and *luxury* were at once to be banished from the nation.

Mandeville shocked his audience with the starkness of the choice he placed before them. A nation could either be very high-minded, spiritually elevated, intellectually refined, and dirt poor, or a slave to luxury and idle consumption, and very rich.

Mandeville's dark thesis went on to convince almost all the great anglophone economists and political thinkers of the eighteenth century. In his essay 'Of Luxury' (1752), the philosopher David Hume repeated Mandeville's defence of an economy built on making and selling unnecessary things: 'In a nation, where there is no demand for superfluities, men sink into indolence, lose all enjoyment of life, and are useless to the public, which cannot maintain or support its fleets and armies.' The 'superfluities' were clearly silly, Hume was in no doubt, but they paved the way for something very important and grand: military and welfare spending.

There were, nevertheless, some occasional departures from the new economic orthodoxy. One of the most spirited and impassioned voices was that of Switzerland's greatest philosopher, Jean-Jacques Rousseau. Shocked by the impact of the consumer revolution on the manners and atmosphere of his native Geneva, he called for a return to a simpler, older way of life, of the sort he had experienced in Alpine villages or read about in travellers' accounts of the native tribes of North America. In the remote corners of Appenzell or the vast forests of Missouri, there was – blessedly – no concern for fashion and no one-upmanship around hair extensions. Rousseau recommended closing Geneva's borders and imposing crippling taxes on luxury goods so that people's energies could be redirected towards non-material values. He looked back with fondness to the austere martial spirit of Sparta and complained, partly with Mandeville and Hume in mind: 'Ancient treatises of politics continually made mention of morals and virtue; ours speak of nothing but commerce and money.' However, even if Rousseau disagreed with Hume and Mandeville, he did not seek to deny the basic premise behind their analyses: it truly appeared to be a choice between decadent consumption and wealth on the one hand, and virtuous restraint and poverty on the other. It was simply that Rousseau – unusually – preferred virtue to wealth.

The parameters of this debate have continued to dominate economic thinking ever since. We re-encounter them in ideological arguments between capitalists and communists and free marketers and environmentalists. But for most of us the debate is no longer pertinent. We simply accept that we will live in consumer economies with some very unfortunate side effects to them (crass advertising, unhealthy foodstuffs, products that are disconnected from any reasonable assessment of our needs, excessive waste . . .) in exchange for economic growth and high employment. We have chosen wealth over virtue.

The one question rarely asked is whether there might be a way to ameliorate the dispiriting choice, to draw on the best aspects of consumerism on the one hand and high-mindedness on the other without suffering their worst consequences: moral decadence and profound poverty. Might it be possible for a society to develop that allows for consumer spending (and therefore provides employment and welfare) yet of a kind directed at something other than 'vanities' and 'superfluities'? Might we shop for something other than nonsense? In other words, might we have wealth *and* (a degree of) virtue?

It is a possibility of which we find some intriguing hints in the work of Adam Smith, an economist too often read as a blunt apologist for all aspects of consumer society, but in fact one of its more subtle and visionary analysts. In his *The Wealth of Nations*, Smith seems at points willing to concede to key aspects of Mandeville's argument: consumer societies do help the poor by providing employment based around satisfying what are often rather suboptimal purchases. Smith was as ready as other Anglophone economists to mock the triviality of some consumer choices, while admiring their consequences. All those embroidered lace handkerchiefs, jewelled snuff boxes and miniature temples made of cream for dessert were frivolous, he conceded, but they encouraged trade, created employment and generated immense wealth, and could be firmly defended on this score alone.

However, Smith offered some fascinating hopes for the future. He pointed out that consumption didn't invariably have to involve the trading of frivolous things. He had seen the expansion of the Edinburgh book trade and knew how large a market higher education might become. He understood how much wealth was being accumulated through the construction of Edinburgh's handsome and noble New Town. He understood that humans have many 'higher' needs that require a lot of labour, intelligence and work to fulfil, but that lie outside capitalist enterprise as conceived by 'realists' like Hume or Mandeville: among them, our need for education, for self-understanding, for beautiful cities and for rewarding social lives. The ultimate goal of capitalism was to tackle 'happiness' in all its complexities, psychological as opposed to merely material.

The capitalism of our times still hasn't entirely come round to resolving the awkward choices that Mandeville and Rousseau circled. But the crucial hope for the future is that we will not forever need to be making money from exploitative or vain consumer

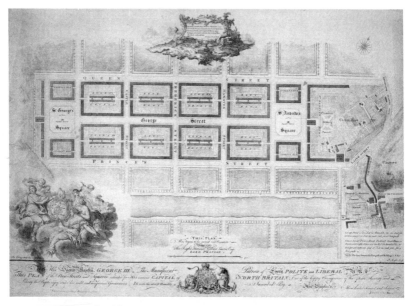

A promise of noble consumption: Patrick Begbie, *James Craig's
Plan of the New Town, Edinburgh*, 1768.

appetites; that we will also learn to generate sizeable profits from helping people – as consumers and producers – in the truly important and ambitious aspects of their lives. The reform of capitalism hinges on an odd-sounding but critical task: the conception of an economy focused around higher needs.

HIGHER NEEDS, A PYRAMID AND CAPITALISM

The idea that capitalism can give us what we need has always been central to its defence. More efficiently than any other system, capitalism has, in theory, been able to identify what we're lacking and deliver it to us with unparalleled efficiency. Capitalism is the most skilled machine we have ever yet constructed for satisfying human needs.

Because businesses have been so extraordinarily productive over the last 200 years, it has become easy to think – in the wealthier parts of the world, at least – that consumer capitalism must by now have reached a stage of exhausted stagnant maturity, which is what may explain both relatively high rates of unemployment and low levels of growth. The heroic period of development, driven in part by breakthroughs in technology, that equipped a mass public in the advanced nations with the basics of food, shelter, hygiene and entertainment, appears to have been brought up against some natural limits. We seem in aggregate to be in the strange position of having rather too much of everything: shoes, dishcloths, televisions, chocolates, woollen hats . . . In the eyes of some, it is normal that we should have arrived at this end point. The earth and its resources are, after all, limited, so we should not expect growth to be unlimited either. Flatlining reflects the attainment of an enviable degree of maturity. We are ceasing to buy quite so much for an understandable reason: we have all we need.

Yet, despite its evident successes, consumer capitalism cannot in truth realistically be credited with having fulfilled a mission of accurately satisfying our needs, because of one evident failing: we aren't happy. Indeed, most of us are, a good deal of the time, properly at sea: burdened by complaints, unfulfilled hopes, barely formulated longings, restlessness, anger and grief – little of which our plethora of shops and services appear remotely equipped to address. Given the range of our outstanding needs and capitalism's theoretical commitment to fulfilling them, it would be profoundly paradoxical to count the economy as in any way mature and beyond expansion. Far from it, it is arguably a good deal too small and desperately undeveloped in relation to what we would truly want from it, having reflected on the full extent of our sorrows and appetites. Despite all the factories, the concrete, the highways and the logistics chains, consumer capitalism has – arguably – not even properly embarked on its tasks. A good future may depend not on minimizing consumer capitalism but on radically extending its reach and depth, via a slightly unfamiliar route: a close study of our unattended needs.

If the proverbial Martian were to attempt to guess what human beings required in order to be satisfied by scanning lists of the top corporations in the leading wealthy countries, they would guess that *Homo sapiens* had immense requirements for food, warmth, shelter, credit, insurance, missiles, packets of data, strips of cotton or wool to wrap around their limbs and, of course, a lot of ketchup. This, the world's stock markets seem to tell us, is what human satisfaction is made up of.

But the reality is naturally more complicated than that. The most concise yet penetrating picture of human needs ever drawn up was the work of a little-known American psychologist called Abraham Maslow. In a paper entitled 'A Theory of Human Motivation' published in *Psychological Review* in 1943, Maslow arranged our longings and appetites in a pyramid-shaped continuum, ranging from what he called the lower needs, largely focused on the body, to the higher needs, largely focused on the psyche and encompassing such elements as the need for status, recognition and friendship. At the apex

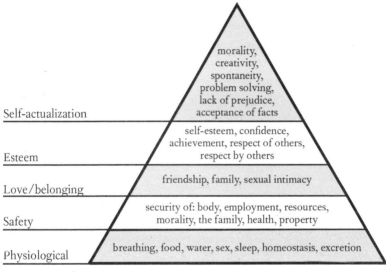

Self-actualization

morality,
creativity,
spontaneity,
problem solving,
lack of prejudice,
acceptance of facts

Esteem

self-esteem, confidence,
achievement, respect of others,
respect by others

Love/belonging

friendship, family, sexual intimacy

Safety

security of: body, employment, resources,
morality, the family, health, property

Physiological

breathing, food, water, sex, sleep, homeostasis, excretion

Abraham Maslow's Pyramid of Needs.

stood the need for a complete development of our potential, of the kind Maslow had seen in the lives of the cultural figures he most admired: Montaigne, Voltaire, Goethe, Tolstoy and Freud.

If we were to align the world's largest corporations with the pyramid, we would find that the needs to which they cater are overwhelmingly those at the bottom of the pyramid. Our most successful businesses are those that aim to satisfy our physical and simpler psychological selves: they operate in oil and gas, mining, construction, agriculture, pharmaceuticals, electronics, telecommunications, insurance, banking and light entertainment.

What's surprising is how little consumer capitalism has, until now, been in any way ambitious about many of the things that deliver higher sorts of satisfaction. Business has helped us to be warm, safe and distracted. It has been markedly indifferent to our flourishing. This is the task ahead of us. The true destiny of and millennial opportunity for consumer capitalism is to travel up the pyramid, to generate ever more of its more profits from the satisfaction of the full range of 'higher needs' that currently lie outside the realm of industrialization and commodification.

Capitalists and companies are seemingly – at least semi-consciously – aware of their failure to engage with many of the elements at the top of the pyramid, among them friendship, belonging, meaningfulness and a sense of agency and autonomy. And the evidence for this lies in a rather surprising place, in one of the key institutions for driving the sales of capitalism's products forwards: advertising.

THE PROMISES OF ADVERTISING

When advertising began in a significant way in the early nineteenth century, it was a relatively straightforward business. It showed you a product, told you what it did, where you could get it and what it cost. Then, in 1960s America, a remarkable new way of advertising

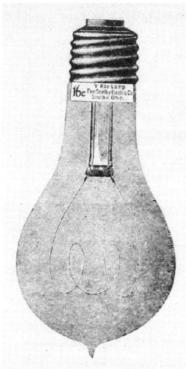

Edison
and
Shelby
Incandescent
Lamps
❧ ❧ ❧ ❧
Electrical
Supplies

Houses Wired
for
Electric

{
Lights
Burglar Alarms
Fire Alarms
Annunciators
Bells

ELECTRIC ENGINEERING & CONSTRUCTION CO.
907 Pacific Ave., TACOMA.

When adverts advertised what they were selling.

emerged, led by such luminaries of Madison Avenue as William Bernbach, David Ogilvy and Mary Wells Lawrence. In their work for brands like Esso, Avis and Life Cereal, adverts ceased to be in a narrow sense about the things they were selling. The focus of an ad might ostensibly be on a car, but our attention was also being directed at the harmonious, handsome couple holding hands beside it. It might on the surface be an advert about soap, but the true emphasis was on the state of calm that accompanied the ablutions. It might be whisky one was being invited to drink, but it was the attitude of reso-luteness and resilience on display that provided the compelling focal point. Madison Avenue had made an extraordinary discovery: how-ever appealing a product might be, there were many other things that were likely to be even more appealing to customers – and by entwining their products with these ingredients, sales could be transformed.

Patek Philippe is one of the giants of the global watchmaking industry. Since 1996, they have been running a very distinctive series of adverts featuring parents and children. It is almost impossible not to have glimpsed one somewhere. In one example, a father and son are together in a motorboat, a scene which tenderly evokes filial and paternal loyalty and love. The son is listening carefully while his kindly dad tells him about aspects of seafaring. We can imagine that the boy will grow up confident and independent, yet also respectful and warm. He'll be keen to follow in his father's footsteps and emu-late his best sides. The father has put a lot of work into the relationship (one senses they've been out on the water a number of times) and now the love is being properly paid back. The advertisement under-stands our deepest hopes around our children. It is moving because what it depicts is so hard to find in real life. We are often brought to tears not so much by what is horrible as by what is beautiful but out of reach.

Father–son relationships tend to be highly ambivalent. Despite a lot of effort, there can be extensive feelings of neglect, rebellion and, on both sides, bitterness. Capitalism doesn't allow dads to be too present. There may not be so many chances to talk. But in the world of Patek Philippe, we glimpse a psychological paradise.

We turn to Calvin Klein. The parents and children have tumbled together in a happy heap. There is laughter; everyone can be silly together. There is no more need to put up a front, because everyone here is trusting and on the same side. No one understands you like these people do. In the anonymous airport lounge, in the lonely hotel room, you'll think back to this cosy group and ache. Alternatively, you might already long for those years, quite a way back, when it was so much easier than it's become. Now the kids are shadowy presences around the house. Your relationship with your spouse has suffered too. Calvin Klein knows this; it too has brilliantly latched on to our deepest and at the same time most elusive inner longings.

Adverts wouldn't work if they didn't operate with a very good understanding of what our real needs are; what we truly require to be happy. Their emotional pull is based on knowing us eerily well. As they recognize, we are creatures who hunger for good family relationships, connections with others, a sense of freedom and joy, a promise of self-development, dignity, calm and the feeling that we are respected.

Yet, armed with this knowledge, they – and the corporations who bankroll them – unwittingly play a cruel trick on us, for while they excite us with reminders of our buried longings, they cannot do anything sincere about satisfying them. The objects adverts send us off to buy fall far short of the hopes that they have aroused. Calvin Klein makes lovely cologne. Patek Philippe's watches are extremely reliable and beautiful agents of timekeeping. But these items cannot by themselves help us secure the psychological possessions our unconscious believed were on offer.

The real crisis of capitalism is that product development lags so far behind the best insights of advertising. Since the 1960s, advertising has worked out just how much we need help with the true challenges of life. It has fathomed how deeply we want to have better careers, stronger relationships, greater confidence. In most adverts, the pain and the hope of our lives have been superbly identified, but the products are almost comically at odds with the problems at hand. Advertisers are hardly to blame. They are, in fact, the victims of an extraordinary problem of modern capitalism. While we have so many complex needs, we have nothing better to offer ourselves, in the face of our troubles, than, perhaps, a slightly more accurate chronometer or a more subtly blended perfume. Business needs to get more ambitious in the creation of new kinds of 'products', in their own way as strange-sounding today as a wristwatch would have been to observers in 1500. We need the drive of commerce to get behind filling the world – and our lives – with goods that really can help us to thrive, flourish, find contentment and manage our relationships well.

To trace the future shape of capitalism, we have only to think of all our needs that currently lie outside commerce. We need help in forming cohesive, interesting, benevolent communities. We need help in bringing up children. We need help in calming down at key moments (the aggregate cost of our high anxiety and rage is appalling). We need immense help in discovering our real talents in the workplace and in understanding where we can best deploy them. We have aesthetic desires that can't seem to get satisfied at scale, especially in relation to housing. Our higher needs are not trivial or minor, insignificant things we could easily survive without. They are, in many ways, central to our lives. We have simply accepted, without adequate protest, that there is nothing business can do to address them, when in fact, being able to structure businesses around these needs would be the commercial equivalent of the discovery of steam power or the invention of the electric light bulb.

We don't know today quite what the businesses of the future will look like, just as half a century ago no one could describe the corporate essence of the current large technology companies. But we do know the direction we need to head in: one where the drive and inventiveness of capitalism tackle the higher, deeper problems of life. This will offer an exit from the failings that attend business today.

In the ideal future for consumer capitalism, our materialism would be refined, our work would be rendered more meaningful and our profits more honourable.

Advertising has at least done us the great service of hinting at the future shape of the economy; it already trades in all the right ingredients. The challenge now is to narrow the gap between the fantasies being offered and what we truly spend our lives doing and our money buying.

ARTISTIC SYMPATHY

One of the most troubling aspects of our world is that it contains such enormous disparities in income. At various times, there have been concerted attempts to correct the injustice. Inspired by Marxism, communist governments forcibly seized private wealth and socialist governments have repeatedly tried imposing severely punitive taxes on rich companies and individuals. There have also been attempts to reform the education system, to create positive discrimination in the workplace and to seize the estates of the wealthiest members of society at their deaths.

But the problem of inequality has not gone away and is indeed unlikely to be solved at any point soon, let alone in the short time frame that is relevant to any of us, for a range of stubbornly embedded, partly logical and partly absurd reasons.

However, there is one important move we can make that might take start to reduce some of the sting of inequality. For this, we need to begin by asking what might sound like an offensively obvious question: why is financial inequality a problem?

There are two very different answers. One kind of harm is material: not being able to get a decent house, quality health care, a proper education and a hopeful future for one's children. But there is also a psychological reason why inequality proves so problematic: because poverty is intricately bound up with humiliation. The punishment of poverty is not limited to money, but extends to the suffering that attends a lack of status: a constant low-level sense that who one is and what one does are of no interest to a world that is punitively unequal in its distribution of honour as well as cash. Poverty not only induces financial harm but damages mental health as well.

Historically, the bulk of political effort has been directed at the first material problem, yet there is also an important move we can make around the psychological issue.

A sketch of a solution to the gap between income and respect lies in a slightly unexpected place: a small painting hanging in a top-floor gallery at London's Wallace Collection called *The Lacemaker*, by a little-known Dutch artist, Caspar Netscher, who painted it in 1662.

The artist has caught the woman making lace at a moment of intense concentration on a difficult task. We can feel the effort she is making and can imagine the skill and intelligence she is devoting to her work. Lace was, at the time the painting was created, highly prized. But because many people knew how to make it, the economic law of supply and demand meant that the reward for exquisite crafts-manship was tiny. Lacemakers were among the poorest in society. Were the artist, Caspar Netscher, to be working today, his portrait would have been equivalent to making a short film about phone fac-tory workers or fruit pickers. It would have been evident to all the painting's viewers that the lacemaker was someone who ordinarily received no respect or prestige at all.

And yet Netscher directed an extraordinary amount of what one might call *artistic sympathy* towards his sitter. Through his eyes and artistry, she is no longer a nobody. She has grown into an individual, full of her own thoughts, sensitive, serious, devoted – entirely deserving of tenderness and consideration. The artist has trans-formed how we might look at a lacemaker.

Netscher isn't lecturing us about respecting the low-paid; we hear this often enough and the lesson rarely sinks in. He's not trying to use guilt, which is rarely an effective tactic. He's helping us, in a representative instance, to actually *feel* respect for his worker rather

Caspar Netscher, *The Lacemaker*, 1662.

than just *know* it might be her due. His picture isn't nagging, grim or forbidding, it's an appealing and pleasurable mechanism for teaching us a very unfamiliar but critically important supra-political emotion.

If lots of people saw the lacemaker in the way the artist did, took the lesson properly to heart and applied it widely and imaginatively at every moment of their lives, it is not an exaggeration to say that the psychological burden of poverty would substantially be lifted. The fate of lacemakers, but also office cleaners, warehouse attendants, delivery workers and manual labourers would be substantially improved. This greater sympathy would not be a replacement for political action, it would be its precondition; the sentiment upon which a material change in the lives of the victims of inequality would be founded.

An artist like Netscher isn't changing how much the low-paid earn; he is changing how the low-paid are judged. This is not an unimportant piece of progress. Netscher was living in an age in which only a very few people might ever see a picture – and of course he was concentrating only on the then current face of poverty. But the process he undertook remains profoundly relevant.

Ideally today our culture would pursue the same project but on a vastly enlarged scale, enticing us via our most successful, popular and widespread art forms to a grand political revolution in feeling, upon which an eventual, firmly based evolution in economic thinking could arise.

V : Culture

ROMANTIC VS. CLASSICAL

As we have seen, we are – each of us – probably a little more one than the other. These categories explain much about us: how we approach nature, what makes us laugh, our political ideas and, of course, our attitudes to love . . . We may not be used to conceiving of ourselves in these terms, but the labels Romantic and Classical, so often alluded to up to this point, usefully bring into focus some of the central themes of our lives and help us to gain a clearer picture of the underlying structure of our enthusiasms and concerns.

It may be helpful to try finally to pin down a few of the central contrasting characteristics of Romantic and Classical personalities.

Intuition vs. Analysis

Romantics are especially aware of all that lies outside rational explanation, all that cannot neatly be summarized in words. They sense, especially late at night or in the vastness of nature, the scale of the mysteries humanity is up against. The impulse to categorize and to master intellectually is for Romantics a distinct form of vanity, like trying to draw up a list in a hurricane. There is a time when we must surrender to emotion, feel rather than try relentlessly to categorize and make sense of things. We can think too much – and grow sick from trying to pass the complexities of existence through the sieve of the conscious mind. We should more often be guided by our instincts and the voice of nature within us.

Decisions must not always be probed too hard, or moods unpacked. We should respect and not tinker with emotions, especially as they relate to love and the spiritual varieties of experience. We need to fall silent – more frequently than we do – and simply listen. Sometimes the best way to honour the ineffable is through unclear language and obscure modes of expression. The supreme Romantic art form is music.

Classicists like order. They may be moved by the sight of a bilaterally symmetrical avenue of trees extending into the distance as far as the eye can see. They reach for their notebooks during emotional tempests. They don't believe there could be anything legitimately termed 'thinking too much'; there is only thinking well or badly. Reason is the sole tool we have available to defend ourselves against primeval chaos.

Classicists know a lot about feelings and intuitions. They have had plenty, often very powerful ones. They just don't respect them. The last thing they are now inclined to do with an emotion is surrender to it. They have committed too many follies to think that following their hearts might be an idea. They know that not all the mysteries can be explained but they are committed to giving it a shot. They don't think that love breaks if you examine it too carefully. They favour clear modes of expression (even about rare and evanescent emotions, like reflecting on the Centaurus A galaxy or looking into a partner's eyes) and a crisp, minimal language that an intelligent twelve-year-old could understand.

Spontaneity vs. Education

Romantics don't like schools. The best kind of education comes from within. The most important capacities are in us from the start. We don't need to learn how to love, how to be kind, how to die . . . Formal learning kills every topic of study. We need to learn to listen to the voice inside us, which will provide us with all we need. There is no greater exemplar of spontaneity than children, and Romantics look upon them with particular tenderness and respect. They are not beasts to be tamed, but gods to be heard. We knew, back then, what mattered. It was school that corrupted us and made us lose our way, which is why it is from the mouths of the very young that we hear truths and sensibilities that the most so-called intelligent adults will have forgotten. To the Romantic, it will always be a child who points out that the emperor is wearing no clothes.

Those of a Classical temperament don't necessarily respect the education system as it stands – there is so much that could be improved – but the abstract idea of education seems essential and the bedrock of civilization. We didn't forget how to live; we just never knew, as no one is ever born knowing. Children aren't any more noble than adults, they just have a particularly hard time containing themselves. The purpose of education is to pass down one or two painfully won insights so that not every generation needs to repeat the same desperate errors.

Honesty vs. Politeness

There is too much hypocrisy already, say the Romantics. We are drowning in our lies and in our compromises. We must do everything to strip away the secrecy our society imposes on us. Authenticity is the highest form of morality. Politeness is a lid that we place upon our real selves to suppress the truths that could free us.

For the Classical person, politeness is the lid we generously place on our inner madness to stop hurting those we care for. Not being ourselves is the kindest thing we can do to someone we claim to love. To give others an uncensored view of our emotions, with their minute-by-minute vagaries and compulsions, is sheer laziness or cruelty. We cannot possibly be good and entirely honest, nor should we try. Strategic inauthenticity is the mark of a kindly soul.

Idealism vs. Realism

The Romantic is excited by how things might ideally be and judges what currently exists in the world by the standard of a better imagined alternative. Most of the time, the current state of society arouses intense disappointment and anger as they consider the injustices, prevarications, compromises and timidity all around. It seems normal to be furious with governments and surprised and outraged by evidence of venal and self-interested conduct in society.

By contrast, the Classical person pays special attention to what can go wrong. They are very concerned to mitigate the downside. They are aware that most things could be a lot worse. Before condemning a government, they consider the standard of governments across history and may regard a current arrangement as bearable, under the circumstances. Their view of people is fundamentally rather dark. They believe that everyone is probably slightly worse than they seem. They feel we have deeply dangerous impulses, lusts and drives and take bad behaviour for granted when it manifests itself. They simply feel this is what humans are prone to. High ideals make them nervous.

Earnestness vs. Irony

Romantics don't believe in how things are. Their attention is fixed on how they should be. They therefore resist the deflationary call of ironic humour, which seems defeatist. They are earnest in their search for a better future.

The Classical conviction is not that the world is a cheerful place, far from it; but rather that a cheerful mood is a good starting point for living in a radically imperfect and deeply unsatisfactory realm where the priority is to not give up, despair and kill oneself. Ironic humour is a standard recourse for them, because it emerges from the constant collision between how one would want things to be and how it seems they in fact are. They are proponents of gallows humour.

The Rare vs. the Everyday

The Romantic rebels against the ordinary. They are keen on the exotic and the rare. They like things which the mass of the population won't yet know about. The fact that something is popular will always be a mark against it. They don't much like routine, especially in domestic life, either. They are anxious about higher things being put under pressure to become 'useful' or commercial. They want heroism, excitement and an end to boredom.

The Classical personality welcomes routine as a defence against chaos. They would very much like good things to be popular. They don't necessarily think that what is presently popular is good, but they see popularity as, in principle, a mark of virtue. They are familiar enough with extremes to welcome things that are a little boring. They can see the charm of doing the laundry.

Purity vs. Ambivalence

The Romantic is dismayed by compromise. They are drawn to either wholehearted endorsement or total rejection. Ideally partners should love everything about each other. A political party should be admirable at every turn. A philanthropist should draw no personal benefit from acts of charity. They feel the attraction of the lost cause. It is very important for the Romantic to feel they are right; winning is, by comparison, not such an urgent matter.

The Classical person takes the view that very few things, and no people, are either wholly good or entirely bad. They assume that there is likely to be some worth in opposing ideas and something to be learned from both sides. It is Classical to think that a decent person might in many areas hold views you find deeply unpalatable.

For a long time now, perhaps since around 1750, Romantic attitudes have been dominant in the Western imagination. The prevailing approach to children, relationships, politics and culture has all been coloured more by a Romantic than by a Classical spirit.

Both Romantic and Classical orientations have important truths to impart. Neither is wholly right or wrong. They need to be balanced. And none of us are in any case ever simply one or the other. But because a good life requires a judicious balance of both positions, at this point in history it might be the Classical attitude whose distinctive claims and wisdom we need to listen to most intently. It is a mode of approaching life which is ripe for rediscovery.

WHY WE HATE CHEAP THINGS

We don't think we hate cheap things, but we frequently behave as if we do. Consider the pineapple. Columbus was the first European to be delighted by the physical grandeur and vibrant sweetness of the pineapple, which is a native of South America but had reached the Caribbean by the time he arrived there. The first meeting between Europeans and pineapples took place in November 1493, in a Carib village on the island of Guadeloupe. Columbus's crew spotted the fruit next to a pot of stewing limbs. The outside reminded them of a pine cone, the interior pulp of an apple.

But pineapples proved extremely difficult to transport and very costly to cultivate. For a long time only royalty could actually afford to eat them. Russia's Catherine the Great was a huge fan, as was Charles II of England. A single fruit in the seventeenth century sold for today's equivalent of £5,000. The pineapple was such a status symbol that, if they could get hold of one, people would keep it for display until it fell apart. In the mid-eighteenth century, at the height of the pineapple craze, whole aristocratic evenings were structured around the ritual display of these fruits. Poems were written in their honour. Savouring a tiny sliver could be the high point of a year. The pineapple was so exciting and so loved that in 1761 the 4th Earl of Dunmore built a temple on his Scottish estate in its honour. And

Charles II being offered the first pineapple ever successfully grown
in England by John Rose, the Royal Gardener, 1675. Hendrick
Danckerts, *Charles II Presented with a Pineapple*, c. 1675–80.

The Dunmore Pineapple, built in 1761, Scotland.

Christopher Wren, south tower of St Paul's Cathedral, London, 1711.

Christopher Wren had no hesitation in topping the south tower of St Paul's Cathedral with this evidently divine fruit.

Then, at the very end of the nineteenth century, two things changed. Large commercial plantations of pineapples were established in Hawaii and there were huge advances in steamship technology. Production and transport costs plummeted and, unwittingly, transformed the psychology of pineapple-eating. Today, you can get a pineapple for around £1.50. It still tastes exactly the same, but now the pineapple is one of the world's least glamorous fruits. It is never served at smart dinner parties and would never be carved on the top of a major civic building.

The pineapple itself has not changed; it is our attitude to it that has. Contemplation of the history of the pineapple suggests a curious overlap between love and economics: when we have to pay a lot for something nice, we appreciate it to the full. Yet as its price in the market falls, passion has a habit of fading away. Naturally, if the object has no merit to begin with, a high price won't be able to do anything for it; but if it has real virtue and yet a low price, then it is in severe danger of falling into grievous neglect.

Why, then, do we associate a cheap price with lack of value? Our response is a hangover from our long pre-industrial past. For most of human history, there truly was a strong correlation between cost and value: the higher the price, the better things tended to be, because there was simply no way both for prices to be low and for quality to be high. Everything had to be made by hand, by expensively trained artisans, with raw materials that were immensely difficult to transport. The expensive sword, jacket, window or wheelbarrow was simply always the better one. This relationship between price and value held true in an uninterrupted way until the end of the eighteenth century, when – thanks to the Industrial Revolution – something extremely unusual happened: human beings worked out how to make high-quality goods at cheap prices, because of technology and new methods of organizing the labour force.

On the back of this long experience, an entrenched cultural

association has formed between the rare, the expensive and the good: each has come to rapidly suggest the other, and the natural-seeming converse is that things which are widely available and inexpensive come to be seen as unimpressive or unexciting.

In principle, industrialization was supposed to undo these connections. The price would fall and widespread happiness would follow. High-quality objects would enter the mass market, excellence would be democratized. However, despite the greatness of these efforts, instead of making wonderful experiences universally available, industrialization has inadvertently produced a different result: it has seemed to rob certain experiences of their loveliness, interest and worth.

It's not – of course – that we refuse to buy inexpensive or cheap things. It's just that getting excited over cheap things has come to seem a little bizarre. How do we reverse this? The answer lies in a slightly unexpected area: the mind of a four-year-old. Imagine him with a puddle. It started raining an hour ago, the street is now full of puddles and there could be nothing better in the world; the riches of the Indies would be nothing compared to the pleasures of being able to see the rippling of the water created by a jump in one's wellingtons, the eddies and whirlpools, the minute waves, the oceans beneath one . . .

Children have two advantages: they don't know what they're supposed to like and they don't understand money, so price is never a guide to value for them. They have to rely instead on their own delight (or lack of it) in the intrinsic merits of the things they're presented with and this can take them in astonishing (and sometimes maddening) directions. They'll spend an hour with one button. We buy them a costly wooden toy made by Swedish artisans who hope to teach lessons in symmetry and find that they prefer the cardboard box that it came in. They become mesmerized by the wonders of turning on the light and therefore proceed to try it 100 times. They'd prefer the nail and screw section of a DIY shop to the fanciest toy department or the national museum.

This attitude allows them to be entranced by objects which have long ago ceased to hold our wonder. If asked to put a price on things, children tend to answer by the utility and charm of an object, not its manufacturing costs. This leads to unusual but – we recognize – more rightful results. A child might guess that a stapler costs £100 and would be deeply surprised, even shocked, to learn that a USB stick can be had for just over £1. Children would be right, if prices were determined by human worth and value, but they're not; they just reflect what things cost to make. The pity is, therefore, that we treat them as a guide to what matters, when this isn't what a financial price should ever be used for.

We have been looking at prices the wrong way. We have fetishized them as tokens of intrinsic value, we have allowed them to set how much excitement we are allowed to have in given areas, how much joy is to be mined in particular places. But prices were never meant to be like this: we are breathing too much life into them and thereby dulling too many of our responses to the inexpensive world.

At a certain age, something very debilitating happens to children (normally around the age of eight). They start to learn about 'expensive' and 'cheap' and absorb the view that the more expensive something is, the better it may be. They are encouraged to think well of saving up pocket money and to see the 'big' toy they are given as much better than the 'cheaper' one.

We can't directly go backwards, we can't forget what we know of prices. However, we can pay less attention to what things cost and more to our own responses. The people who have most to teach us here are artists. They are the experts at recording and communicating their enthusiasms, which, like children, can take them in slightly unexpected directions. The French artist Paul Cézanne spent a good deal of the late nineteenth century painting groups of apples in his studio in Provence. He was thrilled by their texture, shapes and colours. He loved the transitions between the yellowy golds and the deep reds across their skins. He was an expert at noticing how the generic word 'apple' in fact covers an infinity of highly individual examples. Under his gaze, each one becomes its own planet, a veritable universe of distinctive colour and aura – and hence a source of real delight and solace.

The apple that has only a limited life, that will make a slow transition from sweet to sour, that grew patiently on a particular tree, that survived the curiosity of birds and spiders, that weathered the mistral and a particularly blustery May is honoured and properly given its due by the artist (who was himself extremely wealthy, the heir to an enormous banking fortune – it seems important to state this, to make clear that Cézanne wasn't simply making a virtue of necessity and would have worshipped gold bullion if he'd had the chance). Cézanne had all the awe, love and excitement before the apple that Catherine the Great and Charles II had before the pineapple; but Cézanne's wonderful discovery was that these elevated and powerful emotions are just as valid in relation to things which can be purchased for the small change in our pockets. Cézanne in his studio was generating his own revolution, not an industrial revolution that would make once-costly objects available to everyone, but a revolution in appreciation, a far deeper process, that would get us to notice what we already have to hand. Instead of reducing prices, he was raising levels of appreciation – which is a move perhaps more precious to us economically because it means we can all access great value with very little money.

Some of what we find 'moving' in an encounter with the apples is that we're restored to a familiar but forgotten attitude of appreciation that we surely once knew in childhood, when we loved the toggles on our rain jackets and found a paper clip a source of fascination and didn't know what anything cost. Since then life has pushed us into the world of money, where prices loom too large, as we now acknowledge, in our relation to things. While we enjoy Cézanne's work, it might also unexpectedly make us feel a little sad. That sadness is a recognition of how many of our genuine enthusiasms and loves we've had to surrender in the name of the adult world. We've

Paul Cézanne, *The Basket of Apples*, c. 1893.

perhaps given up on too many of our native loves. The apple is one instance of a whole continent we've ceased to marvel at.

Our reluctance to be excited by inexpensive things isn't a fixed debility of human nature. It's just a current cultural misfortune. We all naturally used to know the solution as children. The ingredients of the solution are intrinsically familiar. We need to rethink our relationship to prices. The price of something is principally determined by what it cost to make, not how much human value is potentially to be derived from it.

There are two ways to get richer: one is to make more money and the second is to discover that more of the things we could love are already to hand (thanks to the miracles of the Industrial Revolution). We are, astonishingly, already a good deal richer than we're encouraged to think we are.

IM-PERFECTIONISM

The Netherlands Board of Tourism is responsible for marketing the Dutch countryside. To attract visitors, it employs images of extremely neat windmills bordering pristine canals, with flowers along the banks and permanently sunny skies.

There are occasional places and one or two days of the year – particularly near Leiden in late July – when the Netherlands is exactly like this. But there are many other more typical aspects of the Dutch countryside that the Board of Tourism stays quiet about: it's almost always overcast, there are many places where there's not a flower to be seen, it rains most days and there's always quite a lot of mud. You'll encounter many a wonky old sluice gate and some rickety palings shoring up the banks. In order to avoid an awkward collision with reality, the Board of Tourism would have been wise to consult a painting in the nation's main art gallery, the Rijksmuseum, by the seventeenth-century artist Jacob van Ruisdael. Van Ruisdael loved the Dutch countryside, spending as much time there

Kinderdijk Windmill, Alblasserdam.

Selling the Netherlands: Jacob van Ruisdael, *The Windmill at Wijk bij Duurstede*, c. 1668–70.

as he could, and he was very keen to let everyone know what he liked about it.

Instead of carefully selecting a special (and unrepresentative) spot and waiting for a rare and fleeting moment of bright sunshine, he adopted a very different 'selling' strategy. His most famous painting is an advert for the qualities he discovered. Van Ruisdael loved overcast days and carefully studied the fascinating characteristic movements of stormy skies: he was entranced by the infinite gradations of grey and how one would often see a patch of fluffy white brightness drifting behind a darker, billowing mass of rain-dense clouds. He didn't deny that there was mud or that the river and canal banks were frequently quite messy. Instead he noticed their special kind of beauty and made a case for it.

The Netherlands Board of Tourism, on the other hand, felt that the reality of what it was selling was unacceptable and so resorted – for the nicest reasons, out of a touching modesty – to lies. But the Dutch countryside is filled with merits: it's quiet and solemn; it encourages tranquil contemplation; it's an antidote to stress and forced cheerfulness. These are things we might really need to help us cope with our overloaded and often inauthentic lives.

We should develop the sort of confidence that emerges from understanding a basic fact of human psychology: that we're all very prepared to accept the less than perfect, if only we can be guided to appreciate it with skill, confidence and charm.

Japanese aesthetics in the early modern period can teach us a great deal about this because it managed to create excitement around things which are, on first hearing, extremely unprepossessing, including moss, weeds, aged houses and – especially – broken pots.

Zen philosophers developed the view that pots, cups and bowls that had become damaged shouldn't simply be neglected or thrown away. They should continue to attract our respect and attention and be repaired with enormous care, this process symbolizing a reconciliation with the flaws and accidents of time intended to reinforce

The beauty of resilience: a *kintsugi* bowl.

the underlying themes of Zen. The word given to this tradition of ceramic repair is *kintsugi* (*kin* meaning 'golden', *tsugi* 'joinery', so literally 'to join with gold'). In Zen aesthetics, the broken pieces of an accidentally smashed pot should be carefully picked up, reassembled and then glued together with lacquer inflected with a very expensive gold powder. There should be no attempt to disguise the damage; rather, the point is to render the fault lines beautiful and strong. The precious veins of gold are there to emphasize that breaks have a merit all of their own. The origins of *kintsugi* are said to date to the Muromachi period, when the shogun of Japan, Ashikaga Yoshimitsu (1358–1408), broke his favourite tea bowl and, distraught, sent it to be repaired in China. On its return, he was horrified by the ugly metal staples that had been used to join the broken pieces and charged his craftsmen with devising a more appropriate solution. What they came up with was a method that didn't disguise the damage, but made something properly artful out of it.

Kintsugi belongs to the Zen ideals of *wabi-sabi*, which cherishes what is simple, unpretentious and aged – especially if it has a rustic or weathered quality. A story is told of one of the great proponents of *wabi-sabi*, Sen no Rikyū (1522–91). On a journey through southern Japan, he was once invited to a dinner where the host thought his guest would be impressed by an elaborate and expensive antique tea jar that he had bought from China. But Rikyū didn't even seem to notice this item and instead spent his time chatting and admiring a branch swaying in the breeze outside. In despair at this lack of interest, once Rikyū had left, the devastated host smashed the jar to pieces and retired to his room. But the other guests more wisely gathered the fragments and stuck them together using *kintsugi*. When Rikyū next came to visit, he turned to the repaired jar and, with a knowing smile, exclaimed, 'Now it is magnificent.'

Concepts like *kintsugi* provide case studies that teach us a useful kind of confidence. Things that might easily be thought unworthy of appreciation can, if described in the right way, emerge as deeply worth valuing.

SOLACE

The greatest share of all the art that humans have ever made for one another has had one thing in common: it has dealt, in one form or another, with sorrow. Unhappy love, poverty, discrimination, anxiety, sexual humiliation, rivalry, regret, shame, isolation and longing – these have been the chief constituents of art down the ages.

However, in public discussion we are often unhelpfully coy about the extent of our grief. The chat tends to be upbeat or glib; we are under awesome pressure to keep smiling in order not to shock, provide ammunition for enemies or sap the energy of the vulnerable. We therefore end up not only sad, but sad that we are sad – without much public confirmation of the essential normality of our melancholy. We grow harmfully buttoned up or convinced of the desperate uniqueness of our fate.

All this culture can correct, standing as a record of the tears of humanity, lending legitimacy to despair and replaying our miseries back to us with dignity, shorn of many of their haphazard or trivial particulars. 'A book must be the axe for the frozen sea inside us,' proposed Kafka (though the same could be said of any art form) – in other words, art is a tool that can help release us from our numbness and provide for catharsis in areas where we have for too long been wrong-headedly brave.

Such pessimism is also a corrective to prevailing sentimentality. It provides an acknowledgement that we are inherently flawed creatures, incapable of lasting happiness, beset by troubling sexual desires, obsessed by status, vulnerable to appalling accidents and always – slowly – dying.

The German artist Anselm Kiefer is – running counter to the normal habits of our society – extremely forthright about the essentially sorrowful character of the human condition. Everything we love and care about will come to ruin; all that we put our hope in will fail. In a note accompanying his vast painting *Alkahest*, which is

Life is sorrow: Anselm Kiefer, *Alkahest*, 2011.

nearly four metres across, Kiefer writes that even 'rock that looks as though it will last for ever is dissolved, crushed to sand and mud'. The dramatic scale is not accidental. It's a way of trying to make obvious something that is often repressed and ignored: that dejection, sadness and disappointment are major parts of being human. The work's icy, grey, harsh character summons up equally grim thoughts about our own lives.

It's not an intimate picture because the fact Kiefer is asserting isn't a personal one. He's not attempting to delve into the unique painful details of our individual sorrows. The painting isn't about a relationship that didn't work out, a friendship that went wrong, a dead parent we never fully made peace with, a career choice that led to wasted years. Instead it sums up a feeling and an attitude: lonely, lost, cold, worried, frightened. And instead of denouncing these feelings as worthy only of losers, the work proclaims them as important, serious and worthy. It is as if the picture is beaming out a collective message: 'I understand, I know, I feel the same as you do, you are not alone.' Our own private failings and woes – which may strike us as sordid or shameful or very much our own fault – are transformed; they are now a manifestation of the tragic theme of existence, which is everywhere and immutable. They are, in fact, ennobled, by their kinship to this grand work. It is like the way a national anthem works: by singing it, the individual feels part of a greater community and is strengthened, given confidence, even feeling strangely heroic, irrespective of their circumstances. Kiefer's work is like a visual anthem for sorrow, one that invites us to see ourselves as part of the nation of sufferers, which includes, in fact, everyone who has ever lived.

Jean-Baptiste-Camille Corot described his painting *The Leaning Tree Trunk* as a souvenir or memory. It is filled with the idea of farewell. The moment will pass, light will fade, night will fall – the years will pass and we will wonder what we did with them. Corot was in his sixties when he painted this work: the mood is elegiac, mourning what has gone and will never come back. Ultimately, it is a farewell

Our lives too will pass and fade: Jean-Baptiste-Camille Corot,
The Leaning Tree Trunk, c. 1860–65.

to life, but it is not a bitter or desperate one. The mood is resigned, dignified and, although sad, accepting. Our own personal grief at the passing of our life (if not soon, then some day – but always *too soon*) is set within a much wider context. A tree grows, is bent and twisted by fate, like the one in the background, and eventually dries up and withers, like the one in the foreground. The sunlight illuminates the sky for a while and is then hidden behind the clouds and night descends. We are part of nature. Corot isn't glad that the day is over, that the years have gone and that the tree is dying, but his painting seeks to instil a mood of sad yet tranquil acceptance of our own share in the fate of all living things.

This is a proposition we encounter repeatedly in the arts: other people have had the same sorrows and troubles that we have; it isn't that these don't matter or that we shouldn't have them or that they aren't worth bothering about. What counts is how we perceive them. We encounter the spirit or voice of someone who profoundly sympathizes with suffering, but who allows us to sense that through it we're connecting with something universal and unashamed. We are not robbed of our dignity; we are discovering the deepest truths about being human – and therefore we are not only not degraded by sorrow but also, strangely, elevated.

We can imagine ourselves as a series of concentric circles. On the outside lie all the more obvious things about us: what we do for a living, our age, education, tastes in food and broad social background. We can usually find plenty of people who recognize us at this level. But deeper in are the circles that contain our more intimate selves, involving feelings about parents, secret fears, daydreams, ambitions that might never be realized, the stranger recesses of our sexual imagination and all that we find beautiful and moving.

Though we may long to share the inner circles, too often we seem able only to hover with others around the outer ones, returning home from yet another social gathering with the most sincere parts of us aching for recognition and companionship. Traditionally, religion provided an ideal explanation for and solution to this painful loneliness. The human soul, religious people would say, is made by God and so only God can know its deepest secrets. We are never truly alone, because God is always with us. In their way, religions addressed a universal problem: they recognized the powerful need to be intimately known and appreciated and admitted frankly that this need could not realistically ever be met by other people.

What replaced religion in our imaginations, as we have seen, is the cult of human-to-human love we now know as Romanticism, which bequeathed to us the beautiful but reckless idea that loneliness might be capable of being vanquished, if we are fortunate and determined enough to meet the one exalted being known as our soulmate, someone who will understand everything deep and strange about us, who will see us completely and be enchanted by our totality. But the legacy of Romanticism has been an epidemic of loneliness, as we are repeatedly brought up against the truth: the radical inability of any one other person to wholly grasp who we truly are.

Yet there remains, besides the promises of love and religion, one other – and more solid – resource with which to address our loneliness: culture.

Henri Matisse began painting people reading from his early twenties and continued to do so throughout his life; at least thirty of his canvases tackle the theme. What gives these images their poignancy is that we recognize them as records of loneliness that has at least in part been redeemed through culture. The figures may be on their own, their gaze often distant and melancholy, but they have to hand perhaps the best possible replacement when the immediate community has let us down: books.

The English psychoanalyst Donald Winnicott, working in the middle years of the twentieth century, was fascinated by how certain children coped with the absence of their parents. He identified the use of what he called 'transitional objects' to keep the memory of parental love strong even when the parents weren't there. So a teddy bear or a blanket, he realized, could be a mechanism for activating

Henri Matisse, *Woman Reading at a Small Table*, c. 1923.

Christen Købke, *View of Østerbro from Dosseringen*, 1838.

the memory of being cared for, a mechanism that is usefully mobile and portable and is always accessible when the parents are at bay.

Winnicott proposed that works of art can, for adults, function as more sophisticated versions of just these kinds of transitional objects. What we are at heart looking for in friendship is not necessarily someone we can touch and see in front of us, but a person who shares, and can help us develop, our sensibility and values, someone to whom we can turn and look for a sign that they too feel what we have felt, that they are attracted, amused and repulsed by similar things. And, strangely, it appears that certain imaginary friends drawn from culture can end up feeling more real and in that sense more present to us than any of our real-life acquaintances, even if they have been dead a few centuries and lived on another continent. We can feel honoured to count them among our best friends.

Christen Købke lived in and around Copenhagen in the first half of the nineteenth century (he died of pneumonia in his late thirties in 1848), yet we might count him among our closest friends because of his sensitivity to just the sort of everyday beauty we are deeply fond of but that gets very little mention in the social circles around us. From a great distance, Købke acts like an ideal companion who gently works his way into the quiet, hidden parts of us and helps them grow in strength and self-awareness.

The arts provide a miraculous mechanism whereby a total stranger can offer us many of the things that lie at the core of friendship. And when we find these art friends, we are unpicking the experience of loneliness. We're finding intimacy at a distance. The arts allow us to become the soulmates of people who, despite having been born in 1630 or 1808, are, in limited but crucial ways, our proper companions. The friendship may even be deeper than that we could have enjoyed in person, for it is spared all the normal compromises that attend social interactions. Our cultural friends can't converse fully, of course, and we can't reply (except in our imagination). And yet they travel into the same psychological space, at least in some key respects, as we are in at our most vulnerable and intimate points. They may not know of our latest technology, they have no idea of our families or jobs, but in areas that really matter to us they understand us to a degree that is at once a little shocking and deeply thrilling.

Confronted by the many failings of our real-life communities, culture gives us the option of assembling a tribe for ourselves, drawing their members across the widest ranges of time and space, blending some living friends with some dead authors, architects, musicians and composers, painters and poets.

The fifteenth-century Italian painter Andrea del Verrocchio – one of whose apprentices was Leonardo da Vinci – was deeply attracted to the Bible story of Tobias and the Angel. It tells of a young man, Tobias, who has to go on a long and dangerous journey. But he has two companions: one a little dog, the other an angel who comes to walk by his side, advise him, encourage him and guard him.

The old religious idea was that we are never fully alone; there are always special beings around us upon whose aid we can call. Verrocchio's picture is touching not because it shows a real solution we can count on, but because it points to the kind of companionship we would love to have and yet normally don't feel we can find.

Yet there is an available version. Not, of course, in the form of winged creatures with golden halos round their heads. But rather the imaginary friends that we can call on from the arts. You might feel physically isolated in the car, hanging around at the airport, going into a difficult meeting, having supper alone yet again or going through a tricky phase in a relationship, but you are not psychologically alone. Key figures from your imaginary tribe (the modern version of angels and saints) are with you: their perspective, their habits, their ways of looking at things are in your mind, just as if they were really by your side whispering in your ear. And so we can confront the difficult stretches of existence not simply on the basis of our own small resources but accompanied by the accumulated wisdom of the kindest, most intelligent voices of all ages.

Workshop of Andrea del Verrocchio, *Tobias and the Angel*, c. 1470–75.

Given the enormous role of sadness in our lives, it is one of the greatest emotional skills to know how to arrange around us those cultural works that can best help to turn our panic or sense of persecution into consolation and nurture.

GOOD ENOUGH

High ambitions are noble and important, but there's also a point when they become the sources of terrible trouble and unnecessary panic.

One way of undercutting our more reckless ideals and perfectionism was pioneered by Donald Winnicott in the 1950s. Winnicott specialized in relationships between parents and children. In his clinical practice, he often met with parents who felt like failures: perhaps because their children hadn't got into the best schools, or because there were sometimes arguments around the dinner table or the house wasn't always completely tidy.

Winnicott's crucial insight was that the parents' agony was coming from a particular place: excessive hope. Their despair was a consequence of a cruel and counterproductive perfectionism. To help them reduce this, Winnicott developed a charming phrase: 'the good enough parent'. No child, he insisted, needs an ideal parent. They just need an OK, pretty decent, usually well-intentioned, sometimes grumpy but basically reasonable father or mother. Winnicott wasn't saying this because he liked to settle for second best, but because he knew the toll exacted by perfectionism, and realized that in order to remain more or less sane (which is a very big ambition already) we have to learn not to hate ourselves for failing to be what no ordinary human being ever really is anyway.

The concept of 'good enough' was invented as an escape from dangerous ideals. It began in relation to parenthood, but it can be applied across life more generally, especially around work and love.

A relationship may be good enough even while it has its very dark moments. Perhaps at times there's little sex and a lot of heavy arguments. Maybe there are big areas of loneliness and non-communication. Yet none of this should lead us to feel freakish or unnaturally unlucky. It can be good enough.

Similarly, a good-enough job will be very boring at points, it won't perfectly utilize all our merits or pay a fortune. But we may make some real friends, have times of genuine excitement and finish many days tired but with a sense of true accomplishment.

It takes a great deal of bravery and skill to keep even a very ordinary life going. To persevere through the challenges of love, work and children is quietly heroic. We should perhaps more often sometimes step back in order to acknowledge in a non-starry-eyed but very real way that our lives are good enough – and that this is, in itself, already a very impressive achievement.

GRATITUDE

The standard habit of the mind is to take careful note of what's not right in our lives and obsess about all that is missing. But in a new mood, perhaps after a lot of longing and turmoil, we pause and notice some of what has – remarkably – not gone wrong. The house is looking beautiful at the moment. We're in pretty good health, all things considered. The afternoon sun is deeply reassuring. Sometimes the children are kind. Our partner is – at points – very generous. It's been quite mild lately. Yesterday, we were happy all evening. We're quite enjoying our work at the moment.

Gratitude is a mood that grows with age. It is extremely rare to delight in flowers or a quiet evening at home, a cup of tea or a walk in the woods when one is under twenty-two. There are so many larger, grander things to be concerned about: romantic love, career fulfilment and political change. However, it is rare to be left entirely indifferent by smaller things in time. Gradually, almost all one's earlier, larger aspirations take a hit, perhaps a very large hit. One encounters some of the intractable problems of intimate relationships. One suffers the gap between one's professional hopes and the available realities. One has a chance to observe how slowly and fitfully the world ever alters in a positive direction. One is fully inducted into the extent of human wickedness and folly – and into one's own eccentricity, selfishness and madness.

And so 'little things' start to seem somewhat different: no longer a petty distraction from a mighty destiny, no longer an insult to ambition, but a genuine pleasure amid a litany of troubles, an invitation to bracket anxieties and keep self-criticism at bay, a small resting place for hope in a sea of disappointment. We appreciate the slice of toast, the friendly encounter, the long hot bath, the spring morning – and properly keep in mind how much worse it could, and probably will one day, be.

WISDOM

To teach us how to be wise is the underlying central purpose of philosophy. The word may sound abstract and lofty, but wisdom is something we might plausibly aim to acquire a little more of over the course of our lives, even if true wisdom requires that we always keep in mind the persistent risk of madness and error.

Wisdom can be said to comprise twelve ingredients.

Realism

The wise are, first and foremost, 'realistic' about how challenging many things can be. They are fully conscious of the complexities entailed in any project: for example, raising a child, starting a business, spending an agreeable weekend with the family, changing the nation, falling in love . . . Knowing that something difficult is being attempted doesn't rob the wise of ambition, but it makes them more steadfast, calmer and less prone to panic about the problems that will invariably come their way. The wise rarely expect anything to be wholly easy or to go entirely well.

Appreciation

Properly aware that much can and will go wrong, the wise are unusually alive to moments of calm and beauty, even extremely modest ones, of the kind that those with grander plans rush past. With the dangers and tragedies of existence firmly in mind, they can take pleasure in a single, uneventful sunny day, or some pretty flowers growing by a brick wall, the charm of a three-year-old playing in a garden or an evening of intimate conversation among friends. It isn't that they are sentimental and naive; in fact, precisely the opposite. Because they have seen how hard things can get, they know how to draw the full value from the peaceful and the sweet – whenever and wherever these arise.

Folly

The wise know that all human beings, themselves included, are never far from folly. They have irrational desires and incompatible aims, they are unaware of a lot of what they feel, they are prone to mood swings, they are visited by powerful fantasies and delusions – and are always buffeted by the curious demands of their sexuality. The wise are unsurprised by the ongoing coexistence of deep immaturity and perversity alongside quite adult qualities like intelligence and morality. They know that we are barely evolved apes. Aware that at least half of life is irrational, they try – wherever possible – to budget for madness and are slow to panic when it (reliably) rears its head.

Humour

The wise take the business of laughing at themselves seriously. They hedge their pronouncements and are sceptical in their conclusions.

Their certainties are not as brittle as those of others. They laugh from the constant collisions between the noble way they'd like things to be and the demented way they in fact often turn out.

Politeness

The wise are realistic about social relations, in particular about how difficult it is to change people's minds and have an effect on their lives. They are therefore extremely reticent about telling others too frankly what they think. They have a sense of how seldom it is useful to get censorious with others. They want, above all, things to be nice in social settings, even if this means they are not totally authentic. So they will sit with someone of an opposite political persuasion and not try to convert them; they will hold their tongue with someone who seems to be announcing a wrong-headed plan for reforming the country, educating their child or directing their personal life. They'll be aware of how differently things can look through the eyes of others and will search more for what people have in common than for what separates them.

Self-Acceptance

The wise have made their peace with the yawning gap between how they would ideally want to be and what they are actually like. They have come to terms with their tendencies to idiocy, ugliness and error. They are not fundamentally ashamed of themselves because they have already shed so much of their pride.

Forgiveness

The wise are comparably realistic about other people. They recognize the extraordinary pressure everyone is under to pursue their own ambitions, defend their own interests and seek their own pleasures. It can make others appear extremely mean and purposefully evil, but this would be to overpersonalize the issue. The wise know that most hurt is not intentional but a by-product of the constant collision of blind competing egos in a world of scarce resources.

The wise are therefore slow to anger and judge. They don't leap to the worst conclusions about what is going on in the minds of others. They will be readier to overlook a hurt from a proper sense of how difficult every life is, harbouring as it does so many frustrated ambitions, disappointments and longings. Of course they shouted, of course they were rude, of course they wanted to appear slightly more important . . . The wise are generous as to the reasons why people might not be nice. They feel less persecuted by the aggression and meanness of others, because they have a sense of the place of hurt these feelings come from.

Resilience

The wise have a solid sense of what they can survive. They know just how much can go wrong and things will still be – just about – liveable. The unwise person draws the boundaries of their contentment far too far out, so that it encompasses, and depends upon, fame, money, personal relationships, popularity, health . . . The wise person sees the advantages of all of these, but also knows that they may – before too long, at a time of fate's choosing – have to draw the borders right back and find contentment within a more confined space.

Envy

The wise don't envy idly, realizing that there are some good reasons why they don't have many of the things they really want. They look at the tycoon or the star and have a decent grasp of why they weren't able to succeed at this level. It seems like just an accident, an unfair one, but there were in fact some logical reasons.

At the same time, the wise see that some destinies are truly shaped by nothing more than accident. Some people are promoted randomly. Companies that aren't especially deserving can suddenly make it big. Some people have the right parents. The winners aren't all noble and good. The wise appreciate the role of luck and don't curse themselves overly at those junctures where they have evidently not had as much of it as they would have liked.

Success and Failure

The wise emerge as realistic about the consequences of winning and succeeding. They may want to win as much as the next person, but they are aware of how many fundamentals will remain unchanged, whatever the outcome. They don't exaggerate the transformations available to us. They know how much we remain tethered to some basic dynamics in our personalities, whatever job we have or material possession we acquire. This is both cautionary (for those who succeed) and hopeful (for those who won't). The wise see the continuities between the two categories overemphasized by modern consumer capitalism: success and failure.

Regrets

In our ambitious age, it is common to begin with dreams of being able to pull off an unblemished life, where one can hope to get the major decisions, in love and work, right. But the wise realize that it is impossible to fashion a spotless life. We will make some extremely large and utterly uncorrectable errors in a number of areas. Perfectionism is a wicked illusion. Regret is unavoidable.

But regret lessens the more we see that error is endemic across the species. We can't look at anyone's life story without seeing some devastating mistakes etched across it. These errors are not coincidental but structural. They arise because we all lack the information we need to make choices in time-sensitive situations. We are all, where it counts, steering almost blind.

Calm

The wise know that turmoil is always around the corner – and they have come to fear and sense its approach. That's why they nurture such a strong commitment to calm. A quiet evening feels like an achievement. A day without anxiety is something to be celebrated. They are not afraid of having a somewhat boring time. There could, and will again, be so much worse.

And, finally, of course, the wise know that it will never be possible to be wise every hour, let alone every day, of their lives.

Acknowledgements

For their contributions to this book, we would like to thank the following:

Raul Aparici
John Armstrong
Will Brimmer
Caroline Dawnay
Charlotte Fox Weber
Kathryn Garden
Emma Gordon
Srijana Gurung
Lesley Levene
Marcia Mihotich
Susannah Moore
Charlotte Neser
Joanna Prior
Simon Prosser
Tamzin Simpson
Sarah Stein-Lubrano
Hermione Thompson
Imogen Truphet

Permissions

Photograph of the Reading Room at the British Museum © The Trustees of the British Museum.

Photograph of the Rijksmuseum. Photo credit: Pedro Pegenaute, Pegenaute Studio SL, 2012.

Sandro Botticelli, *Madonna of the Book*, c. 1480. Photo credit: Getty Images.

Lucas Cranach the Elder, *Adam and Eve*. Photo credit: The Courtauld Gallery.

Inkblot by Hermann Rorschach, *Psychodiagnostik*, 1932. First published in English as *Psychodiagnostics: A Diagnostic Test Based on Perception*,1942.

Henry A. Murray, *Thematic Apperception Test*, Cambridge, Mass.: Harvard University Press, copyright © 1943 by the President and Fellows of Harvard College, copyright renewed 1971 by Henry A. Murray.

Saul Rosenzweig, *Picture-Frustration Test*, (1948) from the Saul Rosenzweig Papers, Archives of the History of American Psychology, The Drs Nicholas and Dorothy Cummings Center for the History of Psychology, The University of Akron.

Ludolf Bakhuysen, *Warships in a Heavy Storm*, c. 1695. Photo credit: Rijksmuseum, Amsterdam.

Pieter de Hooch, *Interior with Women beside a Linen Cupboard*, 1663. Photo credit: Rijksmuseum, Amsterdam.

Leonardo da Vinci, *The Madonna Litta*, mid-1490s. Photo credit: Getty Images.

Pieter Bruegel, *Dutch Proverbs*, 1559 © bpk / Gemäldegalerie, SMB / Volker-H. Schneider.

Xu Zhen, *Supermarket*, 2007/2015. Photo credit: Thomas Fuesser. Courtesy the artist and ShanghART Gallery. Exhibition view: 'Xu Zhen Solo Exhibition', Long Museum, Shanghai, 2015.

Xu Zhen, *Supermarket*, 2007/2014. Photo credit: Eric Gregory Powell. Courtesy the artist, ShanghART Gallery, Ullens Center for Contemporary Art. Exhibition view: 'Xu Zhen - A MadeIn Company Production', Ullens Center for Contemporary Art, Beijing, 2014.

Photograph of the Sainsbury Centre, photo credit: David Burton / Alamy Stock Photo.

Photograph of the Sainsbury Centre, photo credit: Sid Frisby / Alamy Stock Photo.

Matthew Darly, *The Extravaganza, or The Mountain Head Dress*, 1776 © The Trustees of the British Museum.

Patrick Begbie, *James Craig's Plan of the New Town, Edinburgh*, 1768, National Galleries of Scotland. Photocredit: © National Galleries of Scotland.

Caspar Netscher, *The Lacemaker*, 1662. Photo credit: Bridgeman Images.

Hendrick Danckerts, *Charles II Presented with a Pineapple, c.* 1675–80, Royal Collection Trust. © Her Majesty Queen Elizabeth II 2019.

The Dunmore Pineapple. Photo credit: Undiscovered Scotland.

Photograph of the South Tower of St Paul's Cathedral © The Chapter of St Paul's Cathedral.

Paul Cézanne, *The Basket of Apples, c.* 1893. Photo credit: Getty Images.

Kinderdijk Windmill, Alblasserdam. Photo credit: Prisma by Dukas/UIG via Getty Images.

Jacob van Ruisdael, *The Windmill at Wijk bij Duurstede, c.* 1668–70. Reproduced by kind permission of the Rijksmuseum, Amsterdam.

Kintsugi bowl © Lia_t/Shutterstock.com.

Anselm Kiefer, *Alkahest*, 2011. Photo credit: Charles Duprat, Galerie Thaddaeus Ropac, Paris/Salzburg.

Jean-Baptiste-Camille Corot, *The Leaning Tree Trunk, c.* 1860–65 © The National Gallery, London. Salting Bequest, 1910.

Henri Matisse, *Woman Reading at a Small Table, c.* 1923. © Succession H. Matisse / DACS 2019. Archives Henri Matisse, all rights reserved.

Christen Købke, *View of Østerbro from Dosseringen*, 1838. Photo credit: INTER-FOTO / Alamy Stock Photo.

Workshop of Andrea del Verrocchio, *Tobias and the Angel, c.* 1470–75 © The National Gallery, London.

Index

Page references in *italic* indicate illustrations.

The School of Life is a global organization committed to emotional education and well-being. It focuses on delivering psychotherapy, as well as drawing upon culture more generally, to illuminate topics of emotional concern. It treats individuals, couples, families and organizations, publishes books, makes films and runs ten centres around the world. For more information, see: www.theschooloflife.com.

read more ⟨penguin logo⟩

ALAIN DE BOTTON

THE CONSOLATIONS OF PHILOSOPHY

Bestselling author Alain de Botton sets six of the finest minds in the history of philosophy to work on the problems of everyday life. Here then are Socrates, Epicurus, Seneca, Montaigne, Schopenhauer and Nietzsche on some of the things that bother us all: lack of money, the pain of love, inadequacy, anxiety, the fear of failure and the pressure to conform.

'Singlehandedly, de Botton has taken philosophy back to its simplest and most important purpose: helping us live our lives' *Independent*

'A pleasure to read. Good writing, like good philosophy, is always a consolation' **John Banville**, *Irish Times*

'Few discussions on the great philosophers can have been so entertaining . . . an ingenious, imaginative book' *Sunday Times*

'Witty, thoughtful, entertaining . . . a stylish book, which manages to make philosophy both enjoyable and relevant' *Literary Review*

ALAIN DE BOTTON

STATUS ANXIETY

Do you worry about how well you're doing? Are you envious of your friends' success? Are you suffering from *status anxiety*?

We all worry about what others think of us. We all long to succeed and fear failure. We all suffer – to a greater or lesser degree, usually privately and with embarrassment – from status anxiety.

For the first time, Alain de Botton gives a name to this universal condition and sets out to investigate both its origins and possible solutions. He looks at history, philosophy, economics, art and politics – and reveals the many ingenious ways that great minds have overcome their worries. The result is a book that is not only entertaining and thought-provoking – but genuinely wise and helpful as well.

'De Botton analyses modern society with great charm, learning and humour. His remedies come as a welcome relief when most books offering solutions to the stresses of life recommend the lotus position' *Daily Mail*

'Clever, wise. De Botton's gift is to prompt us to think about how we live and how we might change things' *The Times*

'Measured, amused, compassionate . . . de Botton is a surefooted discoverer of the pungent but less well-known quote' *Daily Telegraph*

ALAIN DE BOTTON

THE COURSE OF LOVE

Over twenty years after his bestselling debut *Essays in Love*, Alain de Botton returns to the novel and to the subject of love . . .

Rabih and Kirsten's friends always ask them the same question: how did you meet? It's a happy story, one they both love to tell. But there is a second part to the tale, the answer to a question their friends never ask: what happened next?

From the first thrill of lust to the deep problems that surface slowly over two shared lifetimes, this is the story of a marriage. It is the story of modern relationships and how to survive them. It is the story of what happens after happily ever after.

'*The Course of Love* probes the very heart of marriage, its shifts and squalls, its great adventure, with forensic tenderness. I absolutely loved it' Deborah Moggach

'Alain de Botton's gift is to prompt us to think about how we live' Jeanette Winterson